Praise for Ruth Morgan,
Running Out? Water in Western Australia

Lucid and engaging, this book tells a compelling story with vital implications for the nation's future – for the entangled history of water and people in Western Australia is also Australia's story writ large. Ruth Morgan's keen analytical eye never loses sight of the human dimension, the human predicaments of a settler society that dreamed of infinite water on the world's driest continent. Thought-provoking and persuasive, this book tells Western Australia's story from the perspective of its fundamental and most essential element: water. Here is a story of longing and loss; a story shot through with constant anxieties about running out, yet constant, profligate water use; a story about dreams of Big Water and subterranean bounty. What use is experience if we forget it? We need deep histories like this to grasp both our current predicaments and our destiny on this continent. Deeply considered and powerful, this is environmental history at its best.

Grace Karskens,
School of Humanities and Languages, University of New South Wales

In *Running Out?* Ruth Morgan has written a book that wears its scholarship easily and tells its story briskly with grace and skill. She makes Western Australia something more than the canary in the coalmine of anthropogenic climate change. In this case, it appears that the canary helped forge its own cage. Western Australians have created a water regime –'Big Water'– which has inequitably distributed risks and costs and sheltered most urban residents from the region's environmental realities. In an analysis that has relevance well beyond Australia, she examines the history of policies that may very well exacerbate rather than solve climate change while contributing to other environmental and social problems.

Richard White,
Margaret Byrne Professor of American History, Stanford University

RUTH A. MORGAN

RUNNING OUT?

WATER IN WESTERN AUSTRALIA

UWA PUBLISHING

First published in 2015 by
UWA Publishing
Crawley, Western Australia 6009
www.uwap.uwa.edu.au

UWAP is an imprint of UWA Publishing
a division of The University of Western Australia

THE UNIVERSITY OF
WESTERN AUSTRALIA

National Library of Australia
Cataloguing-in-Publication entry:
Morgan, Ruth A., author.
Running out? : water in Western Australia / Ruth A Morgan.
ISBN: 9781742586236 (paperback)
Water-supply—Western Australia—History. Water security—Western Australia—History. Climatic changes—Western Australia—History.
333.911109941

Cover, map and timeline by Xou Creative
Typeset in Bembo by Lasertype
Printed by Lightning Source

The Charles and Joy Staples South West region publications fund was established in 1984 on the basis of a generous donation to The University of Western Australia by Charles and Joy Staples.

The purpose of the Fund was to make the results of research on the South West region of Western Australia widely available so as to assist the people of the South West region and those in government and private organisations concerned with South West projects to appreciate the needs and possibilities of the region in the widest possible historical perspective.

The Fund is administered by a committee whose aims are to make possible the publication (either by full or part funding), by UWA Publishing, of research in any discipline relevant to the South West region.

CONTENTS

CONVERSIONS

This book uses the measurements quoted in primary sources, except where conversions to metric units have been necessary for comparison or clarity.

Conversions are provided below:

Imperial to metric

1 acre	=	0.4 hectares (ha)
1 gallon	=	4.5461 litres (L)
1 mile	=	1.6 kilometres (km)
1 yard	=	0.9 metres (m)

Other measurements

1 kilolitre (kL)	=	1,000 litres
1 megalitre (ML)	=	1 million litres
1 gigalitre (GL)	=	1 billion litres

ACKNOWLEDGEMENTS

This book would not have been possible without the guidance, encouragement, and support of many people. I began this study as a PhD thesis in the History Discipline at the University of Western Australia, where I had the invaluable support of my indefatigable supervisor, Andrea Gaynor. There I had the privilege of working with and learning from Charlie Fox and Jenny Gregory, as well as a vibrant postgraduate community. I am also grateful to my colleagues in the History Department at Monash University, particularly Bain Attwood, Rae Frances, Al Thomson, Graeme Davison, Christina Twomey, David Garrioch, Seamus O'Hanlon, Clare Corbould, Clare Monagle, Julie Kalman, Ernest Koh, Kate Murphy, Michael Hau, Reto Hofmann, Tim Verhoeven, Taylor Spence, Agnieszka Sobocinska and Susie Protschky, for their encouragement and guidance as the thesis became a book.

I have been very fortunate to discuss my research with people who have played, and continue to play, significant roles in the land and water management of southwest Western Australia. Many thanks to Len Baddock, Glenn Cook, Jim Gill, Mal Lamond, Brian Sadler, David Stephens, and Walter R. Stern for giving so freely of their time, experience and assistance. Thanks also to Murray Arnold, David Bennett, Neil Coles, John Cramb, Chris Evans, Tim Kurz, Don McFarlane, Luke Morgan, and Chris Stanley.

My research has benefitted greatly from the friendly assistance of librarians and archivists across the country. I would especially like to thank the staff of the Reid Library Scholars' Centre at the University of Western Australia; the State Records Office of Western Australia; the Battye Library; the Department of Water and the Department of Environment and Conservation; the National Library of Australia, particularly the Petherick Reading Room; the Basser Library of the Australian Academy of Science; and the Perth offices of the National Archives of Australia and the Bureau of Meteorology.

ACKNOWLEDGEMENTS

I am extremely appreciative of the advice, mentoring and moral support I have received over the years from the likes of Richard Aitken, James Beattie, Melissa Bellanta, Nick Breyfogle, Jim Fleming, Jodi Frawley, Don Garden, Heather Goodall, Tom Griffiths, Vlad Jankovic, Emily O'Gorman, Libby Robin, Mike Smith, Pamela Statham-Drew, Will Steffen, Richard White, and Terri-ann White. Terri-ann has steered this book from the outset and I am thankful for the tireless efforts of Kiri Falls and Anna Maley-Fadgyas at UWA Publishing. Thanks also for the generous support of the Charles and Joy Staples fund.

I would like to thank the Water Corporation of WA for allowing reproduction of the water inflow graphs in chapter 6. I am also grateful to the Department of Water (Western Australia) for permitting use of the water consumption data shown in the timeline.

I owe an infinite debt of gratitude to my parents, Carolyn and Keith, for their unending patience and moral support, and to Justin for his unwavering faith in me. Together, they have kept my head above water.

Southwest Western Australia

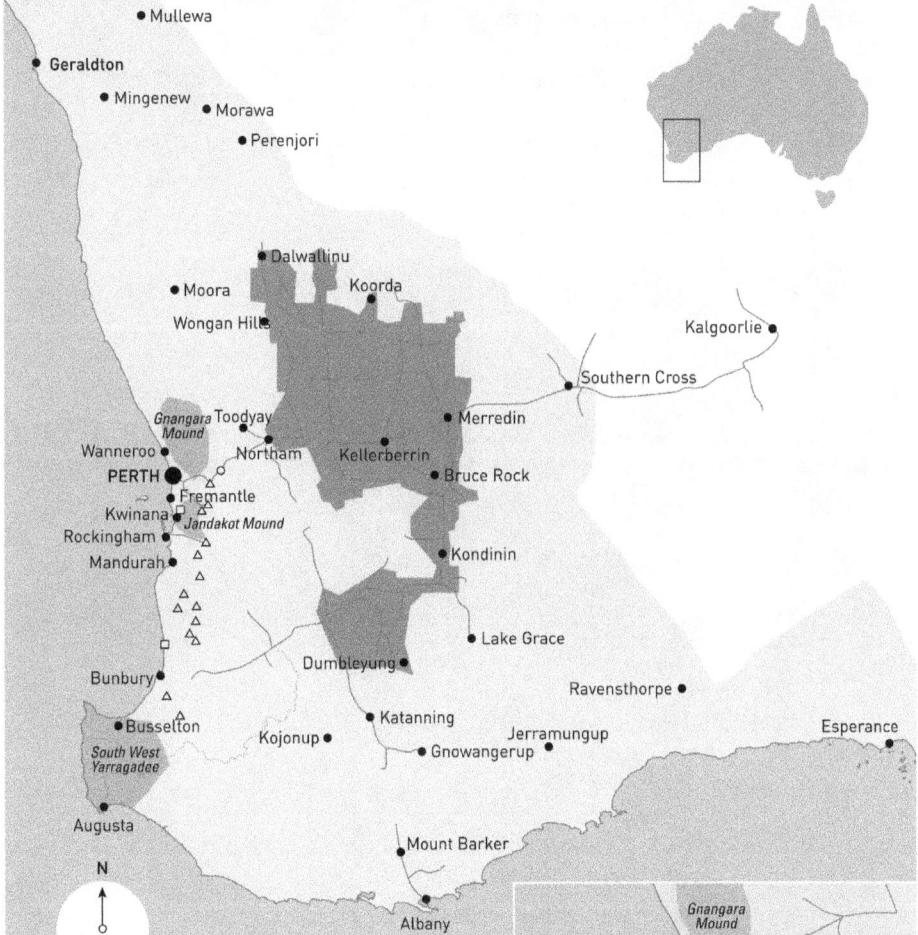

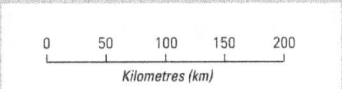

Mullewa

Geraldton

Mingenew
Morawa
Perenjori

Dalwallinu
Moora
Koorda
Wongan Hills

Kalgoorlie

Southern Cross

Gnangara Mound
Toodyay
Merredin
Wanneroo
Northam
Kellerberrin
PERTH
Bruce Rock
Fremantle
Kwinana
Jandakot Mound
Rockingham
Mandurah
Kondinin

Lake Grace
Bunbury
Dumbleyung

Ravensthorpe
Katanning
Busselton
Jerramungup
Kojonup
Gnowangerup
Esperance
South West Yarragadee

Augusta

N

Mount Barker

Albany

0 50 100 150 200	
Kilometres (km)	

△ Dam
□ Desalination plant
○ Weir
‑‑‑ River
— Main pipeline
Southwest region
Groundwater area
Regional water supply schemes

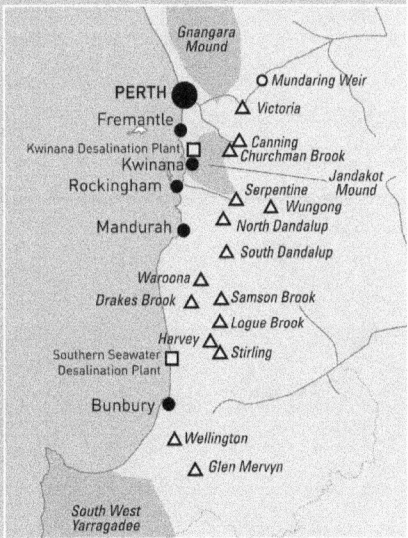

Gnangara Mound

PERTH
Mundaring Weir
Fremantle
Victoria
Kwinana Desalination Plant
Canning
Churchman Brook
Kwinana
Jandakot Mound
Rockingham
Serpentine
Wungong
Mandurah
North Dandalup
South Dandalup
Waroona
Drakes Brook
Samson Brook
Logue Brook
Harvey
Stirling
Southern Seawater Desalination Plant
Bunbury
Wellington
Glen Mervyn
South West Yarragadee

Water use in Western Australia since 1900

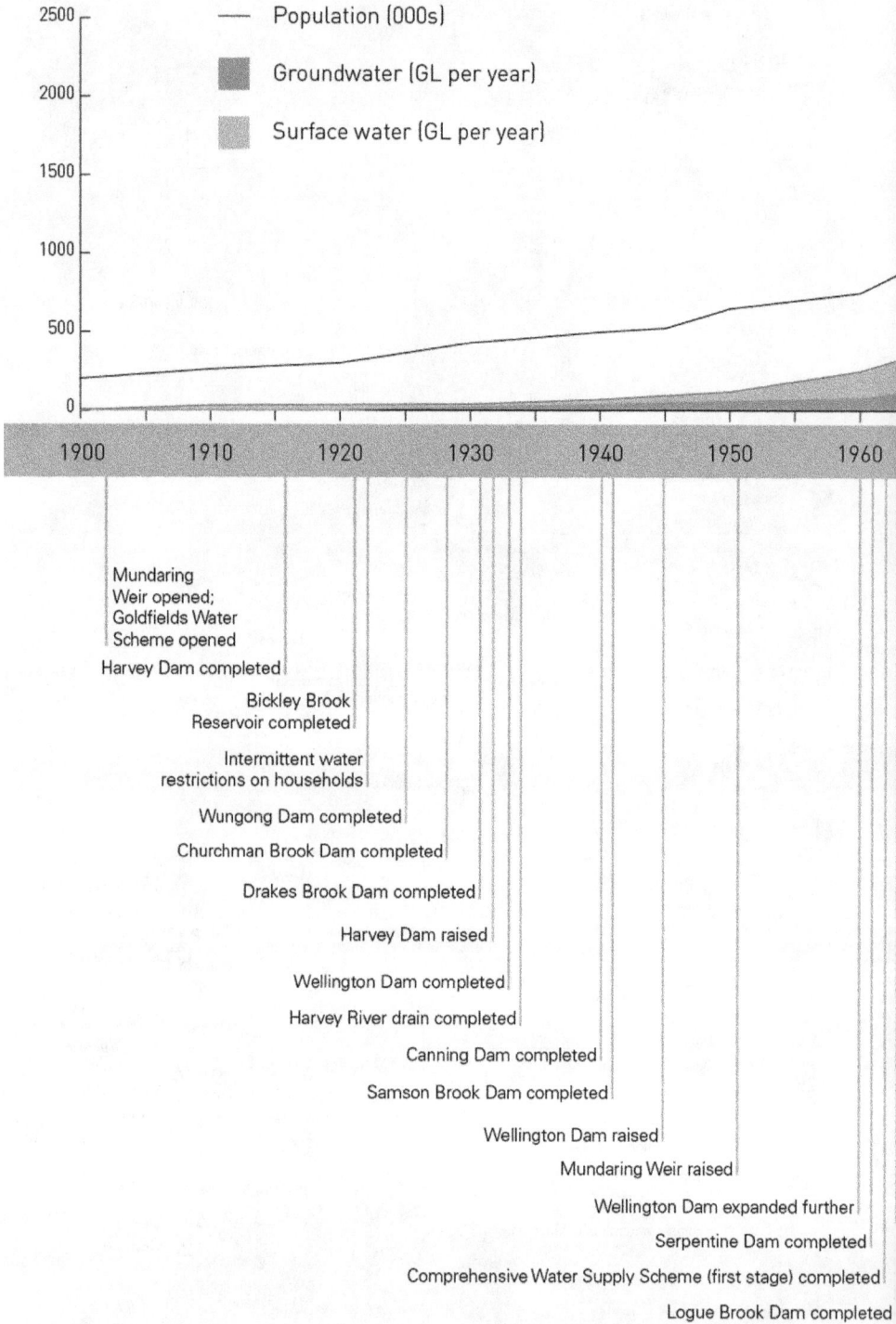

Legend:
- Population (000s)
- Groundwater (GL per year)
- Surface water (GL per year)

Timeline events:

Mundaring Weir opened; Goldfields Water Scheme opened

Harvey Dam completed

Bickley Brook Reservoir completed

Intermittent water restrictions on households

Wungong Dam completed

Churchman Brook Dam completed

Drakes Brook Dam completed

Harvey Dam raised

Wellington Dam completed

Harvey River drain completed

Canning Dam completed

Samson Brook Dam completed

Wellington Dam raised

Mundaring Weir raised

Wellington Dam expanded further

Serpentine Dam completed

Comprehensive Water Supply Scheme (first stage) completed

Logue Brook Dam completed

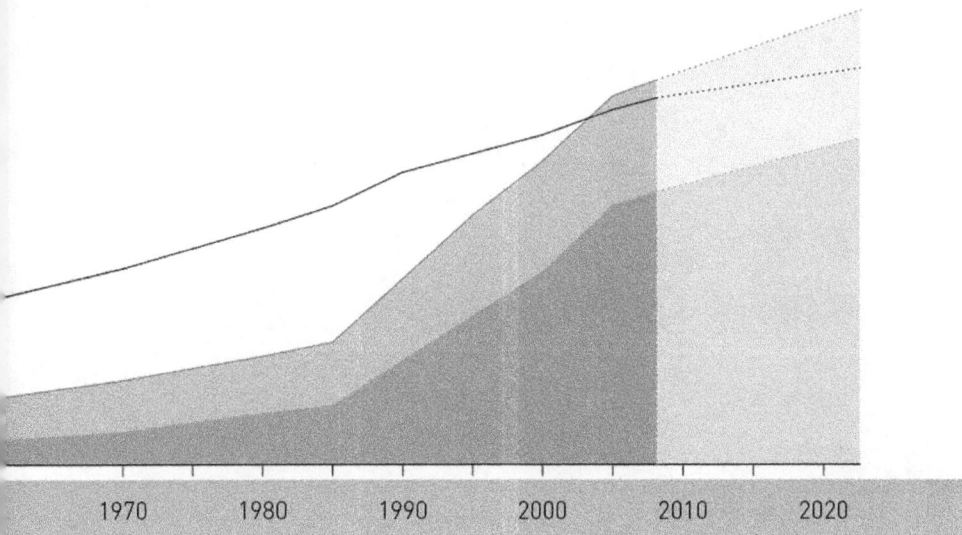

1970   1980   1990   2000   2010   2020

Recycled wastewater
added to water supplies

Southern Seawater
desalination plant opened

Kwinana desalination plant opened

Liberal State Opposition proposes
piping water from the Kimberley

Debate about South West
Yarragadee aquifer

Stirling–Harvey Redevelopment
Scheme completed

North Dandalup Dam expanded

Harris Dam completed

Ernie Bridge's Kimberley Pipeline proposal

Cloud seeding trials in northeastern wheatbelt

Wungong Dam expanded

State Committe of CSIRO investigates iceberg technology
Jandakot Mound groundwater scheme commences

Total household water restrictions in Perth

South Dandalup Dam completed
Voluntary water conservation campaign in Perth

North Dandalup Dam completed

Gnangara groundwater scheme commences

Glen Mervyn Dam completed

CSIRO cloud seeding experiments

Waroona Dam completed

*Water-use information courtesy of the
Department of Water (Western Australia)*

Introduction

There's something about summer in the Australian suburbs: the smell of sweating grass, baking bricks and burning bitumen; the sounds of cicadas humming, magpies warbling, and sprinklers hissing. Most of my summer school holidays in the 1990s were spent at the brick-and-tile home of my grandparents in the southern suburbs of Perth. By the time I was being dropped off for the day, my grandfather would be slipping off his rubber thongs and surveying the morning's lawn watering. The rubber hose would be left snaking from the tap to the roadside verge, too sticky and twisted for coiling up. There was really no need anyway. He would be up before dawn the next day to water the lawns again. He was a man of routine and his dedication could be seen in the bright white stripes left by the thongs on his leathery, brown feet, if not by a green strip of buffalo grass.

The verge aside, he was fairly cautious with his water use. He was a thrifty character, always pointing out waste and pushing for shorter showers. I like to think his frugality was the legacy of growing up in Kalgoorlie after World War I. By the time he was born, C. Y. O'Connor's Kalgoorlie Pipeline was a decade old, but his family seemed to have remembered the worth of water. My grandmother, who he met and married in nearby Boulder on the eve of the Second World War, was the youngest of eight and always last in line for the family's bath water.

My parents weren't quite as frugal when it came to water, but they were hardly profligate either. Pressed for time, they installed an automatic reticulation system to water the garden, yet remained suspicious of the dishwasher. They were always conscious of wastage, and my father maintains that he invented the dual-flush cistern long before they became mainstream. But none of this stopped them from raising a daughter who enjoys a love affair with the washing machine and a penchant for long, hot showers. Not exactly a likely candidate to write about Western Australia's water worries.

When I began this research in 2007, southern Australia was in the grip of drought and climate change was a hot topic. Perth's first desalination plant was a year old, Tim Flannery's *The Weather Makers* had just been published, and Al Gore's *An Inconvenient Truth* was still making headlines. By year's end, Kevin Rudd had declared climate change was the 'great moral challenge of our generation', and his first act as Prime Minister of Australia was signing the Kyoto Protocol to curb greenhouse gas emissions. The drought finally broke in late 2010 and floods took their toll on Queensland, New South Wales, and Victoria. But the dry continued to sap the southwest of the continent.

This drying trend did not go unnoticed among local authors. Stephen Scourfield offered a thinly veiled tale of piping water from the north in *As the River Runs*, while Peter Docker conjured an apocalyptic future of an Australia ravaged by thirst. Meanwhile favourite son, Tim Winton, returned to the characters of *Dirt Music* in his play *Signs of Life*, which he set in 'a future world where there there's no rain and the land's drying up'.[1] Western Australian writers have long been fascinated with water, or the lack of it.[2] Perhaps this arises from a 'sense of being trapped between sea and desert', as Winton puts it.³ George Seddon saw the southwest in similar terms, as an 'island, with sea to the south and west, desert to the north and east, and one cannot leave it without crossing mile and mile of desert'.⁴ Has this isolation provoked a fear of running out of water in the west?

I had grown up in the 1980s and 1990s with the hole in the ozone layer, the dangers of jarrah dieback *(Phytophthora cinnamomi)*, the toll of dryland salinity, the ravages of bauxite mining, and the logging of old-growth forests. But these were problems that were somewhere else, way 'out there', and far beyond my suburban experience. It wasn't really until the introduction of tougher water restrictions in Perth in 2001 and the other capital cities from 2005 that I began to take notice of a national water problem. Here was an issue affecting the suburbs including, literally, my own back yard. Besides, these weren't just any water restrictions. While the use of garden sprinklers in Perth was limited to two days a week, in Melbourne and Brisbane even car washing was forbidden. From the comfort of the city, we spared a thought for the farmers in the wheatbelt and the Murray–Darling Basin, who faced parched paddocks, clear skies, and rising debts.

As the dry dragged on, Australian governments mooted plans to drought-proof their cities. Leading the way was Western Australia with seawater desalination. How had we got to the point where we needed to *manufacture* water? Were we really running out? Finding the answers forced me to look further back than I expected. It required the close examination of the development of Western Australians' relationships with water since the early nineteenth century. It has also prompted questions such as why have some Western Australians had better access to water than others, and to what effect? What is it about water that causes such a stir in Western Australian politics? Could our relationship have developed differently, with different consequences?

In answering these questions, this book provides a Western Australian perspective on the water challenges that have dogged Australians since 1788. It examines how people in the most populated part of the state, the southwest, came to terms with the region's climate, its variability, and its implications for water supplies and agriculture. It is a history that charts the changing degree of Western Australians' resilience in the face of water scarcity, from the foundation of the Swan River Colony in 1829 to the decision to add recycled wastewater to Perth's water supplies in 2013. Since at least the turn of the twentieth century, it seems as if Western Australians have been tormented by recurring fears that sooner or later, they would run out of water. It is largely this anxiety about running out that has prompted support for the near-continuous development of new sources, including ambitious plans to transport water from the north of the state for Perth and the southwest. All the while, many Western Australians have maintained a profligate water culture, living beyond their environmental limits and rendering themselves vulnerable to running out. How this fear of running out has been experienced, and how these experiences have changed over time, is the subject of this book.

Water scarcity means different things to different people. Restrictions on water use in suburban gardens hardly compare to long dry spells in agricultural areas, just as our nineteenth-century forebears would struggle to fathom today's household water use. How we define water scarcity, therefore, is historically contingent on our way of life, our expectations and aspirations, our scientific knowledge, and the changing regional environment. Over time, our needs and desires have evolved from adequate water supplies for health and sanitation, to water for agricultural enterprises, increasingly affluent lifestyles, industry, and the environment. Many factors influence the amount of water available for these purposes, from rainfall and evaporation to the extent of salt encroachment and other threats to water quality. In turn, where and when water scarcity occurs, and who and what it affects, invariably reflects the power dynamics that have developed in the southwest since the nineteenth century and which continue to unfold today.

Among the causes of water scarcity in the region is a changing climate. In the late 1980s, local water managers and climate scientists speculated that the southwest of the continent was undergoing a drying trend. A decade later, they concluded that the region's rainfall had been lower over the previous twenty years than at any point since the 1870s, when official meteorological measurements began. They braced themselves for the worst and made significant adjustments to their plans for infrastructure development. Since then, Tim Flannery has pointed to the region as the first area in Australia to be affected by anthropogenic climate change.[5] The Climate Commission reported in 2013 that the southwest has become drier since 1970 and might become even drier in the future.[6] Once renowned for the most reliable rainfall in the country, the southwest is now the canary in the country's climate change coal mine.

This region's experience of a changing climate is also attracting attention abroad. 'Perth is at the epicentre of global climate change', argues Robert Glennon, a water policy expert from Arizona who visited the city in 2012. 'The city's strategic response offers lessons about climate change mitigation, exacerbation and adaptation. The lessons are acutely relevant to the United States, particularly California'.[7] Like Perth, but on a much grander scale, the southwestern United States has experienced huge population and economic growth in recent years, which has placed an enormous strain on the region's water resources. And like Perth, the North American southwest is getting hotter and drier.[8]

The southwest

Australia's southwest is the most populous region west of Adelaide. Within its boundaries are Western Australia's largest towns and cities, including the capital Perth. The region is home to over 90 per cent of the state's population as well as important sectors of the state's economy, such as the agriculture, horticulture and viticulture industries, as well as some mining operations, service industries, and the finance sector.[9] The largest consumer of water in the region is the Water Corporation's reticulated network, the Integrated Water Supply Scheme, which supplies water to Perth, Mandurah and the goldfields.

The region extends roughly from Geraldton in the north to Esperance on the southeast coast, and creeps inland past the No. 1 Rabbit Proof Fence. It is over 300,000 square km in area, about four times the size of Tasmania, and its waterways, soils and climate are recent products of a long geological history. At present the Yilgarn Block and its younger siblings, the Perth and Bremer Basins, dominate the southwest region. The rifting of the continents, which created the Perth and Bremer Basins, greatly affected the Yilgarn Block's ancient rivers, from which large amounts of sediment had once flowed into these basins. As the rifting processes thrust the Yilgarn Block higher above sea level, rivers that had once threaded across Gondwana were severed, and new rivers and inland drainage patterns were forged. Into these rivers flowed the sediment of the Yilgarn's weathering and this detritus trapped groundwater beneath the surface, a geological feature that both helped and hindered European colonists. Meanwhile, some of these new rivers met with their predecessors so that the oldest stretches of the southwest's larger rivers now lie beyond the Darling Range, and their youngest run through the Scarp.

Nearly seventy million years ago, between the late Cretaceous and early Palaeogene periods, the Perth and Bremer Basins emerged from the ocean. Sea levels began to fluctuate during the Pliocene and the earth entered a cycle of alternating glacial and interglacial periods lasting thousands of years. During the cool glacial periods, sea levels fell and in the warm interglacial periods they rose to their present or slightly higher levels. At about this time, some three to five million years ago, the southwest region's characteristic Mediterranean climate of dry summers and wet winters became established.[10]

The desert and the sea continue to play instrumental roles in the seasonal patterns of this Mediterranean climate. Cool, moist westerly winds pass from west to east across the south of the continent. During the mild, wet winter months of May to September, these westerly winds strengthen as they combine with the low pressure systems over the Southern Ocean to bring rain to the southern areas, including the southwest region.[11] How much rain the westerlies bring depends upon the interaction of oceanic and atmospheric processes, including the Indian Ocean Dipole, the El Niño – Southern Oscillation, and the Leeuwin Current.[12] Tropical cyclones in the northwest are responsible for periods of extreme rainfall during the summer months, which can lead to flooding.[13] During the hot, dry summer, the westerlies usually pass too far south to bring much rain to the southwest, leaving the region at the mercy of the easterlies that blow across the hot, dry inland. Although summer temperatures are high, the sea breeze, the 'Fremantle Doctor', sweeps through the afternoon, bringing with it the cool ocean air.

As little rain falls over the southwest in the summer months, the flows and salinities of the region's rivers are largely seasonal. When the rains eventually come, the moisture in the soil slowly accumulates until the creeks trickle into the rivers and their estuaries, and then into the sea. The salinity of these estuaries depends upon the extent to which the rains flush them out. Freshwater conditions only last in the estuaries until the rain ends and the tides return marine water to them. During extended periods of dry conditions, some are reduced to shallow salt-pans.[14] Although these rivers are significant to the southwest, they carry little water in comparison to those in south-eastern Australia and overseas. They are relatively short, with few extending inland more than 150 km from the coast, making for what Public Works Department engineers described in 1946 as 'hydraulically difficult country'.[15]

Across the southwest, reservoirs of underground water are also at the mercy of the seasons. Throughout the agricultural areas, chains of salt lakes streak the landscape in the hotter months of the year, leaving traces of the groundwater that lies just beneath the undulating hills and valleys. Meanwhile, wetlands of swamps, lakes and floodplains dominate the Swan Coastal Plain, where Perth and its suburbs now lie. In the wetter months, some areas can become locally waterlogged and even flooded when water accumulates in its lower sections. During summer, the lack of rainfall and high temperatures combine to evaporate the water from these shallow wetland areas.[16]

The southwest's rains are highest (at 1,400 mm per year) and most reliable in the far southwest corner, where the Indian Ocean meets the Southern Ocean.[17] As the landscape rolls towards the north and inland, these rains dissipate and become increasingly variable, with higher rates of evaporation. Marooned between the desert and the sea, the region has provided its natural vegetation with what botanists Stephen Hopper and Paul Gioia describe as a 'continental refuge'.[18] The plant life adapted to the southwest's infertile soils and the Mediterranean climate to create a region that is rich in endemic species, and in the year 2000, the region was classified one of the world's twenty-five 'biodiversity hotspots'.[19] But many of these species are under threat, largely as a result of agricultural practices.

Nyoongar country

But these are *wedjela* or whitefella stories.[20] Archaeological evidence suggests that the Nyoongar people have lived in the southwest for at least 50,000 years. Nyoongar have a quite different understanding of the history of the region and their own origins within it.[21] Traditional stories that have been passed down orally from generation to generation explain the southwest origins of the Nyoongar people. For these people, the land is their Mother, forged by the Rainbow Serpent, the *Waakal*.[22] Nyoongar scholar Len Collard explains that the *Waakal* 'came out of the earth' and as it travelled above and beneath the ground, it made the rivers, hills and waterholes, as well as the people themselves.[23] '[T]he *Waakal* is the Creator, the keeper of the freshwater sources', explains Collard. 'He gave us life and our trilogy of belief in the *boodjar* – the land – as our mother and nurturer of the Nyungar *moort* – family relations – and our *katitjin* – knowledge so that we could weave that intricate tapestry known as the "web of life"'.[24] With the *Waakal* as 'guardian' of the 'freshwater springs and rivers of Nyoongar country', the people were the 'keepers of the land'.[25] Nyoongars were and remain spiritually connected to their lands, responsible for maintaining all the life that these lands sustained.

Their primary tool of land care was fire, or what archaeologist Rhys Jones famously called 'firestick farming'.[26] Historian Bill Gammage, using the language of twenty-first century environmental management, argues that through the careful burning of the land, Aborigines made resources 'not merely sustainable, but abundant, convenient and predictable'.[27] This practice, which reinforced enduring connections to country, was largely possible because of the mobility of Aboriginal people through their lands. On the Swan Coastal Plain, for instance, Pindjarup Nyoongar followed an 80 km path from Pinjarra to Fremantle *(Walyalup)* by following the chain of lakes along the coast.[28] This enabled them to fulfil their spiritual responsibilities, while allowing them to maximise their resources, including water. The Nyoongar had developed a way of life that was resilient to 'running out' but they could not be prepared for the changes that colonisation and the colonists wrought.

Historical understandings of water scarcity and climate variability

As anthropogenic climate change forces us all to come to terms with climatic conditions potentially quite different from those we have experienced, environmental histories of Australian climates can shed light on how we have comprehended risk and climate variability in the past. After all, even as anthropogenic climate change destabilises many traditional historical narratives of the land, uncertainty and variability are likely to remain among the continent's signature environmental characteristics. Since the British colonisation of Australia, fluctuating climates and water supplies have challenged settler assumptions about the land, and the associated social and economic toll has demanded the adaptation of these assumptions over time.

The contemporary field of environmental history, which draws on both an imperial legacy and the rise of a new environment movement in North America in the 1970s, has been largely driven by such environmental concerns. Broadly speaking, environmental historians examine the range of interactions between humans and nature over time, from the ways people have thought about the natural world to the ways that humans have produced resources from its parts. Environmental histories can offer tangible human connections to the past, to distant places, and to the complex atmospheric and oceanic mechanisms that control the earth's climate that might otherwise remain beyond our comprehension. By telling stories that reflect careful analysis and rigorous scholarship, historians can help make sense of climate change and inform the ways we approach an uncertain future.

A decade of crippling droughts, cyclones, floods and fires, for example, has prompted historians to look more closely at southeastern Australia, where they have focussed largely on the ways in which settler Australians have tried to understand the climates, hydrologies, and ecologies of the Murray–Darling Basin and the Victorian Mallee, as well as the changes wrought upon these regions, and how these changes have affected and continue to affect them.[29] Building on the pioneering work of historical geographer J. M. Powell, this small but growing group of historians are becoming 'water dreamers' as they engage with Indigenous and non-Indigenous relationships with water and the historic challenges of managing Australia's water resources.[30]

As these works show, when it comes to water scarcity and climate variability in Australia, some people and places have fared better than others. Rather than simply the consequence of misfortune or ill-preparedness, these different experiences arise from differences in vulnerability, or exposure to risk. This degree of vulnerability is a product of complex processes that historians can unravel in order to discern the interactions between humans and their environment over time.[31] The uneven distribution of vulnerability suggests that water scarcity is a more complicated matter than a shortage of water alone. Indeed, it has distinctly human dimensions that account for the changing ways in which running out of water has been perceived, defined, and predicted in southwestern Australia.

Building on the concept of vulnerability, the diverse experiences of water scarcity in Australia might be historically examined through the notion of hydroresilience. Broadly conceived, hydroresilience offers a means to compare and contrast, as well as to account for, the range of ways that Australians have understood and responded to limited water supplies. An individual, group, or society's degree of hydroresilience is the historical product of an interaction of ecological, geographical, cultural, socioeconomic, and political factors, which together shape the extent to which they are adversely affected by a real or perceived lack of water. Changes in those dynamics may improve or diminish a society's hydroresilience over time, and shape the way they understand and respond to future episodes of water scarcity. What is an adverse affect is historically and culturally contingent, and can be deduced from the lived experience evident in the historical record.

Since the 1980s, European theorists such as Ulrich Beck and Anthony Giddens have argued that we are living in a new age of the 'risk society'. Yet our associated fears for the future are not without precedent.[32] Perceptions of environmental change and the potential consequences for economic development and human health have long provoked what New Zealand environmental historian James Beattie calls 'environmental anxiety'.[33] This book argues that among settler Western Australians, their real or perceived vulnerability to water scarcity and climate variability – their hydroresilience – has long fuelled environmental anxieties about running out of water.

In her book *Thirsty Country*, the *Australian* newspaper's rural journalist Åsa Wahlquist suggests that Australians suffer from 'water illiteracy', a lack of understanding and awareness about their nation's water resources.[34] Worse still, many of us seem trapped in what American climatologist Don Wilhite calls the 'hydro-illogical cycle', in which our awareness and concerns about water scarcity soon fade to apathy when abundance, or at least its illusion, returns. In light of the southwest's drying climate, Western Australians can least afford to go on this way. To better understand where we are headed, we need a better understanding of where we have come from. If we are running out, we need all the help we can get.

I

Settling the Seasons?

Sowing the seeds of vulnerability (1829 to 1901)

The foundation of the Swan River Colony, in the southwest of Australia on 1 June 1829, marked Britain's first attempt to establish an agricultural colony of private settlement since the late eighteenth century. It did not take long, however, for the colony – officially renamed 'Western Australia' in 1831 – to earn a reputation as the Cinderella of the Antipodes, with its colonists struggling to establish themselves. For much of the nineteenth century, Western Australia's survival was in the balance and it relied heavily on the Colonial Office to stay afloat. The challenges the colonists faced were more a result of the difficulties of isolation, a small population and limited sources of capital, than the region's climate conditions or its availability of water supplies. Yet as the colonists haltingly expanded their colony, they etched patterns of settlement, governance and resource use across the region, and developed particular understandings of the southwest's environments, which together served to diminish the hydroresilience of the colony.

Putting down roots: settling down in the southwest

Just days after the landing of the first settlers on Garden Island in June 1829, Captain James Stirling elected to locate the administrative centre of the Swan River Colony, Perth, at the midpoint between the port of Fremantle at the river's mouth and the arable farming lands on the upper Swan, near Guildford. Stirling had interpreted the tall jarrah stands and the alluvial soils near the river as a favourable indication of soil fertility, and thus of land suitable for farming and grazing.[1] Other towns soon followed as colonists established settlements along the Avon and Murray valleys and in the southwest corner of the continent. From this dispersal of townships a particular hierarchy of settlement developed in the region in which the capital Perth, while dependent upon its hinterland for wealth, was the locus of socioeconomic and political power. This was an agrarian structure highly reliant on a predictable climate and reliable water supplies, with no place for the southwest's original human inhabitants, the Nyoongar.

As most of these settlements were sited relatively close to water supplies, their vulnerability to water scarcity was less a question of their access to water than their very *permanence*. The intention and purpose of the Swan River Colony was to found an agricultural colony in the temperate climes of the western third of the Australian continent. Land, and therefore property, formed the central pillar of the colonial project: its currency attracted emigrants to the colony, provided the foundation of the colony's socioeconomic and political structures, and spurred the expansion of white settlement. But this realisation of Lockean ideals also formed the basis of the colony's vulnerability to water scarcity: permanent settlement requires permanent infrastructure, particularly reliable (and clean) water supplies.

By contrast, the region's Nyoongar Aboriginal peoples were highly mobile, which had traditionally ensured their resilience to dry periods. Although estimates vary, about 6,000 Nyoongars are thought to have lived in the immediate vicinity of the Swan River at the time of British colonisation, with about 400 near the site of Perth. For the colony's first Governor, James Stirling, however, the Aboriginal presence in the region was of little consequence and he did not attempt to negotiate a treaty with the Nyoongar to occupy their country. After all, Western Australia was a settler colony, implicitly founded on the supplanting of Indigenous peoples on the land and waterways.

For the British colonists, the latter provided important sources of water supplies, as well as the means of transport and communication. Stirling, for instance, had assured prospective settlers that the 'freshwater lagoons' he had observed near the Swan River would provide ample water supplies to the colony.[2] But he had been ignorant of the effects of the Mediterranean rhythms of dry summers and wet winters on the shallow water-table along the coast. During the summer months, the lakes, streams, springs and swamps of the wetlands usually dried up and could not be depended upon for a constant water supply, although they provided valuable sources of food for the Nyoongar people at these times. Colonists had to cart water from the lakes, and supplement these supplies with brackish groundwater drawn from wells. Natural springs close to Perth, such as at Spring Street, Mill Street and Kennedy Fountain, provided colonists with access to groundwater.[3] These public, as well as household, wells remained the major sources of water for Perth until at least the end of the nineteenth century, although water storage tanks later afforded the capital's wealthier residents some measure of comfort.[4]

Vital to the lives and livelihoods of both the colonisers and the colonised, water was a common ground during the colonial period. But rather than presenting places for cooperation, waterways became sites of competition and conflict. Nyoongar relationships with their lands contrasted starkly with the colonists' Lockean attachments to land and property. Theirs was a deeply spiritual connection to country, to the places that guided their way of life. The encroachment of colonial settlement across these tribal territories through property ownership, and restrictions on

Aboriginal movement across country, disrupted the traditional practices of the Nyoongar people.[5] The foundation of Perth on the banks of the Swan River, for instance, pushed some groups to Mongers Lake, 3 km north of the town site. On the Murray River, according to anthropologist and historian Lois Tilbrook, 'soldiers broke down fish traps in the river and fired on the Aborigines who later approached the barracks'.[6] Elsewhere, the competition for resources led to violent clashes between the colonists and the local Nyoongar people, culminating in the bloody battle of Pinjarra in late 1834.

Yet they could not leave their lands. As Captain Frederick Irwin observed in 1835,

> Each tribe has its territory and landmarks. If but one is disturbed it experiences a difficulty in falling back, and retiring upon the tribes in its rear, who are similarly situated in their turn. They continue, therefore, to hover about their ancient grounds and depend for their subsistence upon them.[7]

These opposing approaches to land and property of the British and Nyoongar peoples proved to be irreconcilable. Moreover, the imposition of Western European land ownership on Nyoongar lands rendered them both vulnerable, albeit in different ways and in different levels of magnitude, to environmental change in the southwest.

Farming in the colonial southwest

Owing to the colony's isolation from the other Australasian colonies and the rest of the British Empire, it was imperative that its colonists learnt to farm in order to feed themselves. But it took some time for the colonists to adapt their limited farming knowledge to the foreign conditions of the southwest. After a difficult first year for the colony, its hopes improved when Ensign

Robert Dale crossed the Darling Ranges and found more fertile farming lands east of Guildford along the Avon River, the uppermost part of the Swan.[8]

The colonists of the Swan River were wedded to the Western European belief in the relationship of property and land cultivation to civilisation. Land had long been the main source of wealth in the Old World and its cultivation was a civilising act for both the land and the people. Furthermore, it was cultivation that rendered the land valuable. It followed that societies that did not cultivate their lands in a similar fashion were uncivilised. These bonds between agriculture, civilisation and property provided the foundation for the colonisation of the western third of the continent, and the dispossession of the Nyoongar people of the southwest.

As New Zealand historian James Belich has noted, an 'emigrant joined someone else's society, [whereas] a settler or colonist remade his own'.[9] In terms of the introduction of agricultural and pastoral practices to the southwest, this 'remaking' of British agriculture in Australian conditions contributed to the embedding of vulnerability in the colonial enterprise. With their lack of local knowledge, the colonists' efforts, as historical geographer J. M. Powell has depicted in colonial Victoria and South Australia, were those of a 'gigantic folk experiment'.[10] Many of the colonists were young workers from Britain's industrial cities and lacked the necessary skills to establish successful farms. Although more experienced colonists began to arrive in late 1830, even they struggled to adapt their knowledge to the foreign conditions of the southwest.

Cropping was an especially delicate business and sensitive to the coastal region's distinctive soil and climate conditions. By virtue of the comparatively long period required for germination, and the host of factors aside from the weather that might interfere with the quality and quantity of the harvest, it took the colonists some time to devise a suitable calendar for the planting cycle of their crops. Their English preconceptions and the heavy investment in farming combined to inhibit change, even when their farmlands, equipment, and techniques had proved to be inadequate. Eventually, the colonists realised that their crops had to be planted early in the growing season to make the most of the winter rains – as Lieutenant Henry Bunbury reported in 1836, 'the sooner the seed is in the ground the better'. Yet the timing of these winter rains was highly variable, arriving at any time from early April to the end of May.[11] Herein lay the root of the colonists' farming problems: they were determined to impose a tradition of European agriculture with its rhythms of regularity and reliability, on the seasonal syncopations of the southwest.

As the seasons did not conform to the colonists' expectations, pastoralism offered an alternative, particularly after they had identified plants poisonous to their stock.[12] Prior to the introduction of fencing and heavy stocking, this form of land use was akin in some ways to the mobile Aboriginal hunting economies that colonisation had disrupted.[13] It was a method that allowed livestock to be moved to more hospitable areas if the conditions were poor. During the dry seasons between 1834 and 1838, and those between 1844 and 1846, for instance, crops suffered because of the immovability of that farming system. Pastoralists, meanwhile, had managed to limit the effects of the climatic conditions on their stock.[14] Combined with the lessons of New South Wales and Van Diemen's Land, pastoralists had a vital margin of error. By the late 1830s, Western Australia was self-sufficient in basic foodstuffs, and pastoralism had become a profitable export industry.[15] The lands beyond the eastern boundary of the colony soon beckoned.

'From sojourners to settlers': British bodies and the climate of the Swan River[16]

Much has been written about the 'near collapse' of the British colony at the Swan River during the 1830s and the reasons for its precarious early existence.[17] Historians have paid less attention, however, to the colonists' anxieties about the implications

18

of Western Australia's climate conditions for the progress of permanent white settlement. In the Swan River Colony, the colonists' association of human physiology with the regional climate informed colonial studies of the local weather and climate conditions from colonisation to the late 1870s. Such studies, the colonial authorities hoped, would help to allay the anxieties of vulnerable white settlers over the unfamiliar climes of the region.

Royal Navy Surgeon Frederick R. Clause had accompanied Captain Stirling and botanist Charles Fraser on board the HMS *Success* in March 1827. In his report to the Admiralty, Clause reported, 'I am decided in my opinion that it is the most healthy part of the globe I have visited, having proof positive from the state of my sick list from our arrival off King George's Sound to our return, a lapse of a month, during which time I had only slight cases of colds etc'.[18] Assessments of the colony's salubrious climate conditions for British colonisation rarely wavered from this position. That a surgeon accompanied Captain Stirling and Fraser on their voyage indicates the significance of medicine as a science of exploration in the early nineteenth century. The prospect of permanent settlement, of transforming Britons 'from sojourners to settlers', therefore required medical insight into how whites might fare in potential colonies.

Race and environment were important themes of colonial discourse in the eighteenth and nineteenth centuries. Contemporary medical thought held that each race thrived only in its ancestral environment such that emigration from these lands would lead to their degeneration. In the nineteenth century, physicians considered that the human body was inseparable from its environment and that if this relationship was disturbed, disease would result. Permanent settlement at the Swan River, with its alien environmental conditions, could therefore lead to the eventual demise of the resident white community. Consequently, emigration and colonisation were sources of substantial environmental anxiety for Britons throughout the empire. Hippocratic assessments of the potential healthfulness of a region's climate, such as that proffered by Surgeon Clause, went some way to allay these fears and to offer assurance that Britons could adapt and prosper in other parts of the empire.[19]

Meteorological analyses of newly colonised places served then as a complement to the human body as a barometer of environmental change. En route to the west coast of Australia, Captain Stirling instructed his Colonial Surgeon, Charles Simmons, to maintain a meteorological journal for the colony, documenting barometer and thermometer readings, as well as the wind direction, and 'every circumstance of the weather affecting health'. The collection of meteorological observations at the colony commenced soon after their arrival in May 1829.[20] These measurements at the Surveyor-General's Office were supplemented with observations recorded at other loci of colonial science, the Botanic Gardens and the Colonial Hospital.

For potential emigrants, such meteorological analyses provided unassailable evidence of the suitability of a place for permanent white settlement. With its small population, the promoters of Western Australia were especially attuned to the role that its climate could play in attracting settlers. But it had to compete with other colonies in similarly temperate regions such as the Cape Colony and California. In his report to the Admiralty in 1827, Captain Stirling had recommended the Swan River region as an ideal place of respite for those suffering respiratory illnesses.[21] This approach reflected the prevailing belief that a change of environment might restore 'balance' to a sickly Briton. For instance, William H. Stone of the Brompton Hospital for Consumption, observed in the *Lancet* in 1864 that, 'There are hundreds of Englishmen, many in fair circumstances, or practising useful and lucrative handicrafts, who but for our inclement sky would be healthy, useful members of society' if they emigrated to Western Australia.[22]

This colonial medicalisation of space regularly compared and contrasted the suitability of different climates for European health. As such, the dry and temperate climate of the southwest of Western Australia was contrasted with the tropical climes of India. The

Western medical geography of the nineteenth century attributed high rates of disease and morbidity among Europeans in the tropics to the heat and humidity of these climes, especially when these conditions were made worse by the excesses of the colonists.[23] Stirling had long advocated the temperate Swan River outpost as a convalescent station for British troops serving in tropical India.[24] Three decades after the colony's foundation, he maintained that the region's climate was far superior in its medicinal qualities to the Indian hill stations that the British favoured – after all, he explained, 'The climate of the Hills is only Preservative and not Curative in its effects on Indian maladies'. In defence of Western Australia's long, hot summers, Stirling argued that the 'extreme dryness' of the colony's atmosphere, 'prevents that heat from being injurious to health', and did not inhibit the pursuit of 'agricultural avocations'.[25] During his term as Governor (1883–1889), Sir Frederick Napier Broome revived this agenda, revealing the persistence of physiological understandings of the climate in Western Australia, if only for their promotional value.[26] Although such assessments of the colony's healthy climate were inflated, they went some way to allay settler anxieties about its suitability for permanent settlement.

Eastward bound

White explorers had first ventured inland and along the south coast in the 1830s seeking better pastures beyond the Avon Valley. By the mid-1860s, the likes of Henry Maxwell Lefroy and the Forrest brothers had reached the Yilgarn region, just west of what would later become the eastern goldfields. As the settlers' diaries and the exploration journals of these adventurers reveal, however, these were not unknown lands at all. Rather, these lands were the country of the region's Aboriginal peoples. While some tried to repel the colonists' expansion into their territories, others partnered with colonial explorers as guides on their journeys towards the inland.

The further east the explorers travelled, the fewer sources of permanent water they found amongst the york gums, jam wattles and native grasses. During an expedition with Surveyor-General John Septimus Roe in 1836, George Fletcher Moore wryly observed, 'I fear you will think I am only talking metaphorically when I say throughout the greater part of that vast space we did not see as much water at once as there is in your fishpond'.[27] The only sources of water there, these explorers learned, were to be found at the granite outcrops that dot the landscape. Some of these outcrops stand at over 30 m like tors, while others sprawl flat against the ground, and they had long provided water supplies for local Aboriginal peoples and served as important markers along their trading routes.

To maximise the amount of water they could harvest from these granite outcrops, Aboriginal water managers made the most of natural processes. Weathered sections of granite could be scraped away to form rock or 'gnamma' holes where water could accumulate in shallow depressions in the rock face. Alternatively, lighting fires in cracks in the rock face could fracture the granite and form holes or channels to capture rainwater. Water could also stream down the granite rock face and accumulate at the base of the outcrops, which might form a soak if a rock or clay basin lay beneath the surface. In other dry areas, Aborigines reportedly scooped out holes in the clay to trap water. They would then cover the holes and soaks with branches and soil to prevent their evaporation and pollution.[28] When water supplies were particularly scarce, the local Aboriginal peoples were observed to 'move back west' to better-watered areas.[29]

The white explorers were heavily reliant on the knowledge of local Indigenous peoples to find these precious reserves of water 'hidden' in the landscape. Their dependence on Indigenous knowledge unsettles narratives of colonial domination of the environment and offers insights into the nature of the interactions between Indigenous and non-Indigenous peoples during the nineteenth century. Moore, for instance, was the first European to record and publish his impression of the Aboriginal name for these water sources. In his 1842 *Descriptive Vocabulary of the Language of the Aborigines*, he described them as 'ngamar' and gave the meaning as 'a hole or pool of water in a rock'.[30] Later, on an expedition to the Yilgarn in 1864, Barnard Clarkson, Charles Harper and Lionel Lukin took their guide Gyngich, who had assisted other explorers in the area. In his diary, Clarkson noted that he felt certain that 'we shall not be able to get on well without (a guide), with the country in its present dry state'.[31]

That same year, explorer Charles Cooke Hunt embarked on an expedition to map the watering holes of the pastoral country with four Aboriginal guides – Mundal, Tommy Windich, Jimmy, and Cowitch. His diary entries suggest his amazement at the extent of their local knowledge: 'They all seem to know the direction and names of these places'.[32] Perhaps in recognition of his guides' expertise, Hunt attached Aboriginal names to many of the watering holes he recorded, such as 'Youndegin', 'Dodolokine' and 'Gnarlbine'.[33] Once named, Hunt directed convicts to clean out the waterholes and line them with stones to make them more permanent and accessible to (white) people and stock animals.[34]

The establishment of such watering points throughout the inland areas was important for the development of the region's pastoral industry. Near these points, pastoralists set up their homesteads to ensure that there would be adequate supplies for their family and stock. During 'normal' seasons this pastoral utilisation of these sources was not necessarily problematic. But when the rains failed, these waterways became extremely valuable to both the pastoralists and the local Aborigines, particularly when less reliable sources had dried up. These water sources also provided important opportunities for Aborigines to access food because they attracted thirsty game that could be trapped. But the competition with the pastoralists' stock was exacting a heavy toll on many native species, such the malleefowl, the chudditch (or western quoll) and the bilby.[35] The expansion of pastoralism in the southwest in the mid-nineteenth century was therefore disrupting traditional food and water sources, and diminished the hydroresilience of local Aboriginal people.

Building the sanitary city

Although boosters boasted the salubrity of the region's climate to potential emigrants, the colonial environment remained a source of significant anxiety for its residents. Despite the size and isolation of the colony, disease was not uncommon and its incidence seemed at odds with the prevailing faith in the restorative powers of its temperate climate. Anglican clergyman John Wollaston wondered in 1841, 'I do not think this is so pleasant a climate as has been represented'.[36] But it was not until the 1870s that medical thinking began to move away from climate and related phenomena, such as miasma, to other causes of disease.

Although the major settlements of the southwest remained relatively small compared to other cities and towns in Australasia, the colony was not immune to the social and physiological ills that physicians from the mid-nineteenth century were increasingly associating with urbanisation. In Europe and Great Britain, urban spaces had become sources of anxiety because they harboured bad smells (understood as 'miasma' and believed to cause disease), and these concerns soon emerged in the growing metropolises of southern Australia. Although Aborigines had suffered from the introduction of new diseases such as influenza and measles, Western Australia's isolation had served to protect its colonists from epidemics experienced elsewhere.[37] During the 1870s, however, the death rate among colonists from enteric diseases, such as diarrhoea and dysentery, soared.[38]

Coinciding with these outbreaks of disease was the appointment of the colony's first locally born medical practitioner to the post of Colonial Surgeon (1872–1895). Dr Arthur Waylen had undertaken his training in Britain during the 1840s and 1850s, where it is likely he became aware of the Chadwickian movement for sanitary reform.[39] In his 1842 *Report on the Sanitary Conditions of the Labouring Population of Great Britain*, Edwin Chadwick had advocated the provision of pure, piped water supplies and a water-flushed sewerage network to remove disease-ridden filth and refuse. In light of these recommendations, Waylen identified the colony's 'insufficient and contaminated' water supplies as the source of disease, particularly among the less affluent who could not afford to construct tanks for water storage.[40] Those reliant on wells were especially at risk of disease, as backyard cesspools were prone to leaking and polluting the water supplies.[41] Extensive programs to drain the lakes and swamps around the city in the 1860s and the early 1870s had also contributed to the declining quality of the water drawn from these wells.[42]

Although Perth had been likened to a 'dunghill' at a public meeting of the colony's most prominent citizens in early 1878, progress towards improving sanitary conditions was painfully slow. The following year, a correspondent to the *Inquirer* mused that, 'Perhaps if we lost a Governor or a Bishop, several members of Parliament, and all the City Council, something might be done for the preservation of public health'.[43] Yet Perth was not alone; Waylen was also concerned about the state of the eastern districts, particularly York, Northam, and Newcastle (Toodyay).[44] In York, for instance, he reported that residents 'can hardly expect to escape sickness engendered by foul and insufficient water supply'.[45] He attributed the poor conditions to the complacency of the affluent and the municipal councils, whose legal responsibility it was to carry out sanitary duties. But Waylen's views fell largely on deaf ears, particularly as the drier conditions of the late 1870s helped to reduce the contamination of wells, which in turn, lowered the death rate. It was not until the arrival of Governor Frederick Napier Broome in 1883 that the local champions of Chadwickian sanitary reform could prevail.

Broome's first year of office had been marred by outbreaks of diseases such as measles, influenza, typhoid and diphtheria, which were especially felt by Aborigines and the less affluent.

Waylen was quick to alert the Governor to the source of these diseases – the 'sewerage contamination of air and water' – and blamed this state of affairs on the municipal councils. Broome immediately took charge of the situation and appointed a royal commission under Waylen to inquire into the sanitary conditions of Perth and Fremantle. Also appointed to the commission were Waylen's younger colleague Dr Edward Scott, a fellow campaigner for sanitary reform, and zealous temperance advocate Reverend William Traylen – after all, as historian Geoffrey Bolton has drolly noted, 'A man who urged others to drink water had a particular interest in the quality of public supply'.[46]

The evidence presented to the Commission revealed the extent of the inadequate sanitation in the major towns of the southwest, which had failed to keep pace with the growing population. In 1885, the Commission convinced the Legislative Council and municipal councils of the need to overhaul the storage and disposal of waste and sewage, and to replace the 'antiquated and... impossible wells and tanks as sources of [water] supply' for Perth and Fremantle.[47] In the 1880s, corrugated iron had only been recently introduced to Western Australia so its use for rainwater tanks was still confined to more affluent households, while backyard wells could only provide limited supplies of uncertain quality. Doubts were also cast on the amounts of water that could be abstracted from artesian bores around Perth, even though bores had been drilled previously in its vicinity. Lacking the resources to conduct a thorough exploration of this resource, the Government Geologist concluded that, 'There is no likelihood of obtaining a water supply on such principles here'.[48] Lake Monger could serve as an interim measure but eventually, the commissioners believed, Perth's water supplies would be piped from a dam across one of the rivers of the Darling Range. Transporting water to the capital from 30 km away was, however, beyond the finances and engineering expertise of the colonial government.

The slow pace of government action on the commissioners' report led the Perth City Council to organise a supply of piped water to the colonial capital. To date, engineering works in Western Australia had focussed predominantly on the construction of buildings, bridges, roads and most recently railways – vital projects for the colony's economic development. Roads and railways also required watering points to be constructed alongside to water drays and slake the thirst of the steam locomotives. Two engineers associated with these projects were Henry John Saunders, chief engineer of the Midland Railway Company, and his business partner, civil engineer James Barratt. Like many other colonial engineers across the continent, they had trained in Britain, and were public men, serving on the Perth City Council.[49] In 1887, their firm 'Saunders and Barratt' put to the council a proposal to supply water to the capital and to Fremantle from a dam on Munday's Brook, 25 km southeast of Perth in the Darling Range. This site, the *West Australian* later enthused, had been 'apparently intended by Nature for some such purpose'.[50] The Fremantle Council rejected the scheme because it could cheaply source ample supplies from wells in the nearby Fremantle Prison, which had also provided water for the town since the early 1870s.

The proposal was redrafted and the Perth City Council eventually turned to a private Melbourne-based company to undertake the construction of a modified version of Saunders and Barratt's plan. Construction of the Victoria Reservoir on Munday's Brook, a pipeline, and a storage reservoir on Mount Eliza commenced in February 1890, and the waterworks were opened in October the following year. Meanwhile, concerns about the quality of Perth's shallow groundwater supplies had led to the drilling for deeper artesian groundwater, and water from bores drilled at the Perth railway yards in the early 1880s and late 1890s was used to supplement the city's reticulation. Contamination problems at Victoria Reservoir subsequently ensured that groundwater from bores at Guildford and closer to Perth remained the chief source of supply for the city until the construction of Canning Dam in 1940.[51]

Forecasting the weather

Despite the discovery of lead and copper at Northampton in the 1850s, the Western Australian economy remained dependent on the fortunes of its farming industries. Until the 1870s, the major towns of the settlement clung mostly to the coast where the colonists were more familiar with the climate conditions. Some pastoralists also ventured into the lands east of the Avon Valley, which later became the wheatbelt. Small-scale grain farmers also established crops in the Avon Valley and the Irwin–Greenough district, 400 km north of Perth.[52] This northern district offered fertile tracts on the alluvial flats of the Irwin, Greenough and Champion Rivers around the Champion Bay area, and began to attract farmers from York and Toodyay after a particularly dry year in 1850. The district benefitted from a mild winter climate and a period of unusually good rains, and quickly earned the title of the 'granary of the colony'.[53]

The scientific connections between climate and human health had waned by this time, and climate had since become increasingly associated with concerns about agricultural productivity. 'It is hoped', sighed a weary correspondent to the *Perth Gazette* in 1868, 'that something of practical use to the agriculturalist will come in time from the long tables of figures made up and added to day after day and hour after hour by the many attendants at observatories, but as yet these are little better than accumulations of barren facts'.[54] The development of Western Australia's meteorological services beyond this collection of 'barren facts' would provide, some farmers hoped, forecasts of the coming seasons, which would enable them to prepare accordingly. It was not until the spread of telegraph communication in the southwest, and the appointment of a new Surveyor-General to replace the retired John Septimus Roe that the colony's meteorological services improved.

Although the telegraph was relatively cheap and ideally suited to the long distances of the western third, Western Australians were slow to adopt the technology, waiting over a decade after Australia's first electric telegraph was connected between Melbourne and Williamstown in 1854. Western Australia finally caught up in 1869 when Perth and Fremantle were connected. But the colony remained largely isolated until 1877, when Perth was connected by telegraph with Adelaide and the eastern colonies. Meteorologists situated to the east of Western Australia, particularly Sir Charles Todd, South Australia's Astronomical Observer and Superintendent of Telegraphs, had eagerly awaited this connection. Contrary to prevailing opinion, Sir Charles believed that Australia's weather systems moved across the continent from the west coast to the east. His colleagues believed that if this was correct, the collection and transmission of meteorological observations from the west might allow the derivation of weather forecasts for other parts of the continent, where farmers and mariners would especially benefit.[55] Calls for better climate information and weather prediction had been far louder in the eastern colonies than in the west, as droughts and floods in the 1870s had severely affected farmers, particularly those in the more recently settled marginal areas.[56] But Sir Charles could not confirm his hypothesis until the telegraph extended to the western third of the continent and more systematic meteorological observations were recorded there.

This expansion of the telegraph network coincided with a changing of the guard in the Surveyor-General's office. Western Australia's first Surveyor-General, John Septimus Roe, had presided over its early development but a lack of funding and staff had limited his department's abilities to perform its duties. In 1870, Governor Weld appointed Western Australia's second Surveyor-General, (Sir) Malcolm Fraser, who had worked as a surveyor in New Zealand. The newly appointed Surveyor-General reorganised his department and focussed its energies on improving the mapping of the western third. Sir Malcolm also established a Meteorological Branch within his department to coordinate and collect meteorological observations from around the colony. Although meteorological observations had been kept at Roe's office between 1830 and 1876, these had not documented that variable so crucial to Western Australia's agricultural progress – rainfall. The commencement of official rainfall records coincided with a series of particularly dry winters in the south-west.[57] The *Western Australian Times* hoped this project would help to 'remove the stigma cast upon [Western Australia] at a recent meeting of the Colonial Institute that "it had never spent a shilling upon investigations of its climate"'.[58] In Perth, the Meteorological Record Keeper, M. A. C. Fraser, took measurements twice daily within the grounds of his department until the instruments were moved to the Botanical Gardens (now Government Gardens) in 1885. But it took some time for the department to recruit observers and to equip them with the appropriate meteorological instruments, which had to be supplied from Britain.

The slow pace of improvement drew the ire of Fraser, the Meteorological Record Keeper. In 1881, he complained to Sir Malcolm that, 'Nothing is done to record even the bare outline of its meteorology and climatology, a science which at the present time is fast growing in public estimation and importance'.[59] Although Fraser's report was somewhat exaggerated, meteorological record-keeping remained limited and restricted to the coastal areas: of the seven stations reporting to his office in 1880, only York was situated inland.[60] By contrast, New South Wales had ten times as many observers as Western Australia.[61] Attuned to the important role that meteorology could play in agricultural development, Fraser argued for the 'adoption of the volunteer system of rain observations…to obtain a fuller knowledge of the amount of rain that falls annually, how far inland it reaches, and its effects on the yield of crops, etc'.[62] By 1890, the number of rainfall stations reporting to Perth had increased from two to eighty, thanks to the recruitment of volunteers.[63] Although the network of meteorological observers had expanded, conditions over the vast Indian and Southern Oceans remained unknown. Weather forecasts for the southwest therefore remained out of reach.

This increasingly technocratic approach to understanding the climate of the southwest affected the ways that some Western Australians prepared for, and responded to, dry spells. Until the

1880s, prayer for divine intervention in the weather was a common response among drought-affected colonists. During a dry period on the Victoria Plains in 1870, for instance, a correspondent to the *Perth Gazette* opined, 'I think that in our present calamity and general necessity we ought to have recourse to Him who is the only one who can and will assist us – our common mediator Jesus Christ..."Ask and you shall receive", says He, surely we have only to try'.[64] Such prayers had become common throughout the Australasian colonies as well as in England and Scotland since the early nineteenth century. As the century wore on and understandings of the natural world grew, this practice came under criticism in England and Australia.[65] In its place, they advocated human ingenuity and preparedness.

By the 1880s, such sentiments had reached Western Australia, particularly after the Anglican Bishop of Melbourne, Dr James Moorhouse, refused to support prayers for rain in 1882. Moorhouse had thundered, 'God indicated by His providential arrangements that it was His will that we should conserve the water sent to us in winter'.[66] In light of Moorhouse's comments, 'H.E.V.' advised *West Australian* readers that, 'Although we cannot yet bring [rain] from the clouds at pleasure, nor command its distribution, provision might be made to secure it when it does come, and save all we possibly can, instead of letting it run to waste'.[67] Other local commentators suggested the adoption of practices underway in the eastern colonies and the United States, such as artesian boring and dam construction, while others pointed to the achievements of Indian and Egyptian irrigation.[68] Although calls for improved methods of water conservation and supply in the southwest's pastoral and agricultural areas continued until the end of the century, a lack of public and private funds hindered their widespread adoption in the region. Besides, some farmers and graziers might not have considered such improvements necessary: as a contributor to London's *Daily Chronicle* observed, 'The rainfall is sufficient, even with the carelessness with regard to its conservation which now prevails'.[69]

With the achievement of responsible government came calls, particularly from the new Premier, John Forrest (in office from 1890–1901), for the establishment of an astronomical and meteorological observatory in Perth. A surveyor by training, who had worked under Septimus Roe and later Sir Malcolm, the Premier believed that scientific measurements and observations of Western Australia were necessary for its economic progress, and that it would go some way to overcoming the dearth of scientific inquiry in the state. Science was valued as a means to more fully understand the Australian continent, many parts of which, he noted in 1888, had 'never yet been seen by the white man'.[70]

Despite protests from some of his colleagues, Forrest prevailed and in 1896, Western Australia's first observatory was established: a symbol of wealth, science and intercolonial cooperation overlooking the city from Mount Eliza. At its opening, the Premier proclaimed, 'It would remain for all time an evidence of a liberal-minded and enlightened people, who, while doing all that was necessary to foster the material requirements of the colony, at the same time were anxious to promote and encourage intellectual pursuit'.[71] A new Government Astronomer, William Ernest Cooke, was appointed from the Adelaide Observatory, where he had worked under Sir Charles Todd.

Now in charge of his own observatory, Cooke made every effort to improve the collection of meteorological records from around the state in order to create a hub for the collection of meteorological data. Based on these observations, Cooke issued daily weather maps, rainfall reports and forecasts of the day's weather, which were displayed at prominent locations in Perth and Fremantle and in the local newspapers.[72] He also transmitted these observations to the Australian colonies and overseas. Although the meteorological services in Western Australia had received greater attention at the end of the nineteenth century, there does not appear to have been a commensurate increase in the scientific understandings of local climates. Instead, the benefits of these improvements accrued, arguably, to meteorologists east of the colony because Todd's hypothesis had been proven correct after the extension of the telegraph from Adelaide to Perth. The location of the new Commonwealth Bureau of Meteorology in Melbourne from 1908 only served to deepen Western Australia's peripheral position in the meteorological study of Australia.

By the 1880s, the purpose of meteorological inquiry had shifted away from environmental anxieties about health to anxieties about Western Australia's economic development. Western Australia had struggled to attract and retain both settlers and capital, and farmers and pastoralists had found it difficult to establish themselves in the alien environment of the southwest. The coincidence of agricultural growth and government interest in meteorology in Western Australia initiated, therefore, a highly utilitarian approach to the study of the climates of the western third.

Watering a thirsty city

As Perth's waterworks neared completion, the fortunes of the struggling colony turned with the discovery of gold: first in the Kimberley in 1885 and more famously in Coolgardie and Kalgoorlie in the early 1890s. These finds drew thousands of people seeking the latest El Dorado and precipitated an influx of wealth to the colony. Mirroring Victoria's mid-century gold fever, Western Australia's population trebled during the 1890s, drawing many emigrants from the depressed eastern colonies across the Nullarbor. Once their luck had run out, many settled in Perth. All manner of ramshackle accommodation sprang up to house these hordes, including shanties and tent settlements on the city's outskirts; even stables and outbuildings were used for housing.[73] The local authorities had not expected this surge in numbers or the pressures that a larger population would impose upon the rudimentary water and sanitary services around Perth and the eastern goldfields.

The situation came to a head in early 1897 when the onset of an especially dry summer overwhelmed Perth's basic water supplies, which were already struggling to meet demand. Although the construction of the Queen Victoria Reservoir allowed the reticulation of the city, this service was not uniform throughout Perth and the supply network could not keep up with the sudden growth in demand. The limited availability of piping had delayed the extension of water supplies to the more recently established, less affluent fringe of the city's north. Even after these suburbs were reticulated, there was not enough water to pump to meet demand during the summer months. Although many residents could normally supplement reticulated supplies with water from tanks and wells, the seasonal conditions had left these sources dry. In the unreticulated areas of the city, where hordes of new arrivals had settled in camps in East Perth, Third Swamp (Hyde Park) and Subiaco, the drought put further pressure on the polluted wells and swamps upon which people relied for water.[74] Combined with the inadequate provisions for sewage and sanitation, typhoid inevitably struck.

Just months before the drought crept in, the Forrest government had taken over responsibility for the water supply of Perth and its surrounding suburbs. Besieged by complaints from the city's irate residents, the government hastily made arrangements to take water to the people. In some parts of the city, reticulated supplies were restricted to a few hours at a time and in other areas, the shortages were relieved by a water carting service and pumps, but these measures were not enough. Residents had to collect the carted water in buckets and return home with their burden through the sandy streets. To make matters worse, in some parts of the city, the *West Australian* reported, the cart service was erratic: the carts leaked and could not access unsealed roads, and many carters failed to ring their bell to notify the residents that water was available.[75] So great was the desperation of some residents that a water carter was stoned in East Perth.[76]

Not everyone fared so badly. As one disgruntled correspondent wrote to the *West Australian*, 'I am unfortunately a resident of Lamb-street, and for the last weeks have scarcely been able to get a drop of water from the service pipes on my premises, although I am told…[that] the people in the Terrace are never without a strong supply'.[77] On one particular day, according to the Chairman of the Metropolitan Waterworks Board, about 200 residents on Perth's affluent Adelaide Terrace used nearly 30 per cent of the city's scheme water because they could access it before it reached the Mount Eliza Reservoir. Among these profligate users were the Premier, Sir John Forrest and his politician brother, Alexander, who would become the city's Mayor in 1898. A private supply for residents in the comfortable suburbs of Peppermint Grove and Claremont ensured they too were well-watered.[78] Perth's social elite were thus insulated from an unreliable water supply and the impact of drought, often at the expense of less affluent citizens. The uneven experience of the 'Great Water Famine', as the local press dubbed it, revealed the unequal exposure to risk that historical and socio-economic forces had produced among the residents of late-nineteenth-century Perth. The Great Water Famine was not simply a consequence of drought, an aberration in the weather. Rather, it was a distinctly human event.

How had some Perth residents become more vulnerable to drought than others? The introduction of reticulated water supplies had greatly heightened the disparities between the city's most and least comfortable residents. A correspondent to the *West Australian* complained of this inequity in 1897, 'Those persons who lavish so much on their gardens should be stopped from using water while their fellow creatures are unable to get sufficient to quench their thirst'.[79] Certainly, differences in access to water had been an issue prior to reticulation. In some areas, people sourced water from shared wells, which were subject to over-extraction and pollution, while other residents relied upon private supplies. The introduction of reticulated water supplies, however, widened this gulf. The decision of the Perth City Council to engage the services of a private company to construct the waterworks and provide water for the city meant that ratepayers were charged to deliver a profit. Residents in the reticulated areas of the city paid for a piped water supply for one water closet and one bath.[80] For additional water use, such as for the garden, residents paid for a metered service.

In a society where wealth and privilege enabled better access to water, outward signs of this status, such as cleanliness and the cultivation of gardens, became highly significant. Perth's long dry summers made gardening during those months especially difficult without easy access to water. Only those with private supplies or with enough money to pay for reticulated water could cultivate summer gardens. Admiring Perth's 'only garden', the relatively lush Government Gardens, the *West Australian* explained in 1887,

> The drawbacks during summer and autumn are so great in this country that few people will undergo the trouble or expense of keeping a garden in anything like a presentable and flourishing [state]; besides, people here have little leisure, small means, and are all workers, trying to gain a competency or to make both ends meet.[81]

A year-round garden then was a sign of prosperity, for the garden, like the house, had become an important symbol of middle-class status.

Cleanliness too was a symbol of affluence but without a reliable water supply, it was very burdensome to maintain. Once piped water became available in Perth in the 1890s, many affluent residents invested in bathrooms, which allowed them to bathe more frequently than they had previously.[82] Rising concerns in Britain and the United States about the civic importance of cleanliness had also become apparent in the Australasian colonies and by the late nineteenth century, its absence amounted to moral decay and social decline.[83] In addition to focussing citizens' attentions on their physical and moral hygiene, such anxieties shaped social expectations of what constituted a 'good woman'. In undertaking her primary duties of mothering and housework, she was expected to ensure the upkeep of what historian Jill Julius Matthews describes as those five manifestations of population ideology at the end of the nineteenth century: 'public health, infant welfare, social purity, education and child welfare'.[84] The water and sanitation infrastructure of Australian cities and rural towns were not yet adequate, however, for women to easily attain the standards of domestic cleanliness that these ideals demanded.

During the Great Water Famine in Perth in the summer of 1896/97, a resident of Highgate Hill described her plight in the *West Australian* newspaper: 'No bath; barely any water with which to wash one; no laundry work at home – all put out (expensive and inconvenient); water for cooking, etc., economised to the last degree; scrubbing and cleaning quite impossible. This is a shameful and wicked state of affairs'.[85] Another correspondent reported trudging through Perth's sandy streets to obtain water in heavy tubs and buckets – sometimes late into the evening and often 'when the man of the house is away'.[86] These women would not have been alone in their despair. Furthermore, the difficulties of obtaining water in Perth were undermining their efforts to fulfil their duties and obligations as wives and mothers, as 'good women'. This episode of water scarcity, therefore, exposed the gulf between these women and those from more affluent households, who set the feminine standard in Perth.

Due to the unreliable and expensive scheme water, many people in Perth's suburbs returned to their dependence upon the well as an important source of supply. By 1911, another source had become available: the corrugated iron water tank.[87] Compared to the backyard well, the iron water tank offered households the possibility of clean water supplies. Those with access to a tank were arguably more resilient to climate variability and water scarcity than those who relied on the rudimentary reticulated network. Meanwhile, unrestricted access to water and profligacy in its use remained hallmarks of affluence in Perth well into the twentieth century.

Water for the golden west

As more gold discoveries were made, thousands of treasure seekers established settlements in the area around Kalgoorlie and Coolgardie. Situated on the fringe of the desert, water there was in especially short supply. Rainfall in the area is very variable, evaporation is high, and there are limited sources of potable surface and underground water. Like gold, then, water was precious on the eastern goldfields. Besides its importance to sanitation and health, it was vital for the mines where it was necessary for processing ore, and for the transportation of people, stock and goods to and from the fields, whether by foot, hoof or rail. But what the prospectors perceived as scarce, the Kalamaia Aboriginal people of the Yilgarn region had long found sufficient.[88]

After the discovery of gold on the eastern goldfields, demands for permanent water supplies in the area had waxed and waned with the seasons. Under these variable conditions, water was imported to the goldfields, first via camel train and then, once the railway line had been extended to Coolgardie in 1896, via steam locomotives. Both modes of transportation required clean water supplies along their routes and the water trains were especially thirsty: they consumed at least half their load in the round trip. Another important source was the region's groundwater reserves but these were found to be extremely saline and were purified using condensers. These wood-fired condensing plants ate through vast quantities of timber from the surrounding woodlands, and in many cases exhausted local bore and mine water reserves. Once they were stripped bare, red dust choked the goldfields and even more water was required to keep this scourge at bay.[89]

The government also constructed dams or 'tanks' on the goldfields to collect rainwater but the volatility of the seasons and high rates of evaporation diminished their effectiveness. The rainfall record of the nearby town of Southern Cross demonstrates the extreme climate variability of the region in the early 1890s: both 1889 (258.5 mm) and 1890 were particularly wet years, which were followed by a near drought in 1891 (132.8 mm). The years 1892 (383.5 mm) and 1893 (356.7 mm) were again wet but 1894 (130 mm) and 1895 (137.7 mm) returned the area to drought.[90] Miners and prospectors made do with constructing small dams and exploiting the region's gnamma holes, which had long sustained the local Aboriginal people. As the European population grew and became permanent, and existing water supplies became more expensive and difficult to obtain, the case for seeking alternative sources of water supply strengthened. Without water for the goldfields, Premier Forrest believed, the mines would be abandoned and the flow of funds vital to the state's prosperity would dry up.

The Forrest government had worked especially hard to provide the eastern goldfields with services to overcome their isolation and to ensure their continued prosperity. Investment in such public works, Forrest's government hoped, would ensure that the mining settlements became permanent and that the industry's wealth would continue to grow. By 1896, just a few years after the first finds in the area, railways and telegraph wires criss-crossed the state's inland to connect Perth to the goldfields. This communication and transportation infrastructure had significant structural consequences for the Western Australian economy. They ensured the primacy of Perth and Fremantle as the colony's centres of commerce and trade, at the expense of Albany and Esperance on the south coast. And this economy, in the 'waterless waste' of the eastern goldfields, became dependent on permanent and abundant water supplies.[91]

By early 1896, a plan to water the eastern goldfields was in place. Water would be transported uphill from a dam on the Helena River in the Darling Range near Perth via a pipeline to Coolgardie and Kalgoorlie, nearly 600 km away. The river was dammed at a narrow gorge with a 30 m high wall of solid concrete, which created the world's highest overflow weir at the time. The Mundaring Weir inundated nearly 10 km of the rugged and sparsely populated Helena valley. The pipeline would follow the eastern goldfields railway line and have eight steam-powered pumping stations. Even the engineering schemes of ancient Rome had not been so bold as to pump water such a distance, let alone uphill.[92] The state's chief engineer, Charles Yelverton O'Connor, who had designed this plan, argued that it would supply water to the eastern goldfields quicker and more cheaply than the existing arrangements and other proposals. The other schemes had included sinking deep artesian bores; condensing saline groundwater; and constructing large reservoirs on the creeks running from the northwest. On Thursday 22 January 1903, O'Connor's scheme was opened but he was not present at the ceremony. With his project mired in controversy, and he the subject of vicious criticism from the local press, O'Connor had taken his own life less than a year before his vision was realised.

Even when the scheme was completed, the larger mines continued to use the salty water pumped from the mines or water shafts, which was substantially cheaper than the water from the pipeline. Historian Geoffrey Blainey argues that this preference for local water sources shows that the pipeline was an unwanted and unnecessary enterprise. He also disputes O'Connor's analyses of the rainfall statistics available for the goldfields and asserts that the area was not the 'desert' that the engineer had purported it to be. As a result, Blainey concludes, O'Connor had overestimated the need for water supplies and overcapitalised on the project. Only the insatiable thirst of the growing Kalgoorlie mines, Blainey considers, 'saved the pipeline from becoming an economic failure'.[93] The extent to which the settlements of the eastern goldfields were vulnerable to water scarcity then was perhaps more fear than reality. At the very least, the decision to construct the pipeline reflected an unwillingness to change or a lack of support for adaptation to local conditions. More significantly, it reflected the economic and political importance that the Forrest government attached to the prosperity of the goldfields.

Despite the lingering questions over the need for its construction, the Goldfields Water Supply Scheme is remembered as much for its audacity as for the demise of its protagonist,

O'Connor. It remains one of the only schemes to pump water out of the southwest region and allowed, as the Forrest government hoped, the closer settlement of lands between the Avon Valley and the goldfields in the early twentieth century, which developed the state's wheatbelt. Yet the forging of what Forrest called a 'river in the desert' dramatically altered the ways that people related to water on the goldfields.[94] This engineering feat mitigated the need for settler Australians to adapt to the environment such that extravagance, rather than prudence, became the natural approach to water use on the margins of the desert.

The availability of permanent fresh water supplies swiftly transformed the approach to water use around the homes of many goldfields residents. Such a shift was particularly evident in household gardens and municipal parks. Limited supplies of water on the goldfields had mostly prevented gardening along European lines, and as historian Andrea Gaynor has found, many 'learned to do without', making do with different plants and other pleasures. Once the Golden Pipeline was opened, garden tastes changed dramatically in the direction of a more conventional style with lawns and shrubs.[95] This change in the types of gardens cultivated on the goldfields supports the contention that the availability of water supply mediates patterns of water use in modern homes. From this perspective, the connection of goldfields homes to reticulated supplies served to 'domesticate' water, whereby it became readily available inside the home at the easy turn of the tap. Consequently, many residents became seduced by this seemingly endless supply of water, and more water begat more water use.

Reliant then on water piped over a vast distance, from a dam far away, the people of the goldfields arguably became more vulnerable to water scarcity than ever before. But they were not alone: water now underwrote, and could therefore undermine, the entire colonial economy.

2

Thirst in the Golden West:

Suburban and agricultural expansion (1901 to 1945)

In 1900, the *Western Mail* declared, 'With their colony stronger, sturdier, and more vigorous in its septuagenary than ever it was, the colonists can well look forward to the close of the century exhibiting indications of local development and progress that will place Western Australia in even a more important position than she now holds in the Australasian group'.[1] During the first half of the new century, Western Australians witnessed massive suburban and agricultural expansion that was sustained by political vision, but that was founded on the provision of water supplies. The Western Australian population more than doubled, Perth swelled, and the number of rural holdings increased more than three-fold. But this expansion was not without its costs, as the southwest's vulnerability to climate variability and water scarcity was further entrenched.

These vulnerabilities, arising from permanent settlement, a lack of local knowledge and an economic reliance on water, were exacerbated by an unprecedented passion for development. Writing in the early 1980s, historian Lenore Layman observed, 'From the earliest days of colonial self-government to the present decade, from Sir John Forrest to Sir Charles Court, an ideology of development has been a major characteristic of Western Australia's political culture'.[2] The enduring features of Western Australian developmentalism have included state intervention to initiate, promote and implement development; an anti-Canberra refrain; and, according to Layman, an 'inflated rhetoric which has claimed for Western Australia a "greatness" to match its geographical area'.

The government focus on development was by no means unique: the state has played a particularly central role in economic development in Australian history, as it has in other settler capitalist societies. Moreover, the very notion that development required instigation, as opposed to being something that occurs spontaneously, was first advocated in Wakefieldian tracts from the Australian colonial context in the 1830s and 1840s. Imperial occupation and exploitation provided the ideal environment for scientific experts to flourish. Their role in development had emerged in the context of social unrest in Victorian Britain where liberal thinkers both possessed the means to portray progress as a rational and desirable goal to the populace, and believed they could direct and manage the path to its achievement.[3] Despite the incipience of Western Australia's scientific bureaucracy until after World War I, successive State governments relied upon an emerging faith and credibility invested in science and technology. These governments nonetheless shared an almost reckless optimism about the prospects for managing and achieving economic development. These elements of Western Australian developmentalism and their deployment to engineer the state's wheatbelt, to irrigate the southwest, and to beautify Perth's suburbs in the early twentieth century served to render people in the southwest particularly vulnerable to variations in climate and water supplies – to running out.

Making the last great wheatbelt

Following Western Australia's achievement of self-government in 1890, the state's first Premier, Sir John Forrest, had endeavoured to realise his vision of agricultural expansion throughout the southwest region. The recommendations of the 1887 Venn Commission, appointed to inquire into the stagnant state of colonial agriculture, led the Forrest government to legislate to provide assistance to farmers. This included making more land available to settlers, bank loans to facilitate improvements to their lands, and agricultural advice on farming methods.[4] Forrest envisaged agriculture as the stable foundation for economic development and self-sufficiency that the more volatile mining industry could not provide. The focus of this rural expansion would be the development of a wheat industry between the Darling Ranges and the semi-arid interior of the state. Although this region would be later described as 'hydraulically difficult country', its relatively flat landscape made it ideal for cropping and it became the last of the wheatbelts to spread across the Anglo-world.[5]

Although the colonial government attempted to promote the expansion of farming into new areas through a land grant system, the scale of the endeavour and the difficulties of attracting overseas investment to Western Australia led the government to assume a central role in the development of the wheatbelt region. Its role was not confined only to financing farmers, but also extended to establishing vital infrastructure in the region. The vast distances of the state's emerging agricultural areas from the capital, Perth, and its port, Fremantle, demanded an efficient means to transport goods and people throughout the southwest. Private efforts to establish land grant railways in the 1880s and 1890s had been beset with problems, which had delayed the completion of the arteries vital to 'opening' up new lands and slowed the progress of closer settlement. To spur land settlement after 1901, the government undertook to ensure that all agricultural lands and townships had access to rail services within a radius of fifteen miles (24 km). The emerging pattern of agricultural settlement then aligned closely with the networks of timber and steel snaking across the region. Between Federation and the outbreak of World War I, over 4,000 km of rail were laid in the wheatbelt, which helped to treble the amount of alienated land from nearly 3 million hectares to nearly 9 million hectares.[6] In the age of the steam locomotive, both farmers and their main mode of transport depended on permanent, reliable supplies of fresh water, and were therefore vulnerable to water scarcity in the dry lands of the emerging Western Australian wheatbelt.

Some farming areas and railways benefitted from their proximity to the Kalgoorlie Pipeline. As Premier Sir John Forrest had long envisioned the agricultural development of the state's inland, he and his Chief Engineer, O'Connor, had also seen a role for the 'Golden Pipeline' in supplying water to the state's drier eastern districts. Indeed, Forrest alluded to such intentions in his speech at the official opening of the Eastern Goldfields Water Scheme at Kalgoorlie on 25 January 1903: 'The completion of this beneficent work must have an immense influence in promoting the advancement of these goldfields and *in assisting the settlement of the country through which the pipeline passes*'.[7] The Goldfields Water Supply Scheme became an important source of water for many parts of the wheatbelt in its early development, not least because this expansion of services could help to offset the maintenance costs of the pipeline.[8]

With most wheatbelt farmers undertaking both wheat cropping and sheep rearing, those without access to reticulated water supplies had to find alternative sources to meet their domestic needs and to water their livestock. The government's rail engineers had already encountered the difficulties of sourcing reliable water supplies in the streamless areas of the wheatbelt.[9] They had overcome the lack of surface water by exploiting and excavating the gnamma holes and soaks that had long sustained the region's Nyoongar and Kalamaia Aboriginal peoples. Many farmers developed their own supplies, such as natural reservoirs, wells, and 'earth tanks' or dams, as well as collecting water from their roofs.[10] In his memoir *A Fortunate Life*, Albert Facey recounts digging a soak near Narrogin and later, sinking a dam on a property in Jitarning. Others carted water from government dams that the government had excavated at eight-mile (13 km) intervals.[11]

Although these supplies were sufficient when the seasons were favourable, the slim margin for error in the wheatbelt was exposed when rains fell short of expectation. The winter of 1911, for example, put these supplies to the test, when the wheat-growing districts registered an average of 12.54 inches (318.5 mm) of rain, at least four inches fewer than the preceding four years. These dry conditions resulted in a significant reduction of the average yield of wheat per acre and many farmers in the central and eastern agricultural areas had to cart water over significant distances for their stock.[12] Dependent on run-off from rainfall, dams had proven ineffectual when they were most needed.

The Scaddan government's (1911–16) response to the drought conditions displayed the hallmarks of a technocratic approach to the management of climate variability and water scarcity. Rather than question the historical and social dimensions of natural hazards such as climate variability, a technocratic approach advocates the application of scientific prediction and centralised management of hazards to mitigate disasters. Historical geographer J. M. Powell suggests that the most visible official response to the 1911 drought was a shift away from the reliance on earth tanks to well-boring.[13] The newly established state-wide Water Supply, Sewerage and Drainage Department despatched teams to drill for water in the dry districts and their success was largely dependent on the accessibility and quality of the groundwater. These wells were located near roads at regular intervals for watering travelling stock. The department also improved soaks and rock holes; cleared dam catchments to improve run-off; erected corrugated iron tanks at railway sidings; and ensured these supplies were more accessible to farmers. These were technocratic solutions designed to stave off the abandonment of the agricultural areas and to insure the wheatbelt against future shortages. Although many desperate farmers no doubt welcomed these measures, this hasty provision of water supplies arguably gave farmers and the government the confidence to go on, and to ultimately extend into the most agriculturally marginal areas of the southwest.

These solutions also had ramifications for the resilience of the local Aboriginal people to dry seasons. In early September 1913, Commissioner of the Wheatbelt George L. Sutton presented a lecture to an audience at the Western Australian Museum. Using lantern slides he showed his audience the state's agricultural progress and explained, 'Yesterday our wheat lands were a blacks' camp. To-day they are being broken up with the most suitable implements modern engineering can devise'.[14] Sutton's speech deployed the rhetoric of white development: that agricultural cultivation was a moral act of civilisation, which rendered white Australians superior to Aboriginal peoples, who seemed to lack the ability to till the soil. Yet many Aboriginal people remained in the emerging agricultural areas: historian Anna Haebich estimates that about three-quarters of the southwest's Aboriginal population (possibly 1,500 people) lived in the wheatbelt region at the turn of the twentieth century.[15] The development of Western Australia's wheat industry dramatically transformed Nyoongar and Kalamaia lands and limited the ability of many Aborigines to access country. In turn, these restrictions on Aboriginal mobility constrained their capacities to cope during periods of water scarcity. Consequently, many Aboriginal people were compelled into dependence on white settlements from which they were comprehensively marginalised, and therefore, rendered especially vulnerable to climate variability.

Prior to agricultural development, much of the land that would become the wheatbelt had been held under pastoral lease. The pastoralists had used the waterholes and moved their stock according to the seasons. Many of the region's Aboriginal people had been able to gain employment from the pastoral stations, and the station owners permitted them to hunt and camp on the land. Although the Aborigines had been paid a pittance, this employment had at least allowed them to continue to live on country, to maintain some elements of traditional life, and to access important soaks and waterholes, although many of these had been damaged by stock.

As the wheatbelt slowly began to take shape, however, these opportunities for the region's Aborigines to remain on country were greatly diminished. As the large pastoral properties were broken up, fenced, and cultivated, many farmers prohibited Aboriginal access to their landholdings. Furthermore, employment opportunities for Aboriginies were reduced as their labour was only required for clearing bush and seasonal labour.[16] The extensive land clearing required for agricultural development also affected the water quality of the region's few streams, which became brackish and unsuitable for drinking. The Aborigines who had been granted farms found their efforts subject to stringent conditions. Although they were denied the land titles for their farms, the Lands Department still expected them to carry out a host of improvements to their blocks, such as building a farmhouse and fences, as well as clearing and cultivating portions of the land. If these requirements were not met, the department could reduce the size of their land or resume their properties. But many of these farmers lacked the capital to make these improvements and could not use their properties as security for bank loans.

Such were the constraints on their endeavours that it was nearly impossible for them to survive and with the onset of dry conditions in 1911, many Aborigines were forced to move into camps on the outskirts of the wheatbelt towns. In one town, Katanning, the Aboriginal population increased fivefold in three years, from forty to over 200.[17] Accompanying this shift was a threefold increase in the reliance of Aborigines on government rations, from about 1,000 in 1907 to over 3,000 by the outbreak of World War I. As Haebich explains, the state of the camps quickly degenerated: 'There were no proper shelters, no sanitary or rubbish services, no fresh water, no work and only meagre rations of flour, tea and sugar for the elderly and dependent mothers, issued by the police on behalf of the Aborigines Department'.[18] Many perished as a result of these conditions. The development of the wheatbelt, therefore, forced many Aborigines into a condition of dependency on the state and onto the fringes of the white settlements in the southwest, where their hydroresilience continued to be eroded.

Irrigating the southwest

Other calls to the government to provide additional water supplies came from an unlikely source: the farmers in the coastal districts of the southwest. In the late 1890s when O'Connor's pipeline was under construction, the *Western Mail* had observed, 'Surely it is one of the satires loved of nature, that, while an elaborate scheme is necessary to supply the goldfields with water, a whole district in the South-West is piteously demanding help to get rid of a superabundance of it'.[19] Farmers in the Harvey area had found that they could withstand the dry summer months by irrigating from the drains that had been excavated in the district to alleviate frequent flooding. This water was mostly used for the irrigation of pastures to ensure that cows were in milk throughout the year. In addition to dairy pastures, farmers irrigated orchards, vines, vegetables and lucerne on the productive alluvial soils of the Pinjarra Plain.

Hoping to replicate the perceived successes of the Mildura and Renmark irrigation settlements in Victoria and South Australia, many farmers in the Harvey area were demanding in 1911 that the government provide irrigated water supplies.[20] A government irrigation scheme, these farmers believed, would provide a more efficient and equitable system than using the drains.[21] After government engineer Hugh Oldham surveyed the rivers from the Serpentine to the Collie to gauge their suitability for impounding water, Harvey Dam was constructed on the Harvey River in 1916 and its waters distributed through open, unlined channels. Only time would tell whether it would be the panacea that irrigators had hoped for.

Battling on the home front

'Grim drought stalks almost the length and breadth of the land', reported the *West Australian* on New Year's Day, 1915.[22] Many farmers had had little opportunity to recover from the dry conditions of 1911 and now, the entire agricultural area was affected, with some areas receiving less than half their 'average' rainfall.[23] These conditions caused the state's wheat yield to plummet by 80 per cent in a single year.[24] For many older farmers, it was the worst season they had ever known. John Payne of Perenjori remembered the emotional toll of this drought on his father, who 'put his head in his hands and he cried there for a long time'.[25] The region's Aboriginal farmers were especially affected as they generally lacked the financial resources to persevere and many were forced to leave their properties.[26] The coincidence of the drought with the commencement of World War I saw many young rural men enter the armed services in order to escape economic hardship.[27]

The overwhelming effects of drought and World War I on Western Australian farmers led to grave doubts about the southwest's suitability for agricultural development, particularly regarding wheat farming in the eastern wheatbelt. These were environmental anxieties that questioned the state's economic future. As most of the wheatbelt had only been settled after 1908, many farmers had struggled to establish themselves under difficult climatic and financial conditions. Compared to the longer-established farmers, the more recently established farmers lacked the capital and experience to cope with the dry conditions. In 1916, the State government established a Royal Commission to inquire into the state's agricultural industries; its findings for the wheatbelt and the southwest coastal areas were published the following year. Echoing assessments of the struggling Swan River Colony, the commissioners concluded that, 'The settlers, in brief, have up to the present, conducted a vast experimental farm for the benefit of the State and posterity'.[28]

Evidence to the Royal Commission revealed just how vulnerable some wheatbelt farmers were to climate variability and water scarcity. Witnesses reported that farmers were 'inclined to lose heart' as their debts mounted. In the Victoria district, noted a witness, 'Half of them do not get a decent feed a week'. He wondered, 'It puzzles me to know where the records of rainfalls come from and how it is that people were rushed out into these dry areas'. Of great concern to the commissioners was the amount of rain that the wheatbelt farmers could expect to receive. Farmers at Ajana and Carnamah considered the government had deliberately misled them with promises of 14 and 16 inches of average annual rainfall respectively. The government, argued these farmers, had not only overlooked the drought of 1911 but also assured them that it would be 'absolutely droughtless'.[29] The government had estimated that 12 inches of winter rainfall was sufficient for cropping and rainfall data suggests that, on average, most of the agricultural areas received this amount. But averages can be misleading. Until the end of World War I, this wheatbelt area was 'critically marginal' because of the rudimentary nature of the farming techniques employed at that time.[30]

For the government and the farmers on the wheatbelt's eastern fringe, the drought of 1914 had exposed a mismatch between their ambitions and their knowledge. The testimonies above suggest that at least some farmers blamed the government for the consequences of the drought. This position reflects the prevalence of a technocratic approach to disaster prevention at this time. As this approach fosters the concentration of scientific expertise in government bureaucracy, concern about the preparedness, prediction and control of natural hazards is abrogated to specialists. This process, according to geographer Kenneth Hewitt, 'quarantines disaster in thought as well as in practice', which in turn, places the responsibility to ameliorate disaster squarely on the government.[31] After all, the Western Australian government had promoted farming in the areas that were affected by drought and the state's farmers were vital to its plans for agricultural development. If farming on the margins was to continue, the government would have to do more to improve the hydroresilience of wheatbelt farmers.

Although the commissioners acknowledged the limited climatic knowledge of the outer limits of the wheatbelt, they attempted to impose a 'safe' limit for cultivation. Upon the request of the commissioners, Surveyor-General Frederick Slade Brockman charted a line of 'reliable rainfall' across the western third, recalling Goyder's Line in South Australia. In creating this lesser-known Brockman Line, the Surveyor-General constructed a region in which farmers could safely expect climatic conditions that were suitable for wheat-growing. But it would do little to help farmers avoid or ameliorate droughts in the future; instead, the rainfall limit had 'merely reinforced the prevailing definition of wheat-growing areas'.[32] It served then to support the continued development of these districts that were vulnerable to running out.

After all, drought in the southwest was believed to be an abnormal phenomenon. As the commissioners reported, 'Our rainfall…is more regular than in any of the other States, and we should be able to look forward to regular yields as our methods of cultivation improve'.[33] Failure on the land, therefore, was not seen to be due so much to the land or climate but to the lack of effort and determination of the farmer.[34] The 'land is usually good to those who use it well', observed the commissioners, 'While it rejects infallibly the unfit and the ineffective'.[35] Good farmers were those who applied the latest innovations in wheat growing, such as the new wheat varieties and superphosphate that were helping to support the agricultural expansion into the drier wheatbelt region.

To assist farmers in their endeavours, the Commission demanded better services from the state's Department of Agriculture. To foster the productivity of the inland areas, the Forrest government had established a Bureau of Agriculture in 1894, which later became the Department of Agriculture. The purpose of the Bureau was to regulate the farming industries and their produce, and to communicate scientific developments that could help farmers. Its establishment of experimental farms in the inland areas reflected the pattern of agricultural expansion at this time, with the intention of demonstrating that farming could be successful in these areas if they followed the department's directives.[36]

One of the methods that the department advocated to wheatbelt farmers was dry farming. These techniques had first emerged in the 1870s and 1880s on the Great Plains of the United States.[37] The dry farming concept was based on the idea that cultivating bare fallow left behind a layer of fine dust, which would prevent evaporation and conserve soil moisture. The concept was enthusiastically adopted in eastern Australia at the turn of the century, and later brought to Western Australia by George L. Sutton, the first Commissioner for the Wheatbelt.[38] The fervour for fallow captured the imagination of the agricultural technocracy throughout the nation's cereal regions because it was supposed to make the most of the limited rainfall in these districts. Through technical advice, competitions and Agricultural Bank lending policies, technocrats urged farmers to frequently cultivate bare fallow to increase their yields and improve their ability to withstand dry conditions.[39]

Although the commissioners had found fault with some of the government's more reckless policies, the vital importance of agricultural development remained unquestioned. The definition of a 'safe' rainfall limit counted for little when overseas markets beckoned and allowed farmers to roll the dice when it came to the seasons after the war. Sooner or later, their luck would run out.

The orchardists in the Harvey district, meanwhile, faced the problem of too much water. The predictions of large water losses; the uneven distribution of water through ungraded, established citrus groves; and waterlogging problems were all borne out. Despite their much shorter examination of the challenges facing the Harvey district compared to their study of the wheatbelt, the commissioners were scathing of the state's first large-scale irrigation scheme. 'The application of water to land', they surmised, 'is not an open sesame to profitable production'. The main grievance for the commissioners was the scientific and technical advice, or lack thereof, that had guided the scheme's development: 'There is perhaps no more regrettable feature of the Harvey question than the fact that no attempt was made to show the settlers how to use the water'.[40] The government had deployed inexperienced engineers on the project and failed to address the significant drainage issues affecting the region. Likewise, Oldham's decision to use unlined channels, rather than the piped network that the farmers had wanted, proved a failure. Water could easily escape the channels, causing considerable damage to the poorly drained orchards. Irrigators and their governments continued to face the problems of 'too much' and 'too little' in their ongoing efforts to overcome the summer 'drought' in these districts.

Watering the suburbs

After Federation, Australians across the new nation continued to gravitate toward cities along the coastline. In Western Australia, Perth and its expanding suburbs grew nearly threefold between 1911 and 1941, from 87,000 to 229,700.[41] By the end of World War II, more Western Australians lived in Perth than in the state's agricultural areas, eclipsing the metropolitan dominance in the other states.[42] The expansion of the suburbs transformed the environment of the Swan Coastal Plain as land was cleared to make way for new homes. The water use of suburban householders also underwent a dramatic change, with each Perth resident in 1941 consuming nearly twice as much water per day as they had in 1911. Before World War I Perth residents on average consumed nearly 164 L each per day; by the beginning of World War II, they were consuming nearly 306 L.[43] How did the people of Perth become so thirsty?

Some of this increase in water use can be attributed to the increased domestic availability and accessibility of water, which resulted from the growing reticulation of the suburbs. The opening of the Kalgoorlie Pipeline in 1903 had created a disparity in comfort between those on the eastern goldfields and those in the suburbs of Perth, who remained largely reliant on artesian bores.[44] Even in the early 1920s, the *Daily News* would opine, 'There is no sound reason why the people of the metropolitan area should be treated differently from the rest of the population'.[45] This would later become a complaint from regional residents about the special treatment given to the people of Perth. Reticulation was frequently used as an enticement to prospective residents of the new suburbs and the Metropolitan Water Supply, Sewerage and Drainage Board (MWSSDB) increased its water storages to ensure these supplies would be available. By 1913, all areas serviceable by gravity had been reticulated. Yet nearly a quarter of Perth's homes remained without piped water and they depended on wells and neighbours' taps for their supplies. Many more continued to rely on galvanised iron tanks to supplement the expensive and unreliable reticulated supplies.

In the summer of 1919–20, the State government introduced water restrictions on suburban water use. These restrictions forbade the use of mechanical sprinklers as the tendency of Perth residents to consume more water during the hot summer months threatened to exhaust the city's water supplies. This move was met with a backlash, evident in the local press. The *Daily News* raged:

> The Water Supply Department's order issued to-day is a humiliating confession of incapacity and short-sightedness, and the citizens whose gardens are doomed, and whose pride will very soon be humbled in the hot sand, will be altogether justified if they demand either that the Government...shall either straightway take steps to ensure that no future summer will find us in such evil straits, or will get out of office and give the reins to another set of Ministers who will be...more given to exercise of initiative in big things and capable of administration in the departments which count so largely in our everyday life.[46]

The editor of the *Sunday Times* argued that the government had failed to keep pace with the growing metropolitan population.[47] Although per capita consumption had remained steady, total consumption had doubled since 1911, from about 5,000 ML to over 10,000 ML in 1921.[48]

The press argued that as the 'people [paid] for water, and [paid] dearly', they should be able to use their scheme water when, where, and how they wished.[49] Such an argument suggested a growing consumer activism among Perth water users. In their study of water shortages in London in the 1890s, historians Vanessa Taylor and Frank Trentmann consider that such activism represented a 'politics of entitlement and provision in times of scarcity', which arose from the growing connections between the private and public spheres that reticulated water supplies had helped forge.[50] In both London and Perth, these connections were technical as well as political. The linkage of households to pumping stations and dams, which allowed changes in private routines, became the basis for political mobilisation regarding water services. In Perth, such protests not only reflected public dissatisfaction with the state of the city's water supplies, but also the sense of vulnerability among householders to running out of water. This vulnerability arose from anxieties about the nature of Perth's urban and domestic spaces.

Anxieties about the health and progress of white Australians were important influences on the relationships that people in the growing suburbs of Perth had developed with water supplies and their (natural) surrounds by the first half of the twentieth century. Their anxieties led them to develop dependencies on abundant water supplies to overcome their fears, which in turn, weakened their hydroresilience. The application of the concept of environmental anxiety to the households and suburbs of Perth in the early twentieth century questions the security that Australians have long associated with suburban spaces.

After World War I, concerns were reignited among the British and Australian middle classes about racial degeneration and the decline of the empire.[51] Roused by these worries, reformers from an emergent class of technocrats sought to overcome social ills through the application of principles of science and reason to domestic life. Stimulating this movement were widely held anxieties about the influence of the environmental conditions inside and outside the (middle class) home on the mental and physical health of Western Australians. Meanwhile, the body and its health had come to be seen as a closed system, distinct and separate from its environment. White Western Australians, for instance, no longer perceived the climate characteristics of the temperate southwest as potentially threatening to their health. Likewise, belief in the miasmic theory of disease transmission had been replaced with germ theory.

These ideas point to the paradox that historian Linda Nash has observed in modern public health: 'it insisted on the need for certain environmental changes while denying that the environment played an active role in the production of disease'.[52] In line with the modernist state, advocates of these environmental reforms were mostly male members of an emerging professional middle class seeking to reshape Australian suburbs, homes and families according to their vision of a modern society. Local advocates such as William Saw, Billie Bold, Harold Boas, and also Bessie Rischbeith, called for the improvement of parks and playgrounds to better the lives of Western Australians, particularly children.[53] Water was an important, yet often overlooked, tool to achieve such reform. By the end of the nineteenth century, a constant water supply had come to symbolise modern civilisation and these supplies provided the means to cultivate attractive open spaces. These suburban environmental anxieties, therefore, kindled an ever-growing thirst in many Perth householders and diminished their hydroresilience.

The State government had blamed Perth's avid gardening enthusiasts for the need to implement water restrictions. The Minister for Water Supply, William George, likened their water consumption to 'criminal practice', and considered their behaviour mindless because 'in the sandy soils of Perth this flooding of water simply leached out the plant food'.[54] But without liberal amounts of water, cried one newspaper correspondent, 'the City Beautiful...must quickly become little better than an arid desert'.[55] The government's condemnation was an affront to the city's gardeners who had invested heavily in improving the appearance of their properties. It also revealed the cultural significance that suburban gardens had attained in Perth by the early decades of the twentieth century.

The expansion of Perth's reticulated water supplies had coincided with changing expectations about the appearance of the city and its suburbs. During World War I, Perth's town planning movement emerged and its influence on suburban development in Western Australia was almost immediate. The leaders of the local movement widely advocated the importance of orderly planning, open spaces and aesthetic appeal in town planning.[56] In an address to the Royal Society of Western Australia in 1918, William Saw, the President of the Town Planning Association of Western Australia, argued,

> We must do better than we have done in conserving our baby life by taking greater care of the mothers of the nation...by getting [them]...out...to zones...where the children, in their garden villages, will grow up taller, stronger, deeper in the chest, freer from physical defects, happier, more likely to be stalwart effectives in the wealth-creating forces of the State, and less likely to be a burden on the community.[57]

Attention to these details not only reflected the ideals of the international town planning movement, but was also evidence of the prevailing anxieties about the influence of the environment on the mental and physical health of suburban Western Australians.

Creating the ideal environment for the healthy moral and physical development of Western Australian children was the duty of the state's citizens. Citizenship, therefore, was closely related to the upkeep of the home's outward appearance. The maintenance of the front garden in particular was, according to historian Robert Freestone, 'vital in order to attain the coherence of the garden suburb street picture, which secured a demonstrable sense of community'.[58] Garden fashions called for a large expanse of lawn, with flowering shrubs and annuals. The backyard, in contrast, was a utilitarian space for household tasks.[59] To allow the front garden to deteriorate would undermine the bonds of the community, reflecting imperial anxieties of racial and imperial decline during the interwar period.[60] These middle-class concerns about the appearance of the front garden led to the heavy use of water outside Perth homes, particularly during the long summer months. During the period of water restrictions, some local businesses appealed to these anxieties and encouraged gardeners to invest in windmills and engine pumps to 'be independent' and to ensure 'a free water supply, when you want it, and where you want it'.[61] It was only after this period of water restrictions that locally produced gardening publications for local conditions, such as the *Western Australian Gardening Guide*, advocated methods of water conservation.[62]

Although Perth's gardening enthusiasts were especially outraged at the restrictions on their water use, many householders found their reticulated water supplies had literally dried up. In March 1920, the *Daily News* declared, 'Last night practically the whole city was without water, and the sorry spectacle was witnessed, even in Hay-street West, of mothers taking their pitchers to those who possessed wells, to obtain water with which to wash their children before putting them to bed'.[63] Reminiscent of the Great Water Famine of the late 1890s, this account highlights the domestic relationship between women and water, and the ways in which gender relations shaped water use in suburban Perth in the early twentieth century. At the time of these shortages, nearly half the average household's water consumption took place inside the home.[64] These shortages exposed the dependence of many suburban households on relatively reliable scheme water supplies to maintain the fragile veneer of civility, and in doing so, revealed the vulnerability of the middle class home to running out.

As the account suggests, such episodes of water scarcity interrupted the domestic routines of Perth's housewives and domestic servants, adding to their heavy household burden.[65] After all, argued the local magazine *Western Homes*, they were responsible for making the ideal home: 'The parents of the West must strive to make a home of their house, and create that "Home Influence" which does not distort but beautifies; which makes *good citizens*, and not bad parasites or dangerous criminals'.[66] Despite the improvements in household plumbing and the availability of piped scheme water, the domestic duties of most housewives remained arduous. Even homes that were connected to scheme water supplies did not necessarily have a kitchen sink and its associated drainage system. For instance, on the eve of World War I, a visitor to a comfortable home in suburban Claremont would have found the kitchen tap near to the floor, dishes washed in a bowl, and the dirty water tipped out daily.[67] Although indoor plumbing had become commonplace around World War I, some homes still remained without these conveniences in the 1940s. Nevertheless, these rudimentary technologies helped Perth housewives to conform to middle-class expectations of the domestic sphere. As sociologist Kerreen Reiger notes, their daily chores had become transformed into 'scientific work of national importance' – of creating good citizens.[68] Water scarcity, however, rendered these technologies impotent and exacerbated suburban anxieties of running out.

When restrictions were re-imposed in the following years, newspapers called for lunch-hour demonstrations, warning the government that 'the people [would] not tolerate further fooling. Water must come, or, on the first opportunity, the Government must go'.[69] In 1923, over 2,000 Perth residents attended a meeting at the Rosemount Theatre in North Perth chaired by Premier James Mitchell – a sizable crowd for a city of just under 155,000 people. Their concerns were with both the quality and the quantity of the reticulated water supplies. The disgruntled assembly brought with them specimens of the unpalatable water supply, which they said resembled 'liquid sausage meat' and 'tomato sauce'.[70] Premier Mitchell told the audience, 'It is not the desire of the Government in any way to hamper the laudable desire of the people to beautify their surroundings'.[71] He then announced his government's plan to extend the reticulation system to meet the needs of the city, which would include new service reservoirs on Mt Eliza, Mt Hawthorn and Melville Park in the late 1920s; new catchment dams at Wungong and Churchman's Brooks in 1925 and 1929, respectively; and lastly the Canning River Scheme, which was finally completed in 1940. Until the completion of Canning Dam, however, restrictions were intermittently imposed on garden water use to reduce the draw on the city's limited supplies.

By the end of World War II, nearly all the houses in Perth had running water. In the southwest's agricultural areas, however, fewer than half of the homes had a coldwater tap inside the house.[72] Raising the living standards of the state's farming families became an important project after the war. This post-war project reflected the enduring strength of the environmental reform movement that had shaped the development of Perth's suburbs and homes in the first half of the twentieth century. The movement's emphasis on the role of the suburban and domestic environment in improving the moral and physical health of (white) Western Australians played a significant part in entrenching the thirsty lifestyle that would characterise Perth after the war. It was a lifestyle that would leave the suburbs vulnerable to running out.

Development and depression between the wars

Following the Armistice, James Mitchell's National Party government (1919–24; 1930–33) renewed its support for expanding agricultural settlement throughout the heavily timbered southwest and into the increasingly marginal lands of the eastern wheatbelt. Its policies of group, soldier and unemployed workers' settlement schemes in

Western Australia reflected efforts throughout the British Empire to colonise the dominions with British emigrants, to aid economic recovery, and to reward soldiers for performing their wartime duties. In Western Australia, it was anticipated that the agricultural production of these settlers would offset the decline of the gold industry and overcome the shortage of dairy supplies and associated products in the state. Furthermore, the schemes would relieve post-war unemployment and the influx of migrants would boost the state's prospects for economic development.[73] But the difficulties that the group settlers faced as they attempted to establish a dairy industry in the coastal southwest made success in the wheatbelt vital, for both the state's economy and the government's reputation.

There were doubts within the scientific community regarding the wisdom of Western Australia's agricultural expansion into the eastern districts. Among them was the outspoken physiographer Griffith Taylor, who had worked for the Bureau of Meteorology and participated in Scott's *Terra Nova* expedition to Antarctica prior to his appointment as foundation head of the geography department at the University of Sydney in 1920. In contrast to the resounding call for 'Australia Unlimited' after the war, Taylor counselled caution. He considered that large areas of Australia remained uninhabited by Europeans because these lands were suitable for neither agriculture nor pastoralism. In his 1911 book *Australia* (and its subsequent editions), Taylor had denoted a large portion of inland Western Australia as 'useless'. This description was clearly at odds with the expansionist agenda of the Mitchell government. Perceived then as a poisonous influence, Taylor's textbook was banned from the state's school and university curriculums in 1921.[74] The rejection of Taylor's cautionary message was symptomatic of the revival of long-held anxieties regarding the progress of a White Australia. Moreover, it was representative of the widespread disregard for scientific advice when it conflicted with a political agenda of development and land settlement – a trend that only deepened the vulnerabilities of the southwest to variations in climate and water supplies.[75]

Taylor's former employer, the Bureau of Meteorology, was far more supportive of the Western Australian government's development agenda. In 1929, for instance, the Bureau published the *Results of Rainfall Observations in Western Australia*, the fifth in a six-volume series in which the rainfall statistics of each state were compiled. The Bureau's representation of Western Australian climates complemented the expansionist agenda of the recently elected Collier government (1933–36), which pursued policies similar to its predecessor. In the preface to report, the Commonwealth Meteorologist, Henry A. Hunt, explained:

> The records of past seasons...are...indispensable to the success of most of the young inexperienced men on the land. By a study of his districts' [sic] seasons in the past, a young settler is able to avoid under or over expenditure in increasing his stock or in improvements. The records will show him how many good, bad, or indifferent years he is entitled to expect; and he will not be over optimistic after a good season nor over pessimistic after a bad one. The records, too, are made available for the guidance of the majority of established farmers and graziers, for memory of past seasons can rarely be relied upon.[76]

This passage suggests that the Bureau's system of data collection and recording was closely aligned to agricultural interests. Furthermore, this system could provide more accurate knowledge of the local weather than experience on the land itself and, in time, offer the Bureau the means to 'tame chance' in the state's agricultural areas.

Reflecting its alliance with the development project of the State government, the Bureau of Meteorology directed its advice towards the Western Australian 'Primary Producer'. One of the volume's articles extensively detailed the relationship between rainfall, wheat yield and geographic location. The authors argued that dry fallow practices had the 'virtual effect of increasing total available rainfall for each harvest season'.[77] The eastern limits of the wheatbelt, therefore, could be expanded beyond the existing 10-inch wheat-growing line to the 7.5-inch line. This would embrace towns such as Norseman and Southern Cross.[78] They also assured readers that improvements in agricultural science would provide the means for settlers to develop the eastern margins of the wheatbelt. Indeed, in 1929 after a year of light rainfall, the state's Department of Agriculture had boasted, 'Not many years ago a season such as the last one would have meant disaster to the majority of wheat growers'.[79] This shared belief in the possibilities for settling and indeed cultivating Western Australia's semi-arid inland saw the Bureau of Meteorology and the Department of Agriculture portray the climate of the region's marginal lands as safe and secure for European agriculture, bolstering the government's development aspirations.

Whatever reservations farmers might have had about these districts were easily overcome with the favourable market and climate conditions of the decade following the end of the First World War. With generous government subsidies and scientific advice, wheat farming edged eastwards beyond Brockman's line of reliable rainfall. The government was deaf to the possibility of insufficient rainfall in these increasingly marginal eastern lands, and fortunately for them, the seasons were wet.[80] Historian Geoffrey Bolton has suggested that Mitchell's farming successes in the long-established and better-watered Avon Valley during the 1890s when markets had been more favourable, 'had led him habitually to underestimate the hazards of pioneer farming'.[81] The wheat acreage trebled during the 1920s, as farmers were spared dry conditions like those experienced in 1911 and 1914. The total area under crop grew from nearly 650,000 to nearly 2 million hectares between 1920 and 1930, and in the wake of the Empire Marketing Board's 'Grow more wheat year' of 1929, wheat production reached a record of 53.5 million bushels in 1931.[82] By the 1930s, Bolton explains, the region had become 'the heartland of Western Australia; their creation, from a dry and uncultivated wilderness, was the State's proudest and most recent achievement'.[83]

Building a 'discriminatory sanitary order'[84]

Bringing this land into cultivation, however, came at great cost to the region's Aboriginal population. With few employment opportunities on the land after the war and fewer places to camp, more Aborigines had drifted into the outskirts of wheatbelt towns, particularly in the Midlands, Avon and Great Southern districts. But these towns were unprepared for this growth in the Aboriginal population and few white residents were willing to accommodate their presence. Already forced off country, many of the region's Aborigines were now forced out of the towns and onto local reserves or into native settlements like Carrolup (est. 1915) and Moore River (est. 1918). According to historian Anna Haebich, the number of gazetted town reserves in the area increased from six in 1920, to thirteen by 1925. Among the reasons for their expulsion was the view that Aborigines were carriers of disease, and needed to be kept separate from the otherwise healthy (white) population.[85] As historian Alison Bashford has observed, 'The discourse of public health was always an effective mode for the expression and practice of racism, since health, hygiene and cleanliness were one significant way in which the "whiteness" of white Australia was conceptualised'.[86]

Already considered filthy, Aborigines were forced onto small reserves that were often situated near town rubbish dumps and sanitary depots, where there were inadequate water supplies and sanitation facilities. Aboriginal elder Robert Bropho recalled that in the early 1940s at the Eden Hill camp on the eastern outskirts of Perth, the 'only water supply was from the local tip on the hill near the swamp' or from shallow wells they dug in the ground. In their tin billies they collected water with 'tadpoles and the slime on the top', 'with a bit of flavour in it from human piss and human shit'.[87] In the wheatbelt, future Governor-General Paul Hasluck observed:

> Clothing is seldom washed – how can it be when there are no facilities for doing so or even vessels in which to carry sufficient

water into the dwelling? The human body goes unwashed because there are no baths and often little water, though a swim now and again, in some not too distant waterhole helps a little.[88]

Although Hasluck was sympathetic to their plight, more often than not, white Western Australians blamed the Aborigines themselves for their state of health and living conditions. As historian Linda Nash argues in the Californian context, 'The *habits* rather than the biology of non-white groups would be… frequently cited to explain higher rates of sickness and death'.[89] Confined to the margins of white settlements on reserves, camps and in settlements, Western Australia's Aborigines could be better regulated and controlled under what historian Gyan Prakash has described in nineteenth-century India as 'a discriminatory sanitary order'. Protecting the health of white Western Australians, as in colonial India, required the containment of the putative source of disease – the bodies, habits and homes of Aborigines.[90]

The apparent disregard among Aborigines for hygiene and cleanliness were grounds for their exclusion from the very institutions that could have helped to improve their living standards and employment prospects. After all, according to prevailing middle class ideas about citizenship and environment, unclean people were 'bad citizens'. Across the southwest in towns like Quairading, Katanning and Koogan, parents of white school children demanded the expulsion of Aboriginal children on the grounds that they were an unhealthy physical and moral influence.[91] These demands were finally answered on the eve of the hotly contested state elections of November 1914, when the 'offending' Aboriginal children were expelled from the schools under a provision in the *Education Act 1893*, which authorised the exclusion of children deemed to be 'injurious' to the health, welfare and morality of their classmates. As Haebich observes, the persistence of this practice into the late 1940s denied access to state education for generations of Aboriginal children.

Likewise, Aborigines were denied proper hospital care on the grounds that their lack of hygiene posed a danger to white

patients.[92] Finally in 1915, the government agreed to the demands
of the wheatbelt towns to shut down the town camps and move
Aborigines into segregated settlements.[93] This discriminatory
system trapped the Aborigines of the southwest as surely as in
a prison, where their abilities to uphold their traditional sources
of resilience to climate variability and water scarcity were
systematically eroded. Their lack of access to clean water not only
excluded the southwest's Aborigines from education and health
care, but also initiated a cascade of discriminatory effects that
continued to be realised long after World War I.

High and dry

Despite the heady days of the 1920s, the prosperity of many
Western Australian farmers was coming to an end. During this
decade, wheat farmers in other parts of the world had begun to
reduce their wheat acreages in response to an uncertain economic
outlook. But in Western Australia, wheat remained king. The
state's economy had become heavily reliant on the buoyant
overseas wheat market and the State government was convinced
that Western Australian wheat could continue to compete against
exports from Canada and the United States on British and
European markets.[94] Seduced by the prosperity of the 1920s, many
farmers took on debts to expand their farms. On the eve of the
new decade, however, commodity prices collapsed with disastrous
consequences for the state's wheat farmers.

The severity of these economic conditions had left many
farmers financially exposed to the onset of dry conditions in
the mid-1930s, which lasted until the end of the decade. Aside
from 1939, rains across the state's agricultural areas were below
average and the drought of 1940 rivalled that of 1914 in its severity.
Invasions of ravenous rabbits, grasshoppers, and emus decimated
the surviving crops, exacerbating the farmers' plight. For the
eastern wheatbelt, circumstances were especially dire – farmers

there were over-laden with debt and faced with poor seasons, poor soils and poor prices. Nearly 3,000 abandoned their properties in subsequent years.[95] As Premier Wilcock observed, 'All their labour has gone for nothing, all their hopes have been dashed, and the only result has been disaster'.[96]

In contrast to the Scaddan government's response to the dry conditions during World War I, the Wilcock government (1936–45) decided that it was no longer tenable to encourage wheat farming in the more marginal eastern districts. The human toll had become too great, and the State government lacked the funds to continue to subsidise their agrarian endeavours.[97] In 1940, the Commonwealth joined with the Wilcock government to initiate a 'reconstruction' program to support a shift from wheat to sheep in these 'marginal' areas. The main criteria for 'marginality' were the rainfall and cropping statistics of these areas: about 250 mm (1011 inches) of annual rainfall was classified 'marginal'. Five of these marginal areas were targeted for reconstruction: Ajana to Kalannie; Kalannie to Southern Cross; Dulyalbin; the Lakes/Ravensthorpe District; and Esperance/Salmon Gums. Over a period of four years, about 2,000 farms were reduced to fewer than 800 farms, which now relied on sheep as their main source of income. The Commonwealth assisted with purchasing stock as well as fencing material and water supplies, while the State government helped by reducing land prices, reclassifying soils, increasing acreages by linking abandoned properties, and writing off debts. The intention of these reconstruction efforts had been to reduce the vulnerability of farmers in these marginal areas to variations in climate and the market. Yet when better seasons and prices returned after World War II, along with improvements in soil science, wheat growing resumed in these marginal areas.

Meanwhile, the dire economic circumstances of the 1930s proved to be a windfall for the irrigators of the southwest. After World War I, soldier settlers had struggled to establish themselves in the poorly drained areas around Harvey and Waroona. The Public Works Department had to pump additional irrigation water from the Brunswick and Serpentine Rivers, while irrigators in the Waroona district found that their reliance on drains was inequitable and inefficient.[98] With Commonwealth assistance, the Mitchell government embarked on a scheme to put over 6,000 unemployed men to work on public works around the state, which included irrigation and drainage works at Harvey. At last there was the cheap labour and political will to build the water supply and drainage infrastructure for which irrigators had pressed for a decade.

Construction began on raising the height of the Harvey Dam in late 1930, and the work was completed in 1932. This included expanding the size of the Harvey irrigation district and excavating additional channels. Drakesbrook Dam at Waroona commenced construction in 1930 and finished in 1931. That year, despite protestations from many farmers in the Collie district who were unconvinced of the benefits of irrigation, work began on the Wellington Dam, which was completed in 1933. Finally, the construction of a drain to divert the Harvey River ensured that by 1934, water from the river no longer spread across the plain but ran straight into the Indian Ocean. In the meantime, the irrigation channels were lined with concrete to reduce the loss of water from seepage, and the paddocks underwent grading, to ensure the more even and efficient distribution of water. So successful was irrigated dairy farming during this period that construction began on the damming of Samson Brook in 1939, and surveys commenced for the Stirling Dam on the Harvey River, which was completed after World War II.

For many people in the southwest, the end of the war signalled an end to the hardships of drought and depression, and that an exciting new chapter for the state was about to unfold. Many Western Australians were swept up in the developmentalist zeal of the post-war years. But in their prosperity lay the foundations for running out in the future.

3

A Million Acres a Year:

Engineering post-war prosperity (1945 to 1969)

During the 1960s, the Liberal Brand government proudly declared that a million acres of land was being released to agriculture each year. This pronouncement reflected the spirit of progress and development that had defined post-war Western Australia, particularly in the 1950s and 1960s, and the State government's ongoing role as the shrewd architect of this growth. After World War II, waves of European migrants boosted the state's population and stimulated the construction industry, which was building the new suburbs extending along the Swan Coastal Plain. Western Australia's industrial development was unfolding south of Perth, the Ord River Scheme in the far north was advancing, and lucrative mining projects were underway. For the agricultural areas, the Korean War had also ushered in a boom with soaring wool prices, and farmers benefitted from the mostly wet seasons that followed World War II. These were heady days indeed for many Western Australians.

The Western Australian brand of developmentalism that had emerged in the 1890s and blossomed in the interwar years continued to hold sway after World War II. In the 1950s, however, the characteristics of this brand underwent subtle changes. The conservative State government was now increasingly receptive to large-scale foreign investment in resource development and was willing to relinquish its ownership and control of these ventures.[1] Furthermore, the government offered lucrative incentives to attract this capital, such as generous provision of infrastructure. The allure of development often meant, however, that the benefits of such projects were not adequately evaluated. Guiding all of these elements, argues historian Lenore Layman, was a rhetoric 'centred on the concept of "bigness"', whereby the scale of the state's industrial development in the 1950s and 1960s might at last match Western Australia's geographical area.

Local and national scientific research was also infused with this ethos of development, which shaped both the nature and application of science and technology in the post-war era. Despite the social and economic implications of droughts in Australia, it was not until well after World War II that scientific attention was turned to their study. In 1955, the Chief Scientific Officer of the Bureau of Meteorology, James C. Foley, undertook a continent-wide study of droughts. He concluded that no corner of the continent was safe from drought and warned, 'The rapid expansion of primary industries in Australia in the last fifty years has greatly increased the vulnerability of the economic position of the country to drought'.[2] This direction of scientific and technological research was especially evident in the development of the southwest's water resources and the study of local climates where it was deployed in response to environmental anxieties over aridity and fertility.

In the words of local poet Dorothy Hewett, however, 'The seeds of our destruction have always been imbedded in our brutal innocence'. The post-war pursuit of technocratic solutions to providing water to suburban and rural Western Australians in the southwest encouraged their dependence on plentiful water supplies, which rendered them vulnerable to the shortcomings of a large and inflexible system. Combined with the wet seasons of the 1950s and 1960s, the reticulation of the suburbs and rural areas allowed them to become complacent about the possibilities of climate variability and water scarcity. This post-war faith in the unfettered progress of the state produced a widespread lack of caution – an approach that diminished the hydroresilience of many Western Australians to running out. But none so much as a large proportion of the southwest's Aboriginal population, who were mostly excluded from the government's vision of a prosperous post-war Western Australia.

Big Water in the west

With a renewed emphasis on the ethos of national development in the post-war period, the fruits of the enduring partnership of government and science were particularly evident in the field of water management. Australian governments understood the command of the nation's water resources as vital to the recovery and economic development of the nation. Critics of this landscape authorship later noted the great environmental and economic costs that the grand water projects of the post-war era entailed. After World War II, state and national governments invested heavily in supplying both rural and urban Australians with a seemingly infinite supply of water, creating a system of what cultural theorists Fiona Allon and Zoë Sofoulis have called 'Big Water'. They argue that 'Water authorities (shorthand for a mix of government, corporate and statutory bodies) have evolved to deliver residents a counter-rational (but nation-building) fantasy of an unending, seasonally invariant flow of water'.[3] In the southwest of Western Australia, Big Water comprised the Metropolitan Water Supply, Sewerage and Drainage Department (MWSSDD, later the Metropolitan Water Supply, Sewerage and Drainage Board) in Perth and the Public Works Department (PWD) in rural areas.

The rise of Big Water after the war was a product of the partnership between government and science that had become an important characteristic of the modern Australian technocratic state. The principal architects of Big Water in post-war Western Australia were the engineers of the state's PWD, with the financial and political backing of the state and Commonwealth governments. In the early 1950s, two key players in this nexus of government and science were the engineering head of the PWD, Russell Dumas, and the Minister for Works, David Brand, who later became the state's longest serving Premier (1959–71). They shared a zeal for the state's economic development and focussed their efforts on stimulating both industry and agriculture. For Dumas, as he declared to a meeting of the Institute of Engineers of Western Australia in 1939, 'Engineering is the basis of civilisation'. During the 1930s, he had designed and overseen the construction of Wellington Dam and the Collie irrigation area, as well as the raising of Harvey Weir and the extension of Harvey's irrigation area. He had also played an important role in the development of the controversial Ord River Scheme in the state's far north in the 1940s, which became a monument to the Big Water era. Together Dumas and Brand negotiated for the establishment of the Anglo-Iranian Oil Company's (now BP) refinery at Kwinana, south of Perth, and for the expansion of reticulated water supplies throughout the state's agricultural areas. Big Water was vital to their endeavours to develop Western Australia to its fullest potential. As Sir David later recalled, his colleague 'had undoubted faith in what could be done in Western Australia through water supply'.[4]

Although Big Water was intended to overcome inadequate water supplies in particular locales, it had unforeseen consequences for the vulnerability and resilience of those living in both the reticulated and unreticulated areas of the southwest. In Western Australia, the post-war development and expansion of suburban and rural water supply schemes enabled the enjoyment of higher living standards and greater amenities. However, these local testaments to Big Water also led many consumers and industries into a dependency upon continuous and copious water supplies, which had hitherto been interrupted by water restrictions. Those outside the scope of Big Water relied upon their own private supplies. This independence may have fostered a greater degree of hydroresilience to running out than those who drank from the cup of Big Water. But few took the opportunity to prepare themselves for drier times.

Watering the wheatbelt

Of the potential constraints to Australia's post-war progress, the Commonwealth Rural Reconstruction Commission was especially concerned about the paucity of water in the continent's farming regions. Its *First Report* (1944) warned, 'In the long run water supply will be the limiting factor in Australian expansion. Australian agriculture will in time need all the water which it is possible to conserve'. This environmental anxiety about a natural constraint on the nation's agricultural development recalled interwar concerns about aridity and the future of white settlement. The revival of the state's flagging agricultural industries and the visions of post-war land settlement required the investment of engineering expertise to provide water to the wheatbelt.

The challenge to the nation was not simply one of collecting every falling droplet but of engaging in the enormous task of directing water to thirsty rural regions. This was especially pressing in the wheatbelt region of Western Australia, the home state of the Rural Reconstruction Commission's Chairman, Deputy Premier Frank Wise. His state's PWD engineers had already identified water as a potential limitation on agricultural development in the wheatbelt. In the early 1930s, for instance, PWD engineer B. S. Crimp had reported, 'I am confident...it will be essential to have fresh water from the Darling Ranges to cope with the demands in the Wheat Belt'. His colleague, Edward Tindale, later invoked the state's grandest engineering scheme in support of reticulating the wheatbelt. He argued in 1936 that, 'The proposal may not [seem] economically sound for a start, but I am convinced that it will be ultimately consummated. The Coolgardie Scheme did not look too convincing when it was undertaken'.[5] The post-war agenda of national development helped to breathe life into this nascent vision of Big Water.

Although some wheatbelt towns had been connected to the Kalgoorlie Pipeline before the war, the State government considered these supplies insufficient for its post-war vision of land settlement and agricultural development. In terms of the conditions ideal for European agriculture, the State government considered that the lands east of the Darling Ranges presented 'hydraulically difficult country'.[6] There are no extensive river systems and the streams there are mostly intermittent and brackish, due to the low relief and accumulation of salt over millions of years. In addition, the wheatbelt climate is characterised by wet winters and dry summers, with less rain in the inland areas. Dry seasons during and after the war had renewed environmental anxieties about the likelihood of running out and the consequences of such an event for agricultural production and farming families. Fears of Japanese invasion following the fall of Singapore in early 1942 and the possibility of evacuating coastal populations inland had also highlighted the paucity of potable water supplies in the agricultural areas.

These anxieties could be overcome through the reticulation of the wheatbelt – the inland consolidation of Big Water in Western Australia. In 1946 the State Labor government, now led by Frank Wise (1945–47), announced its intention to bring 'stability to an important area (the wheatbelt), increase production, and most importantly, to bring an essential social amenity to the people' through the Comprehensive Water Supply Scheme (CWSS).[7] Such a technocratic response was necessary to enable increased stocking of sheep in the wheatbelt after the war. Sheep had come to play an increasingly important role in Western Australia's agricultural enterprises and the booming wool prices after the war bolstered this position. These sheep required water supplies during the long summer months, which could not be guaranteed in the dry agricultural areas. A Commonwealth study concluded that, 'There is no prospect of increasing materially the stock–crop ratio for these parts until further supplies can be obtained'.[8]

In addition to its utilitarian purpose, the government also intended the CWSS to improve the standard of living of farming families in the agricultural areas. According to the PWD, many farmers and their families had long been making do with meagre supplies, 'suffering all the discomforts and social disabilities which a shortage of water entails'. The Rural Reconstruction Commission had undertaken a survey of the agricultural areas that had found only about half of the homes surveyed considered they had adequate water for house and garden purposes.[9] Living standards were least adequate in the northeastern districts. The State government and the Commission were primarily concerned with raising the living standards of farming families to those enjoyed by their suburban cousins. These aspirations to replicate the lifestyle of those living in the cooler and wetter coastal suburbs of Perth in the drier agricultural areas contributed to environmental anxieties about water resources and land settlement in the wheatbelt. Without reliable water supplies, the State government correctly argued, it would be difficult to attract and retain a rural population, which would stymie post-war projects of land settlement and population growth.[10]

These concerns reflected a broader theme in post-war political thought of the unique economic, political and cultural value of rural Australia to the nation. This national preoccupation with the livelihoods and lifestyles of those engaged in the agricultural and pastoral industries was the manifestation of what social scientist Don Aitkin has described as 'countrymindedness'. Although the drift to the city was already underway, the persuasiveness of this idea of countrymindedness was bolstered by the fact that nearly half the state's population resided in the rural districts in the mid-1950s. As wool prices peaked thanks to the Korean War, the administrator of the Perth Royal Show, Sir John Dwyer, emphasised this vital role of primary production to all Australians in 1951: 'The wellbeing of all of us depends on the efforts of the man on the land, for the land is the basis of a country's prosperity, and on its wise usage depends the future comfort, wealth and happiness of the nation'.[11] The ideology of countrymindedness not only informed protectionist agricultural policies but also combined with anxieties of a vast and empty land vulnerable to invasion to encourage large-scale migration and land settlement schemes. In many cases these schemes, laced with agrarian mythology, lured inexperienced farmers to marginal lands, and left them vulnerable to running out.

After several rounds of deliberations between the State government and the Commonwealth regarding the extent of federal financial assistance, a slightly smaller, 'Modified' version of the CWSS proceeded in 1946. Under the modified scheme, the reticulated area was reduced by two thirds, from 12 million to 4 million acres, with the number of towns served shrinking from thirty-five to twenty-three, and the population falling from 56,000 to 32,700.[12] To serve the great distances of the southwest's agricultural areas, the scheme operated in two sections. The first section supplemented the Golden Pipeline to create the Goldfields and Agricultural Water Supply, which serviced 1.6 million hectares of the central and northeastern wheatbelt from Mundaring Weir. The second, the Great Southern Towns Water Supply Scheme, pumped water from the Wellington Dam on the Collie River to the southern wheatbelt.[13] The CWSS would provide a metered water supply service to the boundary of every farm holding in the reticulated area. Shortly before the first stage of the scheme was completed in 1962, the State government decided to extend the scheme to the towns of Corrigin, Dalwallinu, Pithara, Ballidu and Kojonup, and soon after with Commonwealth assistance, Gnowangerup, Broomehill, Kalannie, North Koorda, North Bencubbin and Wilgoyne. The existing walls of both the Mundaring and Wellington reservoirs were raised to increase their storage capacities to supply the reticulated lands of the wheatbelt.[14] By the time of its completion in 1960, Wellington Dam was the largest dam in the southwest. For the towns that were connected to the CWSS, their reticulation marked momentous occasions in their local histories.

An Achilles heel

The promise of Big Water was that of continuous, reliable and copious water supplies. Payment for this scheme water then was not just for its supply but also for its ongoing supply and quality – for the guarantee of permanency. To deliver this promise, water reserves had to be stored and their quality protected. Those who used Big Water were therefore vulnerable to fluctuations in the quality and quantity of supplies through their reliance on a distant source over which they had little personal control. Although Big Water reflected the interests of powerful players in the State government and PWD, it came under threat from another consequence of developmentalism: secondary salinity. The same developmentalist ethos that had given birth to Big Water had also fostered a lack of caution, particularly with regard to agricultural land settlement. As historian Geoffrey Bolton has noted, 'Agricultural scientists tended to be damned when they brought bad news and praised only when they brought good'.[15] This was especially evident in the persistence of land clearing in the Wellington Dam catchment.

By the early 1950s, the PWD had become concerned about the growing levels of salinity in the Wellington Dam as a result of land clearing in its catchment. But its warnings fell on deaf ears amid the din of developmentalism. In 1961, the PWD wrote to the Department of Agriculture requesting that 'no further land be alienated' and suggested that 'clearing control of land already alienated will assuredly be necessary'. Although the relationship between land clearing and salinity had been recognised at the turn of the century, the Department of Agriculture dismissed the notion of restricting land release 'because of the large areas that would have to be left uncleared'.[16]

The PWD's warnings were voiced at the height of the Brand government's program to clear 'a million acres a year' and went unheeded. By the end of the 1960s, the area of land under cultivation in Western Australia had nearly doubled from 14 million to 25 million acres, which was unprecedented in national history. This disregard for salinity was even more disturbing, given that the paucity of potable water supplies in the agricultural areas had been a significant factor in the post-war development of the CWSS. By the 1980s, the deterioration of the catchment had become so severe that Wellington Dam ceased to supply water to the Great Southern Towns Scheme and was replaced by the Harris Dam on the Harris River, north of Collie, in 1990. This disregard for scientific advice when it conflicted with the ideology of developmentalism threatened to undermine Big Water and render those who relied upon its function vulnerable to running out.

At the 35th State Conference of the Country Women's Association in 1959, State President Lilian Higgins declared, 'If I was asked to assess the value of any Government to this country I would do so according to the number of miles of water pipe lines that were laid during their term of government'.[17] The extension of Big Water across the wheatbelt was indeed a feat to be celebrated, representing a testament to Australian engineering expertise and a commitment to the future of rural Western Australia. When the Minister for Works and Water Supplies John Tonkin officially opened Brookton's connection to the CWSS in December 1958, the district's schoolchildren were given a holiday to mark the occasion. Likewise, in Kulin, the connection to the eastern goldfields line in 1966 supported the town's growth and allowed for the building of a local swimming pool. The secretary of the Dowerin museum, Gwen Friend, later remembered that the town's connection to the scheme was the 'most important event in the history of the town'. The arrival of piped water to these towns brought an end to pan toilets and allowed many households to nurture more sophisticated gardens. Yet it also rendered them vulnerable to running out because they were now dependent on a distant source of water supplies.

Drowning the southwest

With the growing post-war demand for dairy products in Perth, the southwest's irrigators joined the wheatbelt farmers' clamour for 'water, water everywhere!'[18] They needed more water for their irrigated summer pastures of paspalum, rye grass and cocksfoot. Amid prevailing anxieties that Western Australia was 'every year menaced by the fear of drought' because 'she cannot, at present, store enough from one year's end to another to afford water security', the engineers of Big Water complied with the irrigators' demands.[19] There were several choices available for increasing the water supplies available to the Harvey District: the Harvey Dam could be raised; a new dam could be built on the Harvey River downstream of the existing dam; or a new dam could be built on Logue Brook. This latter option was favoured because of its close proximity to irrigable lands between Yarloop and Wagerup, which reduced the costs of distribution. It was also the cheapest scheme. Construction of the dam on Logue Brook was commenced in 1960 and completed in 1963, bringing an end to a four-year period during which the rationing of irrigation water had been necessary. Three years later, engineers completed the construction of Waroona Dam, which provided water for the Waroona Irrigation District. Finally, in 1969, work finished on the small Glen Mervyn Dam on a tributary of the Preston River, which stored water for controlled release down the river during summer.

Interestingly, the large gains in terms of water storage since the 1930s were not accompanied by a corresponding increase in the area covered by the irrigation districts. Irrigators had instead shifted to a more intensive system of watering their pastures.[20] Such a method of cultivation not only required large water storages, but also resulted in the application of large quantities of water to swampy lands. Big Water was required then to ensure both abundant water supplies and sophisticated drainage systems to remove it. In the Collie District at least, dependent as it was on water supplied from the Wellington Dam, this intensive watering added vast quantities of increasingly saline water to the soil and the watertable, contributing to secondary salinity in the area. These large soakings also combined with phosphatic fertilisers to produce algal blooms and nutrient pollution in the Peel–Harvey estuary: problems which were already emerging in the late 1940s and early 1950s.[21] Big Water, therefore, helped facilitate the development of water-intensive methods of cultivation, which had significant implications for the land and water resources, as well as the ecologies, of the southwest irrigation districts.

Slaking the suburbs

In addition to the rural expressions of Big Water in the post-war era, its snaking networks of water supply were also facilitating Australia's evolution into a suburban nation. Although Perth was the smallest of the mainland capital cities, it was the fastest-growing metropolitan area in the nation, swelling by 22 per cent from 1947 to 1954.[22] By 1959, over 60 per cent of the state's population was living in the suburbs along the Swan Coastal Plain.

This suburban growth was not without its costs. For instance, Aboriginal camps were forced, sometimes violently, to make way for housing estates lest they offend suburban ratepayers.[23] The steady march of the suburbs also took its toll on nearby bushland. As Frank Crowley lamented in his 1962 history of South Perth,

> Almost everywhere the bulldozer, the builder, and the bitumen have obliterated the last signs of the state of nature. Gone forever are the banksia, the sheoaks, the blackboys, and the Christmas trees. And in their place stand the neatly built, wholesome-looking homes of brick, fibro or asbestos.[24]

Less visible was the growing impact of the suburbs on the south-west's water resources. By the mid-1970s, water consumption in Perth had almost tripled since the end of the war – increasing from about 60 to nearly 170 ML per day.[25] The post-war affluence of suburban Western Australians had combined with political rhetoric to 'conceal' Big Water, encouraging Perth households to indulge in the fantasy of endless water supplies. The sole dependence on these water supplies that suburban Western Australians were able to develop left many of them unprepared and vulnerable to running out in the dry 1970s.

Post-war political aspirations for the economic growth of Western Australia shaped the development of Big Water along the Swan Coastal Plain. Dry seasons after the war had highlighted the limits of the region's existing sources of water supply and the expected post-war growth of the metropolitan population would only stretch these supplies further.[26] Furthermore, ambitions for the state's industrial development around Kwinana also demanded the provision of ample water supplies to attract investment.[27] In early 1951, the Minister for Water Supplies, David Brand, announced the government's program to increase the scheme water available to the people of Perth. These public works, which provided employment to many returning soldiers and New Australians, included further storage reservoirs, the sinking of an additional bore in the southern suburbs, and the damming of the Serpentine River near Jarrahdale. After all, a Big City had a thirst that needed to be slaked, and Perth's Big Water was born.

In July 1953 the *West Australian* declared, 'High water consumption creates storage problem'.[28] The journalist assured readers, however, that, 'At the rate of progress the department has made so far in the supplying of water, it seems unlikely that any day we turn on the tap in our bathroom or kitchen, no water will appear'. The 'high water consumption' of the article's headline was simply a natural consequence of efforts to maintain the appearance of traditional lawns and gardens in Perth's long dry summers and sandy soils. Although this custom had made Perth's water consumption per head the highest among the capital cities (except Canberra), it went largely unquestioned. According to the journalist, suburban supplies were adequate to meet the growing demands of Perth households, so long as there were sufficient rains to fill the dams. Less than a decade after the war, a situation of path dependency had emerged in the suburbs of Perth, whereby the existing infrastructure was shaping and directing future water resource development. As a result, anxieties about running out combined with the supply of more water to beget demands for more water and so on, which diminished their resilience to fluctuating water supplies.

Improving technology was not the sole cause of the post-war profligacy of the people of Perth. The development of the domestic sphere as an important political space after the war played a significant role in shaping suburban attitudes and behaviours regarding water use around the home. The detached, single-storey homes of the Australian suburbs had long been what historian Mark Peel calls 'projects for privacy', sanctuaries from the outside world. Under Prime Minister Robert Menzies, this vision of the home was developed further, as the home became shaped as a site of 'independent individualism' in contrast to the mass organisation, impersonal rationality and bureaucracy that Menzies associated with the Labor Party.

As historian Andrea Gaynor has suggested, the diminishing social value of the communal qualities of interdependence not only affected relationships between Australians but also fostered a widespread sense of an independence from natural processes in the suburbs. The vagaries of the natural world, with its own cycles and constraints on the household's ambitions, were relegated beyond the boundary line of the suburban property (or perhaps even further), which reinforced the ideological construction of the domestic space as an impenetrable, clean and private sanctuary for its residents.[29] In the post-war era, the increasing availability of consumer products and a culture of suburban consumerism fostered the impression that the necessities of nature could be circumvented. Advertisements in gardening magazines and newspapers offered readers tempting solutions to the problems that nature's hand had seemingly dealt them. Poor soils? Add an artificial fertiliser. Unwanted insects? Spray one of the new organochlorine or organophosphate insecticides. Too dry? Just turn on the sprinklers. This sense of independence from nature, at the expense of interdependence, combined with Big Water to shape household water consumption in post-war Perth.

Inside the home, the post-war boom and introduction of new household appliances had revolutionised the lifestyles of suburban Australians. Hot water could now be obtained by the turn of a tap, which allowed the introduction of appliances like washing machines and dishwashers, as well as more luxurious bathrooms for more frequent bathing.[30] Many of these household appliances were marketed to Australian wives, who had become the purchasing managers for the household. In the more affluent 1950s and 1960s, as historian Jill Julius Matthews argues, more money was now available for family consumption, not least because more Australian women were part of the paid workforce. The use of these technologies could help Australian housewives more easily overcome their anxieties about the cleanliness and hygiene of both their homes and families. By maintaining a pristine and sterile domestic space, the Australian housewife was 'doing her bit' for the moral defence of the nation. She was, after all, a domestic scientist moulding modern Australian citizens. These changes helped to triple water consumption in Perth after the war and entrenched a suburban reliance on Big Water to maintain a high standard of living.

Although other mainland capital cities exhibited this trend towards higher water use, the rate of consumption of water in Perth domestic gardens was unusual. Only residents in Perth and Adelaide had increased the use of water per capita in their gardens since the end of the war. In the post-war era, over half of Perth's water consumption took place in suburban gardens and in the dry summer months, this proportion rose to about 70 per cent of water use. This increase had occurred in spite of some households' access to private water supplies through backyard bores.[31] Perth gardeners had long appreciated the benefits of applying copious quantities of water on their gardens to defy the natural constraints of dry summers and sandy soils. The Nylex plastic garden hose and improved sprinklers were a panacea to Perth's keen gardeners, who could now soak their couch or buffalo lawns and flower beds more easily. After all, watering Perth's gardens was widely considered, as one wit put it, 'as necessary a daily routine as regular breathing is to the survival of man'.[32] Maintaining the appearance of the front garden had always been important to Perth gardeners but the increasingly aesthetic and recreational roles of the back garden also required additional watering for its upkeep. This profligate water use in Perth's suburbs led scholar George Seddon to warn Western Australians in 1970 to 'fear the hose', as 'once you start using the hose, your garden becomes dependent on it, and you are hooked forever'.[33]

In his 1969 poem, 'The way we live now', local poet William Grono observed a complacent air in the suburbs of Perth. He penned, 'Yes, we like it here. Sometimes the shrewdest of us find the time, after the gardening, before television, sipping beer on enclosed verandahs, to speculate on the future'.[34] But only the 'shrewdest' of Western Australians — those who could perhaps see that these halcyon days could not last. Big Water had combined with post-war affluence and home ownership to foster a sense of independence from the constraints of natural processes and a seemingly unslakeable thirst in the suburbs of Perth. The dry seasons of the 1970s would serve to remind Western Australians in the southwest that they were not separate from nature after all — they were vulnerable to running out.

Beyond Big Water

Big Water was not extended to all Western Australians in the southwest. Despite the State government's aim to reticulate the wheatbelt, the geographical span of the agricultural areas had prevented the expansion of the CWSS to all farming families. For those who were connected, the cost of consuming scheme water was often prohibitive, which encouraged some families to develop their own supplies. But even this option was beyond the reach of many of the region's Aboriginal families.

Those who could not access the CWSS remained wholly reliant on their own supplies and on carting water from government dams. In subsequent years, some districts pushed for extensions to the CWSS to protect them from running out. However, even in the reticulated areas, farmers did not necessarily depend entirely on these supplies. As farmers were responsible for connecting to the service and paid for the amount of water their farms consumed, it remained cheaper for many farmers to continue to rely on their own supplies, such as farm dams and bores. For many, the scheme served then as a supplement to existing measures, as a safeguard, in the wheatbelt.

As a consequence of dry conditions and engineering advances, the excavation of earth tanks (or dams) in the agricultural areas had undergone significant changes in the post-war years. For instance, the drought conditions of 1944 and 1945 had prompted the PWD to repair older excavated dams as well as to construct new ones, particularly in areas outside the boundaries of the CWSS. The larger and more effective earth-moving equipment that had become available after World War II enabled the construction of much bigger and deeper dams for both towns and farms. Although these measures may have contributed to improving the resilience of some farmers to running out, more reliable water supplies could also reduce the drought-relief burden on the government during periods of water scarcity. Like the CWSS, the government's investment in improved farm water supplies, therefore, might be understood as a means to sustain permanent settlement in climatically marginal areas in the post-war era.

These new approaches to water conservation also extended to farmers' private supplies. After World War II, the scourge of soil erosion was a matter of great national public and political concern. One of its causes was water, which swept away precious topsoil as it flowed into farm dams. A Department of Agriculture survey undertaken during the war had found that this form of soil erosion affected nearly two-thirds of wheatbelt farmers and that the extent of this erosion on their properties was increasing.[35] To overcome this problem, the engineers of the PWD devised what one called the 'greatest single advance in water conservation that has been made in this state': the roaded catchment for farm dams.[36] To create a roaded catchment, engineers used heavy rolling machinery to compact a series of parallel 'roads', which were designed to direct water run-off into troughs or channels that drained water into a nearby dam. Compacting the soil in this manner prevented soil erosion and maximised the collection of rain. Nevertheless, some farmers complained that this method consumed too much land that could be put to better use under crop or pasture.[37] By the 1970s, however, farmers had constructed roaded catchments for over 40 per cent of the farm dams in the southern agricultural areas.[38]

To encourage farmers to adopt these measures, the government established the Farm Water Supply Loans Scheme in 1965 to provide finance for bores and dams in the southern, northern and northeastern areas of the wheatbelt, including non-reticulated properties within the area of the CWSS.[39] But the Advisory Committee for the Loans Scheme was 'disappointed' and 'disturbed' to find that many eligible farmers were not interested in applying for these loans. They concluded that 'generally farmers are not sufficiently water conservation conscious'.[40] The committee attributed this lack of interest to the 'excellent winters' of recent years; a false sense of security provided by generally low stocking rates; to the reluctance to invest in infrastructure for which there was no immediate return; a lack of understanding about the Loans Scheme; and the false hope that the CWSS might eventually extend to provide for their future needs. Similar reasons were also likely to have discouraged farmers to store fodder for the dry summer period. As one Meckering farmer earlier observed in 1957, 'This

State enjoys such a consistent rainfall that the fodder conservation side of our farming operations has been sadly neglected'.[41] The widespread faith in the persistence of the prevailing conditions allayed any environmental anxieties about the 'hydraulically difficult country' of the wheatbelt, leaving many unprepared for the dry seasons of the 1970s.

Although Big Water did not extend reticulated water supplies to all of Western Australia's farming families, there was extensive technical and financial support available to improve their resilience to climate variability and water scarcity in the post-war era. After all, the ethos of development and ideology of countrymindedness had shaped the expansion of Big Water and their influence ensured that the government would provide assistance to those outside its scope. But not to everyone, for Big Water was also White Water.

In 1948, the McLarty Liberal government (1947–53) introduced the policy of assimilation for the state's Aboriginal population, 17 per cent of whom resided in the southwest.[42] The intention of this policy, led by the newly-appointed Commissioner for Native Affairs Stanley G. Middleton, was to enhance the political rights of Aboriginal people; to improve their living standards; and to effectively break down the political, cultural and socioeconomic barriers that prevented their advancement in white society. A significant component of this policy was to alleviate Aboriginal poverty through the provision of better housing and sanitation facilities, and through the education of Aboriginal children.[43] But these keys to white society, including access to Big Water, were not freely given – they had to be earned. As historian Anna Haebich observes, 'The step of seeking acceptance as an assimilated individual demanded the greatest price: to abandon the old, accept the superiority of the new, and remain permanently on trial in a world where the goalposts for acceptance were continually being shifted'.[44] Despite Middleton's best intentions, the assimilation policies of his department served only to perpetuate the discriminatory sanitary order that had prevailed since the turn of the twentieth century. The exclusion of Aboriginal people from Big Water undermined the policy of assimilation, contributed to the fragmentation of Aboriginal families, and ultimately helped to perpetuate the dependence of many Aboriginal people on the state into the late twentieth century.

Under the policy of assimilation, it had become compulsory for Aboriginal children to attend state schools or other education facilities. To facilitate the acceptance of Aboriginal children in the classroom, the government made half-hearted attempts to improve the domestic environments of Aboriginal families. Encouraging these families into 'conventional' (or white) homes would, in theory, not only raise their living standards but also serve to fragment extended families into the more conventional living arrangements of the nuclear family, and provide an important political sign of the progress of the assimilation policy. Not surprisingly, this housing policy was met with both white and black resistance. Some white Western Australians protested the accommodation of Aboriginal families in their towns, while many Aborigines resented the greater surveillance of their daily lives that this policy seemed to entail. There was also an official reluctance to significantly invest in the improvement of the living standards of Aboriginal families. For instance, in contrast to its assistance to New Australians and other families, the Commonwealth government provided no funding to the state for the provision of better housing for Aborigines. It was clear, as Haebich observes, that 'Aboriginal families were not included in the national imaginary of a nation of homeowners'.[45]

With the State Housing Commission, the Department of Native Affairs resorted to a program of transitional housing, by which Aboriginal people could advance from camps to homes in State housing estates. A lack of funding, however, hampered this progression. In the Great Southern district, for instance, only five of the twenty-two reserves had full access to water, laundry, shower and toilet facilities. At least ten had no facilities at all.[46] According to an officer of the department, these services 'were a fair approximation of similar necessities provided at, for example, caravan parks'.[47] By the end of the 1960s, nearly two-thirds of the houses built were equivalent to just the first stage, and fewer than 5 per cent were of the standard of conventional housing.[48] Such conditions were hardly conducive to the assimilated lifestyles to which Aboriginal families were supposed to aspire.

Departmental officials conducted regular inspections of these facilities and their residents to monitor the progress of Aboriginal families towards the official goal of assimilation. Families were expected to demonstrate signs of their assimilation by displaying clean and tidy homes with the mother and father playing their designated parental roles and without the presence of the extended family. Department officials also provided extensive training – what Haebich calls 'assimilation's "Trojan horse"' – to guide Aboriginal people, especially women, in the management of the home, including cleaning, child care, health, budgeting and liaison with local authorities.[49] But as nearly 85 per cent of the southwest's Aborigines still lived on reserves for most of the year, where infrastructure was poorly maintained, it was extremely difficult for Aborigines to maintain these standards.[50] In many cases, a failure to meet the department's standards was grounds for the removal of Aboriginal children from their families. As one department officer noted in 1968, 'A thorough examination was not made as the father was not present. From what I saw however, I am satisfied that the children are "neglected", if for no other reason than the shack they live in'.[51] Deprived of access to the standard of living that Big Water could provide, Aboriginal people were ill-equipped to advance towards the 'conventional' Australian way of life.

Despite citizenship and greater freedoms in the post-war era, many Aborigines in the state's southwest remained governed by a discriminatory sanitary order and these conditions persisted into the 1970s. As Robert Bropho rued, 'We have given up hope of being accepted for what we are, and my children are scarred for life...Their home now, as fringedwellers, is living under canvas'.[52]

A climate for growth

Mirroring the post-war expansion of Big Water in the southwest was the burgeoning scientific bureaucracy focussed on the nation's economic development. The contributions of meteorologists to Australia's war effort had served to reinforce their close relationship with the nation's governments. This relationship continued after the war and significantly influenced the nature and direction of climate research during peacetime. The nation's meteorologists served among the 'officer corps' of government scientists deployed for the post-war battle with the land.[53]

Upon the recommendation of the Rural Reconstruction Commission, the Commonwealth Bureau of Meteorology established climatological sections in each state after the war. Their role was to provide climate information on the suitability of particular regions for the economic development of agricultural and pastoral industries. This decentralisation of data collection was a significant change in the Bureau's operations, which had previously taken place in Melbourne. This devolution was particularly celebrated in Western Australia, where the Perth observatory's isolation from Melbourne had hampered efforts to provide meteorological records when required.[54] The developmentalist focus of the State government and the applied nature of post-war meteorology ensured that scientific studies of the unique climates of Western Australia remained inherently focussed on the state's agricultural areas.

In addition to this Commonwealth scientific expertise, the study of (Western) Australian climates was also a subject of local interest. At the forefront of local research was an Italian geographer at the state's university, who had fled Europe on the eve of World War II. Soon after his arrival in Fremantle in September 1939, Joseph Gentilli was appointed to a lectureship in economics and just two years later, established a new course in economic geography. From the outset, Gentilli's project was to 'transform bare statistics (of which there were many) into maps (of which there were none)' in order to improve scientific understandings of Australian environmental conditions, particularly its climates.[55] These studies provided the framework for Gentilli to compare Australia's regions to others around the world using the Köppen system of climate classification.

The purpose of such comparisons was to provide insights into the possibilities of economic development in the seemingly 'under-developed' regions of Australia. And Gentilli embraced this developmentalist ethos in his work. In 1941 he declared, 'Western Australia's key problem is how to increase her population; nearly all other problems are mere corollaries of this one great question'.[56] Determining the climate suitability of different areas for closer settlement in Western Australia was regarded as a key to the state's post-war progress and prosperity. According to Gentilli's calculations, most of the wheatbelt was only expected to experience fewer than thirty drought years in a century and was therefore well-suited for closer settlement.[57] This estimate was not based on 'natural' conditions, but instead on the agrarian use of the region. For his focus on agricultural development, Gentilli was roundly applauded, including a commendation from the state's former Premier and then Governor, Sir James Mitchell.[58]

In the early 1950s, scientists reported that temperatures in the northern hemisphere had risen since the nineteenth century. These findings prompted lay anxieties, both in the United States and Australia, about a changing climate and the extent to which the use of nuclear weapons had contributed to these changes. Already the residents in Perth had begun to wonder whether seasonal conditions differed from those they had experienced in the past. These concerns led Gentilli to study whether any such changes in climate could be observed in the southwest region. He and his ornithologist colleague Dominic Serventy had already noticed that, despite extensive efforts to drain swamps around Perth, the watertable in these areas had risen since the end of World War I, much to the benefit of many aquatic bird species.[59]

A study of the rainfall records revealed to Gentilli that between 1877 and 1945 winter rainfall in Perth had increased.[60]

This confirmed the explanations that Water Supply Department engineers had offered for the sodden conditions in the early 1930s.[61] Gentilli was uncertain, however, as to the cause of these changes and whether they would continue. Despite this uncertainty, Gentilli, like many other climate scientists, was quite unconcerned about this trend, as neither its direction nor its magnitude appeared to pose a serious threat to livelihoods. Wetter conditions would reduce the likelihood of drought and potentially benefit the wheatbelt's farmers. Had the meteorological record revealed a drying trend, however, Gentilli might have been more alarmed, as he had recently concluded that, 'The Western Australian environment is...much more deeply affected by movements of the arid margin and by a decrease than by an increase in the rainfall'.[62] The drier climate conditions that developed later in the twentieth century confirmed his fears.

Despite the scientific interest in the climates of Western Australia after the war, this research had not progressed sufficiently to convince the State government to experiment with the emerging technology of cloud seeding. Western Australian governments had followed the growing profile of cloud seeding with close interest from the late 1940s. After the first Australian trials of cloud seeding were conducted near Sydney in 1947, it did not take long for the idea to travel across the Nullarbor to Western Australia. But the Brand government was reluctant to commit its resources to a science untested in Western Australia's unique climate conditions. The exact reasons for its unwillingness to trial cloud seeding are not explicitly stated in the documentary record. It is likely, however, that the government considered the prevailing climatic conditions adequate for agricultural growth. Premier Brand relented only in 1966, after receiving a letter from the Acting Prime Minister Jack McEwen that impressed upon him the importance of cloud seeding for overcoming climatic limits to agricultural production.[63] From the mid-1960s, therefore, Western Australia joined New South Wales, Victoria, Queensland, and South Australia in undertaking local cloud seeding operations under the advice of CSIRO.

Across the Nullarbor, these cloud seeding operations had been triggered by widespread drought conditions. These severe droughts, particularly in New South Wales and Queensland, prompted the Bureau of Meteorology to increase its research into the causes and patterns of these conditions. It was only in the wake of the droughts of the mid-1960s that the Bureau's director Bill Gibbs ventured a definition for drought in Australia: a 'severe water shortage'.[64] But what 'shortage' meant for the farmer might be different to the market gardener, the pastoralist, and the gardening enthusiast. Although CSIRO considered it had the technology to beat droughts, the Bureau's meteorologists were struggling to define and measure them, let alone predict their onset.

Meanwhile, the Western Australian government's engineers remained sceptical about the cloud seeding experiments. Some considered too little was known about the atmospheric and oceanic systems shaping the state's climate. They were also concerned about public opposition to the trials, particularly the fear that rainmaking in one area might deprive another area of its rain.[65] In other words, they did not want to disrupt the climate status quo. As CSIRO was willing to shoulder half of the financial burden, the Brand government decided to give the technology the benefit of the doubt. In May and June 1967, the PWD conducted a cloud seeding experiment in the southwest, aiming to stimulate rainfall in the Avon River region. But with only seven hours of seeding, researchers were left unconvinced as to whether the experiments had increased rainfall in the area. It was not until the dry spells of the early 1970s that Western Australian scientists returned to rainmaking as a possible means to change the weather.

The state's engineers may have lacked confidence in the depth of scientific knowledge about Western Australian climates, but successive State governments were sufficiently convinced of the suitability and reliability of the southwest climate conditions to continue to promote extensive land settlement programs across the region. Although the Rural Reconstruction Commission had advocated a cautious approach to post-war land settlement, the state's Land Settlement Board declared in 1951 that,

> It may be sound policy under normal conditions to examine every new project most critically and ascertain – if necessary – by experiment the answer to every question of management or soil use, as a pre-requisite to settlement. Such information, however, may take years to obtain, during which the vital factor of 'timing' may be lost.[66]

The board members were confident that land settlement would be a great success and considered it reasonable to take a calculated risk.

Such was the enthusiasm for agricultural development in Western Australia that 60 per cent of qualified applicants were allotted farms, compared to just 10 per cent in other states.[67] By the mid-1960s, thanks to a host of technological advances in the agricultural sciences, wheat growing had resumed in areas that had been deemed 'marginal' prior to the war. The combination of the sanguine seasons of the post-war decades with a faith in the ability of science and technology to overcome natural limits had assuaged most environmental anxieties about the reliability of Western Australia's agricultural areas by the late 1960s.

The luckiest state?

In his 1987 book *From the Ground Up*, historian Bryce Moore scathingly observed that 'the contented and prosperous citizens of mineral-rich Western Australia during the 1960s really believed that theirs was the Lucky Country, and that Western Australia was its luckiest state'.[68] The post-war era had been particularly kind to the residents of the western third – farmers had enjoyed a run of reasonable seasons, the suburbs had swelled, industrialisation was underway, and mineral exports were fuelling a boom. Giddy with this prosperity, as Moore suggests, they were not prepared for the time when their luck would run out. The following decade put them to the test.

4

The 'Age of Anxiety':

Reaching the limits of settlement (1969 to 1983)

On the eve of a new decade, Western Australians in 1969 farewelled the prosperity of the post-war years and entered, with trepidation, a new era. The onset of drought conditions in 1969, which severely affected farmers, foreshadowed the dry seasons that characterised the following decade and shaped the ways that suburban and rural Western Australians related to water in the southwest. Accompanying this climatic volatility was economic instability overseas and at home, which added to the difficulties facing many local farmers. Across the nation, agriculture was undergoing a decline in importance, and in Western Australia, this trend combined with the burgeoning resource development in the state's northwest.[1] Meanwhile, as environmental problems like salinity took an increasing toll on the southwest's land and water resources, the promise of unfettered development lost some of its appeal.

The poor seasons of the late 1960s and their persistence during the 1970s combined with erratic markets to usher in an 'Age of Anxiety', which exposed the vulnerability of many suburban and rural Western Australians to running out of water.[2] Naturally, some fared better than others in these circumstances, owing largely to their geographical position, their affluence, and their preparedness for periods of climate variability and water scarcity. In contrast to earlier government responses, the onus was now on consumers, rather than the government, to improve their hydroresilience.

A change in the weather

'I heard twice on the radio news that the warm, fine weather should continue for the present but that it should deteriorate soon', wrote a Kojonup farmer to the *West Australian* in April 1969. 'I don't know who thought of the word "deteriorate" in this instance, but I do know that all farmers hope the weather deteriorates very soon'.[3] The situation in the state's wheatbelt did deteriorate as the months passed by, but not in the way that this correspondent had hoped. By the end of the year, a large proportion of the agricultural areas had been declared 'drought affected'.[4] The extent and severity of the conditions were comparable to the disastrous seasons of 1914 and 1940, which had called into question the wisdom of prevailing land settlement and agricultural policies. The severity of this drought for many farmers was a result of a long-standing belief in the 'reliability' of the rains of the southwest, which had fostered a sense of complacency towards running out. The dry conditions of 1969 dashed these illusions and contributed to reinterpretations of the seasons of the southwest.

The long run of moist seasons after World War II had reinforced official and lay belief in the reliability of the rains of the agricultural areas. As the Chairman of the Farm Water Supply Committee Jack Gabbedy later conceded, 'Farmers generally had become quite complacent as to the need for guarding against drought years and this complacency probably resulted from the series of very wet years in the decade preceding 1969'.[5] Their faith that these conditions would continue had been bolstered by scientific research, such as that undertaken by local geographer Joseph Gentilli. Furthermore, most farmers had not experienced the extent of variability in the region because they had only settled there recently. Others had not experienced such dry conditions since the devastating drought of 1914. Across the southwest, farmers generally believed that 'things like that (the 1969 drought) *should not* happen here'.[6] These ideas had led many farmers to inadequately bolster their fodder and water supplies for the increased stock levels they were carrying in the late 1960s.[7] Relatively confident that drought would spare the southwest, few farmers had taken advantage of Public Works Department (PWD) and Department of Agriculture initiatives to improve their resilience to variations in climate and water supplies.

As the dry conditions continued, the Brand government was also accused of 'taking the punt' that drought would not afflict the state's agricultural and pastoral areas.[8] The Labor Opposition and rural press criticised the government for failing to respond more quickly. But the government's response was hampered by the reluctance of farming shires to proclaim their area drought-stricken. As Minister for Agriculture Crawford Nalder reported to Parliament in early August 1969, 'Not one local authority will admit that drought conditions exist'.[9] Although such a proclamation entitled farmers to drought assistance from both the Commonwealth and State governments, these shires were concerned that the stigma associated with the label of 'drought-affected' might damage their shire's reputation as a profitable farming area and cause land prices to plummet.[10] The reality of drought clearly conflicted with long-held official and lay ideas about the nature of the southwest's climate.

Once a local council conceded the extent of their shire's dire situation, the Brand government implemented emergency efforts to relieve the affected areas. These measures included financial assistance, water carting, searching for alternative water sources, and drilling for underground water to boost supplies.[11] The future expansion of Big Water, the State government, farmers and rural press believed, would 'drought proof' the agricultural areas and ensure their return to prosperity. Just a year earlier, the State government had presented a proposal to the Commonwealth for funds to expand the scope of the Comprehensive Water Supply Scheme (CWSS) to include the York–Greenhills and Corrigin–Bullaring areas.[12] As the *West Australian* declared in October 1969, 'Australia reaps big national dividends, even in times of wheat surplus and falling wool prices from the areas the CWSS serves. Those dividends would be bigger in these adverse times if there were more water to sustain the sheep'.[13] Nevertheless, in 1972, the Commonwealth rejected Western Australia's proposals. Another request for assistance to reticulate districts with severe water problems, including the West Midlands, Eradu and the areas east of Merredin, was also turned down in 1975. These decisions contributed to a reorientation in the State government's approach to watering the wheatbelt and to the study of its climate.

Although meteorological interest in drought had grown in eastern Australia after the war, far less attention had been paid to such conditions in Western Australia. Forecasters there faced the difficulty of calculating their predictions with little weather information from the Indian Ocean. Even in the late 1970s, local meteorologist Bob Southern noted, the Indian Ocean remained 'very much a "no-man's land" in global meteorology' and forecasters relied upon observations from ships and Amsterdam Island in the central Indian Ocean.[14] The development of mineral and oil resources in the state's northwest during the 1960s had led the Perth office of the Bureau of Meteorology to focus its attentions on the study of weather phenomena that might disrupt northern development, such as tropical cyclones.[15] In contrast, few efforts seem to have been devoted to developing a method of long-range forecasting for the southwest. This was likely a result of the widely held idea of the reliability of the southwest climate, the relatively wet conditions of the post-war decades, and the seemingly accurate forecasting by local Bureau of Meteorology forecasters. Besides, as it was rare for both sides of the continent to be drought-affected at the same time, agricultural production in unaffected areas could compensate for the losses in affected regions.[16] It was left then to the University of Western Australia's Institute of Agriculture and the state's Department of Agriculture to examine Western Australian climates more closely.

On the eve of the drought of 1969, researchers at the Institute had been influenced by the recent encouragement of the Director of the Bureau of Meteorology, Bill Gibbs, at an Australian & New Zealand Association for the Advancement of Science (ANZAAS) meeting on drought to 'ascertain the frequency with which droughts may be expected'.[17] Consecutive years of poor rainfall would have a more devastating impact on farmers than a single bad year as they would not be in a position to either recover financially from the previous season or to ensure adequate supplies of water and fodder for the coming year. Knowledge of how often droughts might occur could direct farmers to plan their agricultural and pastoral practices accordingly. Their research found that the likelihood of drought in the southwest had been underestimated – there was a one in seven chance of a serious drought developing between the break of the season and at the end of July.[18] Since these findings were concerned with the timing of rains, rather than total rainfall, they were more precise and applicable to wheat-growing than Gentilli's earlier estimation of drought probability in the southwest.

Meanwhile, similar research was being undertaken at the state's Department of Agriculture. At the height of the 1969 drought, the Assistant Director of the Department, George H. Burvill, had observed, 'A few years ago it was forecast that the cleared area could rise to fifty million acres. But the drought has shown us that we should perhaps look more closely at whether we have been expanding too far into the low rainfall areas'.[19] This statement was particularly striking in light of the fact that just two years earlier, the government was still releasing a million acres of Crown land a year, particularly along the south coast.[20] At a meeting on water supplies in Mukinbudin in early 1970, Burvill revealed his department's estimates for the upcoming seasons in the eastern and northeastern areas of the wheatbelt based on long-term rainfall averages. In contrast to earlier glowing assessments of the southwest's climates, Burvill concluded that in these areas at least, there had been 'more dry years than wet years'. The drought of 1969, he warned, was the beginning of a 'period of five to eight years of below-average rainfall'. As that drought had 'revealed some chinks in our armour', farmers in these areas, with government assistance, needed to undertake measures to improve their hydroresilience.[21]

These revisions of official ideas about the climate variability of the agricultural areas and the diminishing likelihood of further Commonwealth funding for extending the CWSS combined to prompt government efforts to help farmers protect themselves from dry conditions. Although the Farm Water Supplies Committee had been in operation since the mid-1960s, relatively few farmers had taken advantage of its assistance, as the 1969 drought had revealed. In the central and northeastern wheatbelt – those areas the Department of Agriculture expected to be worst affected by poor seasons over the next decade – just 15 per cent of farm dams were regarded as 'drought proof'. Meanwhile, farm dams were the only source of stock water on most farms in the southern and southeastern wheatbelt, as well as in the Mallee and Esperance areas. Although the PWD had hailed its development of the roaded catchment after the war, by 1969 very few farmers in the agricultural areas had adopted this technique to improve the runoff into their dams. Plentiful rains in the 1950s and 1960s had made such investments in infrastructure seem wasteful so they had relied instead on natural catchments of sloping pastures. The need to cart water during the 1969 drought exposed their misplaced faith in the weather. The Committee considered that over half of the wheatbelt's dams could benefit from the addition of roaded catchments, which was a more sustainable alternative than digging bigger and deeper dams.[22]

Unfortunately for many southwest farmers, the estimations of the Department of Agriculture were borne out by the dry conditions of the 1970s. Although cyclones Glynis and Ingrid in January and February of 1970 brought with them heavy rains and strong winds, the dry summer conditions prevented the replenishment of water storages across the areas afflicted by the 1969 drought and in some southern districts, the dry conditions persisted well into the following year.[23] For many farmers, the impact of the drought was deepened by the changing fortunes of agriculture in the Australian economy. Fewer farmers could look forward with 'unbridled optimism' to 'unlimited opportunities', and many more saw 'uncertainty and scepticism' on the horizon. In Western Australia at least, government advisors considered, 'This change in outlook has occurred rapidly and, if any specific time is to be identified as the turning point, it might be from the beginning of 1969'.[24]

Seeking supplies

On the eve of the drought of 1969, *Choice* magazine had observed, 'The amount of garden hose in Australia could, like Puck, put a girdle around the earth with very little difficulty'. Wielding their new plastic garden hoses and with their supplies assured by the post-war growth of Big Water, the people of Perth embraced the suburban ritual of watering their gardens with gusto. After the war, Perth householders had become prodigious users of water, outstripping the residents of the other capitals.[25] Total water consumption in Perth had been doubling almost every fifteen years since 1920.[26] With the economic development of the 1950s and 1960s, the state's population had soared and was increasingly concentrated in the suburbs of Perth. The city had swelled from 62 per cent of the state's population in 1954, to 68 per cent in 1971.[27] At the dawn of the 'Age of Anxiety', the Metropolitan Water Board was struggling to keep pace with the growth in demand, which fuelled engineers' concerns about running out by the end of the century. How would Big Water continue to slake the thirst of the suburbs? From where would it drink next?

In late 1969, construction began on the Dandalup River Scheme near Pinjarra to provide water to the suburbs of Perth. Under this scheme, a pipehead dam was built across the North Dandalup River and a major dam constructed at Lake Banksiadale on the South Dandalup River. The damming of the North Dandalup River had been earmarked during the war as a possible supplement to the Mundaring Weir in the plan to reticulate the agricultural areas. The rapid post-war growth of Perth and its thirst for water soon led to the consideration of the site as a water source for the city. The prospect of piping water away from a district that supported dairying, orcharding, livestock, and timber milling raised the ire of rural shires.[28] At the 1960 South West Conference of the Country Party in Bunbury, the delegates resolved, "'that no further catchments should be provided to create new supplies for the metropolitan area", especially in that area south of Pinjarra'.[29] Local politicians outside Perth argued that damming the Dandalup Rivers was at odds with political rhetoric of decentralisation and regional development.[30] And where would it stop, they wondered? But the thirst of the suburbs had to be quenched – as engineer Ian O'Hara noted in 1967, 'It seems to be quite well-established that the garden suburb is part of the accepted way of life'.[31]

By 1971, water from the North Dandalup pipehead dam was supplying water to Perth. The South Dandalup Dam was completed in 1974 and became the largest of the reservoirs supplying the city. But the fears of running out remained. Even in the late 1960s, Big Water's engineers considered that Perth's dams would only be able to supply two-thirds of the water necessary to slake suburban thirsts by the end of the century. Further calculations in the early 1970s only confirmed these anxieties: demand for water would exceed the available supplies by the mid-1980s.[32] Although suburban householders had responded well to campaigns to voluntarily conserve water in the summer of 1972/73, Big Water's engineers were convinced that more water was needed.[33] In 1973,

PWD engineers calculated the long-range demand for water and their findings gave colleagues further cause for concern.

Compared to Canada and the United States, water planning in Australia was very rudimentary at this time. Estimations of future demand tended to assume that population and per capita consumption would continue to increase at existing rates, and water would have to be supplied accordingly. This approach reflected the relatively high level of available water resources per head in Australia's cities.[34] But in Perth this abundance was now in doubt – the most accessible and cheapest sources had already been developed and some of these were being threatened by salinity. Big Water was running out of options.

It was in this context of looming scarcity for Perth that Big Water and the State government addressed growing demands from irrigators in the Harvey district for more water. Irrigators argued that the Harvey Dam was no longer adequate for their needs and that a new dam was necessary to support their farm planning and to ensure the reliable supply of dairy products to Perth.[35] Reflecting the Whitlam government's recent withdrawal of the dairy industry subsidy, economists, including the author of *Australia: wet or dry*, Bruce R. Davidson, argued that it was not in the State government's interest to continue providing cheap water to irrigators. Instead, they recommended that irrigators compete with other consumers (particularly those in Perth) under free market conditions for water supplies, or shift to dryland milk production, which did not require as much water.[36] But support for this radical change was not unanimous. As one commentator asked, 'Is the human suffering, ghost towns and farms created by following such a policy warranted for a saving of this small magnitude?'[37]

A compromise presented itself: the piping of the Harvey irrigation district. Some 50 km of dilapidated open channels continued to supply water to irrigators, a system that allowed up to a quarter of the water released from dam storages to be lost in the process of delivery. This deficit, engineers calculated, was equivalent to the amount released from Logue Brook Dam and Harvey Dam combined.[38] The savings achieved through piping the district would conserve enough water to meet some of the irrigators' demands. The construction of the piped scheme commenced in 1977 and was finally completed in the late 1980s. Nearly seventy years after government engineer Hugh Oldham had dismissed the idea, the irrigators of Harvey finally had their vision realised. Water for Perth had to be found elsewhere.

In the search to secure water for the southwest, some members of the community looked to sources beyond the region. The Western Mining Corporation was especially concerned that limited water supplies might restrict industrial development and mining activities in the eastern goldfields.[39] Following a 1970 PWD report on the state's exploitable surface water resources, the Corporation undertook a feasibility study of the possibility of establishing a dam site on the Fitzroy River in the state's northwest and pumping the water to Perth and Kalgoorlie.[40] Although the Corporation envisioned the Fitzroy pipeline proposal as a descendant of 'O'Connor's (Kalgoorlie) pipedream', Premier Sir Charles Court was less enthusiastic about the prospect. Seeing a conflict with his visions for northern development, he argued in 1975, 'We cannot expect to reach too far with our pipelines to bring to Perth water that might be needed elsewhere'.[41] Besides, the Water Board's engineers calculated that it would cost the government nearly sixty times more to supply water from the northwest than some of the other available options.[42] Although the return of dry conditions in the late 1970s renewed this pipedream, Sir Charles remained unmoved.[43] The rivers were simply too far and expensive to tap, and these plans to pipe water from the state's northwest were shelved, at least temporarily.

Far closer and far cheaper were the groundwater resources of the Swan Coastal Plain. International efforts to further global hydrological studies in the early 1960s had encouraged Australian endeavours to undertake the long-awaited measurement of the continent's water resources.[44] As part of its assessments of the underground water resources of Western Australia, the PWD undertook exploration of the groundwater reserves between Gingin in the north and Mandurah in the south. These studies revealed extensive stocks within two superficial formations about 70 m below the ground that the Water Board considered could be cheaply used for scheme water supplies.[45] They had found two shallow formations: the Gnangara Mound, located between Gingin Brook and the Swan River; and the Jandakot Mound, between the Swan River and the Serpentine River flats. Composed of late Tertiary to Quaternary age sediments, such as sand, silt, clay and limestone, these aquifers are recharged by rains percolating through the watertable.

Conveniently, this subterranean treasure trove was almost exactly aligned with the coastal ribbon of Perth's post-war suburban development. No longer associating them with disease, more and more Western Australians were beginning to appreciate the wetlands, lakes and swamps (the portals to these groundwater reserves), not only in terms of their value as water supplies for local market gardens and pine plantations but as places for recreation and as habitats for local flora and fauna. These changing perceptions of Perth's wetlands were characteristic of the growing environmental awareness and concerns among suburban Western Australians. In the early 1970s, for instance, many residents of the suburb of North Beach campaigned to prevent the clearing of the wetlands and bushland of Star Swamp for housing development, reflecting the spread of urban environmental protests around the country at this time.[46]

These lay concerns combined with scientific interest in the complex ecologies of these areas to prompt public scrutiny of Big Water's subterranean expansion. Local ecologists were especially concerned about the combination of dry years and the extraction of groundwater on the ecological health of the wetlands. Already some 50 per cent of the Swan Coastal Plain's wetlands had been destroyed, reported ecologists, and further deterioration could affect migratory birds and cause the loss of swamp and lake vegetation.[47] The recently created Environmental Protection

Authority (EPA) had the task of overseeing the monitoring of groundwater levels and ensuring that this vital source was not contaminated. These community concerns added an ecological aspect to the developmentalist approach to the management of Perth's water supplies.

The focus on monitoring and measurement by local scientists and engineers as a means to limit the effects of groundwater abstraction on the ecologies of the Swan Coastal Plain conform to the notion of engineered resilience. According to Cameron Muir, Deborah Bird Rose and Philip Sullivan, this form of resilience suggests a meeting of 'ecological science informed by the biological sciences, and environmental science informed by the physical sciences and engineering'.[48] The aims of engineered resilience reflect its engineering origins: 'efficiency, constancy and predictability'.

The application of these principles to the abstraction of groundwater was all-important to preventing Big Water from running out and to protecting the wetlands. Yet such a focus on the constant production of water over other elements of the ground-water ecologies could come at a cost. As ecologist Buzz Holling explains, 'Productivity or yield is often increased over short time periods due to management efficiency and optimisation but suffers in the long run as ecological surprises exceed the diminished resilience of the system'.[49] By concentrating on ensuring the stability of water levels, scientific measurement and monitoring could affect the intricate processes and functions of ecologies, and therefore affect their resilience to periods of climate variability and water scarcity. Furthermore, local critics were concerned that Big Water had not adequately defined the consequences of groundwater abstraction and whether it was undesirable for wetland environments.[50] In the absence of clear definitions, these critics argued, it would be difficult for Big Water to make decisive and transparent choices about the management of the groundwater resources of the Swan Coastal Plain. Only time would tell just how much Big Water would be allowed to transform these areas.

Concerns about the effects of groundwater abstraction on Perth's wetlands did not extend, however, to considerations of the possible consequences that this might have for Nyoongar country. This was in spite of the recent introduction of the *Aboriginal Heritage Act 1972*, which was designed to protect places and objects of significance to Aboriginal people.[51] In the same year as the first symposium convened on the 'Groundwater Resources of the Swan Coastal Plain' in late 1975, local archaeologist Sylvia Hallam documented many colonial accounts of Aboriginal use of Perth's wetlands in her important book, *Fire and Hearth*. Each of these accounts attest to the significance of these sites to Nyoongar people, particularly owing to the spiritual importance of fresh water. The enduring significance of Perth's wetlands to local Aboriginal people may have been overlooked because of a lack of appreciation for the ongoing connections of Nyoongar people to country. Even Hallam noted, 'One might not expect much evidence of [the *Waakal's*] importance or his association with water...to survive in the South-west'. This position reflects contemporary misconceptions about the identities of Australian Aborigines living in urban settings. As anthropologist Sandy Toussaint explains, 'It was generally believed that by their very presence in an urban context, Aboriginal people would ultimately come to deny, or shed, their Aboriginal heritage', that they were 'without culture'.[52] Worse, they were not regarded as '"real" Aborigines'.[53]

If only non-urban Aboriginal people had connections to country, only non-urban places and objects of significance required protection. In light of the mineral resources boom of the 1960s, it follows that the Aboriginal Heritage Act was intended for objects and sites in the state's north, not in the more densely populated and developed southwest.[54] It was not until the mid-1980s that the Western Australian Museum commissioned a site survey of metropolitan Perth. Nyoongars in the suburbs of Perth, however, had retained many practices and beliefs from the past: many Nyoongars living in Perth in the 1970s did know about the *Waakal*, even if they were unsure of the exact path of its

Dreamtime journey.[55] As one elder later recalled, 'We used to travel all through there [the Gnangara Pine Plantation] and we could get water from the swamps'.[56] The ongoing connections of many Nyoongar people to the wetland areas of the Swan Coastal Plain were just one of the many ways that they continued their spiritual associations with country in the late twentieth century. The State government's apparent disregard for the significance of the wetlands to Nyoongar people, therefore, served to undermine their ecologies and connections to country. Despite these sacrifices for the development of water supplies in the southwest, Nyoongars continued to benefit the least from the expansion of Big Water.

The Water Board's development of underground resources commenced with the commissioning of groundwater schemes on the Gnangara Mound with Mirrabooka in December 1970, followed by Gwelup (1974), Wanneroo (1976) and East Mirrabooka (1980), and on the Jandakot Mound in 1979. By the mid-1970s, the aquifers provided about 10 per cent of Perth's water supply and the city's reliance on this source was expected to grow.[57]

Blocked from Big Water

The post-war Age of Innocence may have looked 'a little like Eden' to many Western Australians but for the Aboriginal people living outside Big Water, it was anything but paradisiacal.[58] Despite some improvements to their political status in the late 1960s, Aborigines in the southwest remained largely on the fringes of white society. Many continued to live in squalid camps both in the suburbs and in country towns such as Moora, Kellerberrin and Narrogin.[59]

The legacy of discriminatory housing and welfare policies took on a new guise in the 1970s. New federal policies of self-determination and Aboriginal housing emphasised raising living standards of Australian Aborigines to those enjoyed by non-Indigenous Australians. In 1975, for instance, the House of Representatives Standing Committee on Aboriginal Housing declared, 'All Aborigines should be housed in conventional houses to the standards as those of the European community'.[60] But this rhetoric was not reflecting reality. In 1971, the Department of Native Welfare was abolished and its housing responsibilities transferred to the State Housing Commission, which established an Aboriginal Housing Board (AHB) under its auspices in 1978. As anthropologist Sandy Toussaint observes, the ability of the AHB to influence Commission planning appears to have been slight. For instance, the Commission allocated three-quarters of Commonwealth housing assistance to village programs in the state's northwest in the early 1980s, against the recommendations of the AHB.[61] Consequently, few homes could be built around Perth, where over three-quarters of the state's Aboriginal population lived below the poverty line and were among the lowest income earners in the nation.[62]

Despite these administrative changes and the rhetoric of self-determination, assimilationist ideas persisted in the management of Aboriginal housing. These ideas echoed earlier environmental anxieties surrounding race and health in the southwest. For instance, the Commission implemented a 'salt and pepper' approach to the distribution of Aboriginal families in the suburbs. This was designed to assist their assimilation, to prevent 'ghettoisation' and to assuage widespread (white) concerns about the accommodation of Aboriginal people in the suburbs of Perth.[63] Similarly, the commission initiated a 'saturation point' policy in the mid-1970s to limit the number of families of Aboriginal descent who could be accommodated in an area. If the 'saturation point' had been reached, no additional Aboriginal families could be housed in that area – even if there were vacant lodgings available. Moreover, the commission's policy was to accommodate Aboriginal families in detached dwellings only, where they could be kept at arm's length from their neighbours.[64] With nearly three-quarters of Aboriginal families in Western Australia dependent on public housing, these assimilationist policies served to hinder the government's provision of accommodation for Aboriginal people.

With limited public housing available to the southwest's Aboriginal people, many had to seek alternative accommodation. But where? The private rental market was hardly accessible and in the early 1980s, fewer than a quarter of Aboriginal people living in Perth were tenants in 'conventional' housing. The rest lived in circumstances ranging from 'semi-conventional housing' to 'improvised dwellings'.[65] Others found shelter in even less conventional surrounds, such as refuges, relatives' homes, and parks as well as camps such as the 'bull paddock' in East Perth. But even those who resided in conventional housing had a tenuous hold on this accommodation. Aboriginal families living in public housing were often subject to inspections without prior notice to ensure they were meeting the Commission's standards of housekeeping. These standards, of course, were based on suburban expectations of cleanliness, neatness and order, to overcome anxieties about citizens' moral and physical health in domestic spaces. More often than not, Aboriginal tenants were found wanting. Many were simply unprepared for conventional living arrangements. As Aboriginal activist Ken Colbung argued in 1974, 'Sure you say "we put them into good houses and they don't even know how to look after them". If you had been living for years on the rubbish tips…you wouldn't know how to look after a house either'.[66] These tenants were again branded with the stigma of 'bad standards', which justified eviction and even the removal of their children.[67] Furthermore, this stigma made it unlikely that they would be reconsidered for public housing. Rather than helping to improve the lives of Aboriginal families, the state's housing policies tended to perpetuate the discriminatory sanitary order and to deny many families access to the very means – scheme water – to raise their standard of living and social position. The exclusion of many Aborigines from access to the benefits of Big Water, therefore, continued to shape their lives in the southwest and served to continue their marginalisation from 'conventional' white society into the 1980s.

A vulnerable city

In a 1977 issue of the Australian Conservation Foundation's journal *Habitat*, George Seddon described Perth as an 'exceptionally vulnerable city' owing to 'its almost total dependence on stored water'.[68] Even Big Water's subterranean expansion could not forestall the introduction of water restrictions in mid-1977 to cope with dry conditions. The restrictions lasted from July 1977 to October 1978, and were then eased to partial restrictions to May 1979. Meanwhile, the Water Board also embarked on a publicity campaign to reinforce the importance of water conservation and to show the severity of the situation.[69] But water restrictions could not continue indefinitely, as they were proving both financially and politically costly to the Court government. The emerging influence of market principles in water resource management overseas led the State government to implement a 'user pays' water rating system in July 1978, which finally rewarded consumers who used less water.

Although Perth's water use had been restricted in the past, the government's policies to curb suburban water consumption during the 1970s reflected new approaches to managing water resources. After nearly a decade without water restrictions, the particularly hot summer of 1971/72 led the Water Board to experiment with a voluntary conservation campaign. This was an attempt to promote more water-efficient behaviour in the home and garden and so relieve pressures on the limited supplies of Big Water. The program lasted from December 1972 to March 1973 with the Board publishing details of domestic water consumption in a daily 'Water Gauge' in the *West Australian* newspaper. Yet the pattern of water consumption for this period suggests that householders were more responsive to temperatures than the Board's campaign.[70] The voluntary conservation campaign of 1972/73 may therefore have improved community awareness of domestic scheme consumption, with few alterations to household behaviour.

Just a year later, however, the Water Board implemented restrictions in January 1974. During heatwave conditions, the Board complained that householders were not co-operating with their calls to reduce consumption. The responses from Perth householders published in the local newspapers apportioned most of the blame for the January restrictions to those who watered their gardens excessively. These correspondents urged the Water Board to carry out 'spot checks' on the suburbs to catch such householders, who were said to be watering 'roofs, paths, roads and people next door'. Indeed, the Water Board received a record 350 complaints from residents concerned about their neighbours' water use. This response represents a marked departure from the Australian stereotype of collective defiance in the face of authority and state interference. Perhaps these complaints represented a sign of a growing public awareness of the problems associated with excess water consumption. Alternatively, householders might have resented neighbours flouting the restrictions to maintain a handsome garden or to avoid the inconveniences of hand-watering. A more likely explanation is that complainants believed in sharing the burden of government intrusions fairly and equally.

Although the Water Board implemented another voluntary water conservation campaign in late 1976, ongoing dry conditions necessitated the introduction of water restrictions in mid-1977. The Board also embarked on a publicity campaign to reinforce the importance of water conservation. The publicity to encourage the reduction of household water consumption generally focused residents' attention on their gardens, where prying neighbours and Water Board inspectors could most easily observe their abstinence or extravagance with scheme water. The campaign thus publicised the work of the Board's inspectors, as well as publishing images of reservoirs at low levels. This emphasised the importance of conserving water in each home and garden in the metropolitan area, and encouraged householders to monitor their own consumption and that of others. Through this publicity campaign, then, the

Water Board aimed to make the 'public aware of the seriousness of the water shortage'.[71]

Over the course of the decade, meanwhile, a transformation had occurred in the ways that overseas and Australian governments perceived the provision of water supplies. In the United Kingdom and United States, water managers had become increasingly aware that water consumption was not merely for the purposes of public health – the 'sanitary revolution [was] over'.[72] A gulf had emerged between needs and demands.[73] Meanwhile, the cost of Big Water, of sustaining the illusion of endless supplies, had grown exponentially since the war and other public works were competing for these funds. Those demands had to be curtailed. The Western Australian government recognised that it too faced these challenges regarding water supply and demand and invited overseas experts to help it reduce the pressures on Perth's limited water supplies.

These experts advocated the shift away from traditional, development-oriented engineering approaches to the management of water supplies. According to policy analyst John Pigram, managing water resources now required the creation of 'conditions which will bring about optimum use of water resources' through the 'adoption of measures to modify water needs and to maximise efficiency in water use'.[74] The primary tool to achieve this efficiency, argued the experts, was the price mechanism, that is, user pays. It was a policy that reflected the growing influence of neo-liberal laissez faire thinking in Australian politics, which advocated the market over state intervention. In the wake of the political instability of the Whitlam government, the emergence of stagflation, and the well-publicised visit of Milton Friedman, conservative Australian politicians in the mid-1970s saw in these principles a viable alternative to what they perceived to be the failed Keynesian policies of the post-war era.[75]

In Perth, Big Water sought to implement a shift to user pays, under which household water rates now reflected more closely the costs of providing this service. As for the people of Perth, the new pricing policy recast their identities as consumers. Before, they had been citizens with a right to water and the government determined their ability to pay for this water through the valuation of their property, which provided a proxy measure of the wealth and income of the consumer and their 'capacity to pay'. Now, under user pays, they were customers, who could purchase different quantities of the commodity, water, according to their willingness to pay.[76] This changing consumer identity resembled the process underway in England and Wales following the nationalisation of the water industry in 1974. There, pricing policies had developed to ensure the recovery of the cost of supplies, whilst in Perth, it was a means to manage demand by linking price to consumption.[77] Although the introduction of user pays in Perth helped to reduce water consumption in the late 1970s, some households bore the brunt of this reduction more heavily than others.

The Metropolitan Water Board implemented a system of user–pays water rating for the domestic sector on 1 July 1978. It stipulated a fixed charge for households ($36), an allowance of 150 kL per annum, and a further charge for each kilolitre used in excess of the 150 kL allowance (at 17c per kL).[78] The most significant difference between the new and old systems was the introduction of a water allowance for each household. In the past, property values had determined the household's water rates, which were independent of the quantity of water consumed. Under the new system, all households had the same allowance (150 kL), regardless of house value, family size, or block size.

Although there appeared to be general support for the philosophy behind the new scheme, some aspects of the system raised the ire of householders, not least its retrospective application. Taking up the cause of those worst affected, the editor of the *West Australian* noted in August 1978, 'Depleted water storages are now not the Government's only worry. An enormous reservoir of public goodwill is drying up rapidly. It will continue to dry up unless some corrective action about retrospectivity is taken.'[79] To appease its irate customers, the Water Board increased the 1978 allowance to 210 kL, which saved households $10.20 on the water bill. For those customers whose meters had been read prior to July 1, the Board also granted a pro-rata additional allowance of 12.5 kL for each month between the meter reading and the July implementation of the new scheme.

The Opposition viewed 'pay for use' as an opportunity for the Water Board to increase rates.[80] Some residents estimated that this new flat rate was nearly double the cost of 150 kL under the previous system (in cents per kilolitre), and decried its impact on poor families.[81] Newspaper correspondents also complained of large increases in their total water bill.[82] Others, meanwhile, found the new system had a negligible impact on their bills, probably because the new allowance was not significantly different from their usage under the previous system.[83]

The loudest opposition came from Perth's keen gardeners, who considered that the new rating system discriminated especially against them. They believed the Court government had 'unmercifully slug[ged] thousands of people' who did 'an environmental job in keeping Perth pleasant and presentable'.[84] One asked, 'Is our choice only to be brown lawns, wood chips or paving bricks?'[85] Others accused the Water Board of turning Western Australia from the 'State of Excitement' into the 'State of Dehydration'.[86]

Despite this initial controversy, the new system combined with the cultural effects of the water restrictions and publicity campaigns to bring about a reduction in the consumption of scheme water by the end of the 1970s.[87] When restrictions were lifted in 1979, a major rise in scheme water use did not occur. Total and average water use in 1981/82 remained well below 1975/76 levels, even though the number of properties serviced by the Water Board had increased by over 20 per cent during this period. The Board's 1985 Domestic Water Use Study of consumer attitudes and behaviours regarding scheme water – itself a reflection of growing interest in demand management – observed that that the economic pressures of 'pay for use' rating were most accountable for this change in behaviour, particularly among non-bore users. Furthermore, the study found that this reduction in scheme water use had most likely occurred outside the home, as indoor water use was very insensitive to price changes. Indeed, the study established that in contrast to the mid-1970s, over half of the average household's scheme water consumption occurred inside the home in the mid-1980s.[88]

The persistence of lower levels of household water consumption into the 1980s suggests that these elements helped to shape a broader cultural change towards water use in Perth's suburbs. The dry 1970s had exposed the cultural dependence of Perth residents on the illusion of endless water supplies that had developed with the ascendance of Big Water after World War II. The voracious growth of Big Water had both fostered and facilitated their escalating demands for water in the post-war era. With this façade stripped away by the introduction of water restrictions and conservation campaigns, many households became cognisant that they could maintain their lifestyles with less (scheme) water. The implementation of user pays at last provided these consumers with the financial incentive to lower their scheme water use and to shape a less thirsty water culture in the suburbs of Perth.

This cultural change manifested itself differently throughout the suburbs. Some of the board's water conservation publicity had specifically targeted women, linking the image of the enthusiastic and competent housewife to a range of conservation messages regarding water use inside the home. These included turning off taps in the kitchen and bathroom to reduce household expenditure and waste. Even though an increasing proportion of women were engaging in paid work outside the home by this time, the Board's publicity assumed that women could and should take primary responsibility for water conservation inside the home.[89]

In a forerunner to the 'Water Wally' campaigns of the 1980s, water conservation publicity also reinforced the different roles of men and women outside their homes. Although images of men and women in their homes and gardens were prevalent in local gardening literature, there is very little evidence of conservation campaigns involving characters and photographs prior to the 1970s. The Water Board's 1977 'Save Water' campaign, however, clarified certain gender roles. The cover of a water conservation brochure featured a barefoot Test bowler Dennis Lillee 'guiding a lawnmower over a suburban lawn as green and as flat as a billiard table'.[90] Meanwhile, model Elizabeth Fisher raked the flowerbed. Here, the garden was a distinctly masculine sphere, where men were responsible for watering, maintenance, and lawn upkeep. Women were beautiful accessories to this male gardening experience, confined to the lesser role of tending the flowers. As many suburban gardens transformed into domestic spaces of leisure and recreation during the 1950s and 1960s, the domestic role of women inside the home had now extended beyond the sliding doors and into the back garden. Out there, as historian Katie Holmes notes, 'She remained the housewife...while the man became the gardener'.[91]

Although men and women were depicted as enjoying different relationships to their gardens, many of them shared a desire to preserve their traditional gardens, even at great financial cost. Indeed, the financial relationship of householders to their homes tended to guide their approach to domestic water conservation. The Domestic Water Use Study found that owner–occupied homes consumed twice as much as rental properties, probably because tenants were less likely to invest in 'someone else's' garden. Likewise, wealthier householders tended to consume more water and were able to afford the higher charges associated with excess water use under the user pays system.[92]

Those householders who did not want, or could not afford, to install private bores could opt to make landscaping changes to their gardens. The establishment of the Society for Growing Australian Plants and the Western Australian Wildflower Society in the 1950s had signalled that urban Australians were taking an interest in native plants for their appearance and practicality. After the war, Australian garden writers and designers had encouraged gardeners to use native flora as a means to protect vulnerable species from suburban and agricultural expansion. Writers like Betty Maloney and Jean Walker urged their readers to embrace, rather than fear, the bush and its flora. The increased enthusiasm for native plants may also be seen as a sign of Australia's burgeoning national confidence in the 1970s and the emergence of a broader environmentalism, perhaps even a sign of respect for the genius loci (or the spirit of the place).[93] By the 1970s, in Perth at least, gardening with native plants was becoming a more mainstream activity, particularly after the long-awaited opening of Western Australia's Botanic Gardens at Kings Park in 1965.

In Perth, the State government and gardening experts urged residents to replace their exotic plants and lawns with more hardy, drought-resistant Australian natives to cope with the below average rainfall of the late 1970s. Since the 1950s, proponents of gardening with native flora had assured gardeners that these plants were maintenance-free and more Western Australian species became commercially available from the late 1960s. Local businesses encouraged this apparent shift in favour of less thirsty plants and landscaping designs. Advertisements and gardening columns featured references to Perth's water restrictions and 'pay for use', emphasising the availability of alternative, native garden designs and landscaping features, such as brick paving and wooden railway sleepers. Nurseries advertised a wide range of native plants, including callistemon, grevillea, banksia, and boronia, reminding shoppers to 'Go Native, Save Water'. To appeal to those gardeners who were reluctant to forgo their traditional garden, native plants were marketed as able to 'enhance the appearance of their homes' and 'provide a splash of colour with minimum maintenance'.[94]

The 1985 Domestic Water Use Study found that many Perth gardens had undergone marked landscaping changes in the late 1970s. A significant proportion of householders reduced their lawn area, and increased their use of native plants, woodchips, and brick paving. Affluent households, which invested heavily in their gardens, were more likely to make such changes than less affluent ones. It is worth noting that affluent households could have afforded excess water and bores, but many chose to make significant landscaping changes to their gardens. These garden alterations, however, did not necessarily lead to a reduction in water use.[95] A lack of knowledge of the water needs of native plants might have limited the impact of native gardens on householders' water use.[96] A more likely explanation, however, is that landscaping choices were influenced more by garden fashions and the desire to reduce the expenditure of time, labour and money on the garden, than the push to reduce domestic water consumption.[97] It therefore appears that the shift towards native plants in some Perth gardens was partly a result of pressures regarding water use as well a product of fashion and nationalism.

Of course some households rejected the trend towards native plants in Perth gardens: Australian plants were widely perceived as dry, brown and ugly.[98] Some households resisted any change at all. This was more than merely an aesthetic preference for a traditional garden. Western Australia has historically attracted a high number of British migrants compared to the other states and their presence has strongly influenced the taste and character of Perth's suburbs. Perth households were therefore especially inclined towards the English-style garden. In all Australian capital cities, however, such gardens were important cultural sites, invested with suburban meanings of civility and social status.[99] This consensus on the significance of the traditional garden could only have emerged after decades of reliable water supplies across the nation's urban centres. Suburban standards of social duty and conformity were most prominently displayed in the front garden where their maintenance was vital to the suburban streetscape. The large amounts of water required to maintain this traditional image of suburban respectability may have hindered the practical success of the Water Board's efforts to promote water conservation. Furthermore, landscaping changes that significantly altered the traditional garden were not an option for those householders who placed a high value on the aesthetic and social values of such gardens. The historic commitment to the traditional garden in suburban Perth, which was symptomatic of the enduring profligate water culture, prevented many gardeners from improving their hydroresilience.

For households that valued their traditional gardens and were fortunate enough to be financially and geographically well-situated, private bores and wells could be installed, giving access to virtually unlimited water for garden use. Although private bores have a long history in Perth's suburbs, bore ownership trebled between 1976 and 1982. Although bore users were found to consume significantly less scheme water than non-bore users at the end of the period, the Domestic Water Use Study estimated that the volume of groundwater extracted from the shallow aquifer by domestic bores was over seven times the average household scheme water irrigation of non-bore users.[100] Private bores were clearly installed so that householders could continue (or even extend) their existing consumption behaviour while reducing their scheme water use. This trend persisted into the 1980s, when the Water Board estimated that up to 45 per cent of total water used for domestic consumption in Perth came from private bores.[101] Many consumers therefore interpreted the Water Board's efforts to encourage water conservation as relating only to *scheme* water use, rather than water in general.

The increased household tapping of groundwater sources suggests that there was a dearth of information and knowledge in the community regarding the environmental impact of groundwater use. Prior to the mid-1970s there was very little public comment from the government or householders regarding the effects of groundwater use and during earlier periods of restriction, the Water Board had recommended residents install private bores to reduce public demand for scheme water. As these backyard bores tapped the same source of groundwater as Big Water, some residents expressed concerns about the ecological consequences of this supplementary supply.[102] Big Water's engineers believed, however, that private abstraction had little effect on groundwater levels because it generally involved small abstractions from a large number of widely distributed wells. Furthermore, the engineers reasoned, more water permeated to the shallow aquifers beneath the residential block, compared to the undeveloped Gnangara Mound so the watertable would hardly decline.[103]

Consequently, although the Water Board made information regarding groundwater use available, there was not the same level of urgency to conserve this water resource that had accompanied voluntary and enforced restrictions on scheme water. Furthermore, attempts to licence and meter private bores in the early 1970s had been met with staunch opposition from the community. Bore owners believed they were reducing pressure on scheme water supplies and thus helping the Water Board conserve water.[104] In spite of public education campaigns encouraging the reduction of scheme water, the widespread acceptance of groundwater as an alternative or supplement to scheme water suggests that both Big Water and its customers were reluctant to significantly reduce the *total* demand for water or to question Perth's profligate water culture. Although bore-owners could reduce their dependence on Big Water to slake their thirst, access to unfettered water supplies did little to improve their long-term hydroresilience.

The responses to the water demand management policies of the late 1970s may also be examined in the context of the rising profile of local and overseas environmental issues as part of a broader trend of increasing international ecological awareness and the emergence of the new environment movement. Geographer Maria Kaïka argues that in western societies, the home operates as a means of separating 'the inside from the outside, nature from human beings, [and] the public from the private sphere'.[105] Although Kaïka refers to Western European trends, her ideas fit a long-held Australian notion of the domestic space, house and garden, as an impenetrable private sphere, a sanctuary for its residents.

In the 1970s, when public awareness of environmental problems was concerned largely with 'green' issues, such as conserving bushland, the issue of water scarcity did not appear to be woven into the emerging environmental consciousness. Furthermore, Perth residents often understood the broader environment as somehow independent of or distanced from the household, geographically and politically. This exclusivity of the domestic space reflected a cultural attachment of many householders to their homes as places to retreat from the outside world.[106] As private gardens were usually not seen in this sense as part of nature but part of the home, water use in the garden was not widely considered to have environmental implications.

Enforced restrictions and user pays posed a threat to this sociocultural isolation of the home, rendering visible those social processes that had scripted nature as 'the other'. More precisely, as access to water was restricted Perth residents started to experience some of the consequences of their thirsty lifestyles; they were increasingly subject to the vagaries of 'nature'. The intermittent periods of enforced and voluntary restrictions from the early 1920s to the late 1970s, combined with the additional measure of user pays, thus exposed the fragility of suburban standards of civility and domestic bliss.[107] Although suburban anxieties about running out continued into the 1980s, the demand management strategies deployed in the late 1970s helped to temper the profligate (scheme) water culture of the people of Perth.

Protecting Big Water

Despite the curtailment of water consumption through restrictions and user pays, the government's anxieties about running out persisted. Although the State government had already dismissed plans to pipe water from the northwest, another grand project presented itself as the means to attain endless water supplies for Perth. This was a vision that was far grander in scale: Antarctic icebergs. International scientific and political interest in the possibility of using Antarctic icebergs to alleviate water scarcity was first sparked at a conference of the International Glaciological Society in Cambridge, England in 1969. Research continued into the early 1970s, primarily under the auspices of the RAND Corporation and also at the behest of Prince Mohamed Al Faisal Al Saud of Saudi Arabia. In 1974, the Australian Academy of Science (AAS) established a special committee to consider the possibilities of using this technology in southern Australia. The *Financial Review* reported that 'with two thirds of the world's fresh water bailed up on the continent it is inevitable that technological improvements will eventually allow this immense reservoir to be harvested on a large scale'.[108] No one seemed to note the irony inherent in taking water from one desert to another.

In 1978, Foundation Professor of Meteorology at Flinders University, Peter Schwerdtfeger, approached the Western Australian State Committee of CSIRO with regard to employing iceberg technology in Western Australia. Schwerdtfeger had been closely involved in the AAS study and had recently become the Australian coordinator for Iceberg Transport International, an international consortium sponsored largely by Saudi Arabia that was considering Western Australia for its iceberg experiments.[109] According to these plans, an iceberg would be towed from Antarctica and moored off the Western Australian coast near Fremantle. A pipeline would be constructed to transport the iceberg water to land. Despite enthusiastic negotiations between Schwerdtfeger and the State Committee, especially its secretary John Brophy, local scientists and engineers dismissed the idea. The PWD Director of Engineering, Bob Hillman, and the Water Board Chief Engineer, Harold Hunt, declared that the financial cost of the plan made the proposal unfeasible.[110] It was just another pipedream.

Meanwhile, Big Water had become increasingly reliant on the groundwater resources of the Swan Coastal Plain. In the late 1970s, for instance, up to 50 per cent of Big Water's supplies were drawn from its groundwater schemes on the Gnangara Mound.[111] Although groundwater reserves had softened the severity of water restrictions in the late 1970s, their use was not without cost. Ecologists, for instance, noted the stress that the tapping of these reserves had put on nearby native vegetation, which was already under strain in the dry conditions.[112] Both the quality and quantity of Perth's groundwater resources needed protection to ensure that this valuable stopgap for Big Water would not run out. Already the EPA had recommended against the proposed Pacminex Alumina refinery in Upper Swan because of the risk it posed to groundwater supplies.[113] Mining was not the only threat, however, to the groundwater reserves of the Swan Coastal Plain. The region's market gardeners also competed with Big Water's claim to these supplies.

The Water Board had introduced restrictions on water and land use near its groundwater schemes since the early 1970s. But as these applied to the Gnangara Mound, where the landscape was relatively undeveloped, there had been few, if any, complaints from the public. This was not the case in 1977 when the Board revealed its intention to control and tap the groundwater reserves of the Jandakot Mound south of Perth. At that time, market gardeners were using this area for the cultivation of fruit and vegetables, and animal husbandry. Under the new regulations, farmers faced restrictions on the use of insecticides and animal manure on market gardens and cattle farms, as well as licensing on their private bores. Not only were they concerned that their farming methods would be curtailed without compensation but they also feared a drop in the watertable. This would reduce the availability of water close to the surface, which these farmers relied upon to water their pastures and crops during the summer without irrigation. If the watertable fell, farmers would have to invest in drilling and irrigation equipment to supply their properties with water during the annual dry season.[114]

Outraged that they were not offered compensation, some Jandakot farmers joined forces with the Cockburn Town Council to take legal action against the Water Board, and a bloodthirsty rural press closely followed their case. The farmers unsuccessfully alleged that the Board had failed to comply with a section of the Metropolitan Water Supply Sewerage and Drainage Act that required the Board 'to make certain details of its plans public for objections before obtaining the approval of the Governor' to develop the water resources.[115] The rural newspaper *Western Farmer* seized upon the story and presented the Jandakot situation as a conflict between both rural and urban interests, and productive and unproductive uses of water, as well as an issue of ecological destruction.

According to the *Western Farmer*, the Water Board's treatment of the Jandakot farmers represented yet another example of the State government favouring its suburban constituents over rural areas. Although the Jandakot area was ostensibly suburban by this time, the landholders subscribed to a rural identity, which stemmed from its development as an agricultural area at the turn of the century.[116] The *Western Farmer* asked, 'Is it right to threaten a region's agricultural future for the comfort of city and town dwellers?'[117] This perspective argued that because the water use of Jandakot farmers was intended for horticulture and animal husbandry, it was justifiable and 'right'. The diversion of the groundwater resources for suburban use was inherently (morally) flawed. For instance, the newspaper reported, 'Landholders question why their water supplies to grow food should be restricted for the benefit of urban lawns and gardens'.[118]

In its support of the Jandakot farmers, the *Western Farmer* also argued that the Water Board development of the area's groundwater reserves would be detrimental to the local wetland areas. The toll of the successive dry years of the late 1970s on the shallow lakes and native vegetation had not gone unnoticed. According to the newspaper, increasing the draw on the groundwater resources would only deplete them further.[119] The use of this water by farmers, the newspaper suggested, was not contributing to lowering the watertable. As one farmer argued, 'The water we use goes back into the ground. When it's pumped to the city it will be gone forever'.[120] For the market gardeners on the outskirts of Perth, these restrictions raised anxieties about their livelihoods — the vulnerability of the suburbs, they considered, would be reduced at their expense.

Although groundwater had become an important supplement to the hills sources, these surface water storages remained vital components of both the urban and rural water supply networks. It was therefore necessary to protect the quality and quantity of the water supplied from the dams in the Darling Ranges. Although there had been PWD concerns about the rising salt levels in Perth's water supplies since at least the 1950s, the issue did not come to the attention of the suburban public until the mid-1970s. The local media and the Campaign to Save Native Forests conservation group stirred up community concern about the quality of the urban water supply, citing the links between saline water and health problems. Keen to downplay these anxieties, the government attributed the salt levels to the prevailing drought conditions and assured the public that the water quality had improved following winter rains. But the weight of research conducted by government scientists suggested otherwise: the clearing of native vegetation was the real cause of the rising salinity.[121] And it was endangering Big Water.

Nearly seventy years after government scientists first identified a relationship between the clearing of native vegetation and salinity, the State government undertook measures to limit the spread of salt. In January 1979, the government introduced legislation to ban land clearing in the Mundaring Weir and Denmark River catchment areas and the Warren and Kent River Water Reserves.[122] This legislation was enacted without consultation with the affected farmers to avoid a rush of clearing before the ban commenced, which resulted in protests from farmers and their representatives that they had been unfairly treated. Again, the rural press seized upon the issue as yet another example of the suburbs profiting from the expense of rural communities — they would be 'strangled' by a 'thirsty metropolis'.[123] Despite the backlash from affected farmers, the government maintained its position on the clearing bans to ensure that the region's water supplies were protected. The stage was set for a clash between the city and its hinterland, between misuse and use, frivolity and utility. The subsequent curtailment of farming practices reflected a change in the weather for the southwest's agricultural areas.

Paying the piper

Although many southwest farmers had found the seasonal conditions of the early 1970s difficult, the series of dry years later in the decade were unprecedented in their severity and impact. Unusually low winter rains in 1976 brought drought conditions to many areas of the southwest region, which lasted into the early 1980s for many farmers, particularly in the northeastern wheatbelt. The severity of the drought shocked farmers across the region, with old-timers like Dalwallinu farmer Ted Black noting that he had 'never seen it as dry'.[124] As these conditions lingered, farmers in the northeastern wheatbelt suffered four consecutive years of drought. Even areas like Kondinin and Katanning, where rainfall had been considered safe and reliable, were affected. As Perenjori farmer Bill Bestry recalled, 'They were our hardest years...They set us back a lot, set us back a long way, those years'.[125] By the end of the decade, the drought-affected area extended from the northeastern wheatbelt and upper central region down into the southern wheatbelt.[126]

The same economic turn that had transformed Big Water in the suburbs was affecting the ways that both farmers and the government prepared for, and responded to, climate variability and water scarcity. By the late 1970s, it had become increasingly likely that the farmers in unreticulated parts of the wheatbelt would remain outside the scope of Big Water. In 1978, the State government proposed the development of reticulated water supplies to farmlands north of the boundary of the area served by the CWSS, where it had been difficult to establish farm supplies. This scheme involved the development of groundwater resources at Agaton to supplement the CWSS to alleviate the burden on the

Mundaring source. But the cost of the project was its downfall. The Commonwealth government refused to support the program in 1981 and the State government was unable to fund the scheme alone. This failure to attain Commonwealth funding for the expansion of the CWSS revealed the growing fiscal constraints on the provision of public water supplies in the 1970s and 1980s.

The earlier rejection of plans to extend the CWSS and the failure of Agaton demonstrated to the government, at least, that Big Water in its rural form was unlikely to undergo further expansion. As the Department of Agriculture reported in 1981, 'Economic forces have moved against projects involving water transfer over great distances, and in favour of maximum local development of supplies'.[127] Big Water had always run at a loss in the agricultural areas, because the government subsidised the supply of scheme water to farms. Besides, improvements in technology had reduced the cost and difficulty of constructing dams and sinking bores. Greater development of local supplies, whether in towns or on farms, would not only protect agricultural production from drought, but also reduce the financial burden of government subsidies for the CWSS and alleviate the mounting public debts of drought assistance. It seems that whatever enhancements farmers had made to their water supplies since 1969 had not been sufficient to improve their hydroresilience. Further efforts were required to prepare themselves for future periods of water scarcity and the government provided assistance to these ends through low-cost loans as well as fodder and agistment subsidies. More than ever before, the onus was on farmers to protect themselves from running out.

Yet in the areas of the wheatbelt most affected by drought, the government's campaigns to improve water conservation on farms must have seemed frustrating. The Department of Agriculture had urged farmers to access underground water if possible; enlarge dam catchments and use contour drains to capture water; prevent dam leakages; and excavate 'flat batter' dams, which combine a circular, artificial catchment with a central storage dam. Although these were sensible strategies for the future, if underground water was not available, they provided no remedy for the immediate problem at hand: a severe shortfall of rain. As the drought wore on, the prospect of making the heavens open appeared very attractive. In July 1977 nearly 200 farmers from Morawa and Perenjori formed the Northern Rainmakers Committee and were prepared to finance a cloud seeding operation if CSIRO could provide the equipment.[128] Reports of successful experimentation elsewhere in Australia and overseas gave these desperate farmers hope that their situations could improve. As CSIRO and the Federal and State governments were responsible for funding and conducting the cloud seeding missions in other states, the affected farmers naturally turned to the Court government for assistance in establishing their own program.

The unconvincing results of previous attempts to modify the region's weather made the State government and CSIRO particularly reluctant to support the farmers' efforts. Although the State government sympathised with their position, the idea of investing in an unproven technique for uncertain results was at odds with the growing influence of laissez faire principles among decision-makers. As a result, the Agriculture Minister Dick Old stressed the need for further research on local weather conditions before any action could be undertaken. Neither CSIRO nor the Bureau of Meteorology wanted to be involved 'in a trial that was doomed from the start'.[129]

But as the dry wore on, the farmers of the northeastern wheatbelt persevered with their cause. In 1979, the Northern Rainmakers (now with over 500 members) joined with Northampton's Elsewhere Rain Inducement Committee and other groups in nearby Dalwallinu and Mount Marshall to form the Western Australian Weather Research Association (WRA). The Association managed to convince the government of the need for funding and with this assistance, it could afford to sponsor a cloud study of the northern wheatbelt by physicists at the Western Australian Institute of Technology. The purpose of the three-year study (1980 to 1982) was to determine the nature of the local atmospheric conditions and to commence a cloud seeding program based on this information.[130] But the tests were inconclusive: the study found that although the northern wheatbelt region was probably suitable, it would be difficult to identify a noticeable increase in rainfall in the short term. As a result, a long-term commitment of funding was necessary. Yet this commitment did not eventuate. In late 1981, CSIRO announced the end of its cloud seeding program because it was no longer economically feasible.

The inability of the Bureau of Meteorology to provide long-term or seasonal forecasts to southwest farmers was also a source of discontent. In July 1976, the *Western Farmer* began to publish the predictions of private weather forecaster, Lennox Walker – the successor to the controversial weather prophet, Inigo Jones. The Bureau of Meteorology declined to comment on the accuracy and effectiveness of his forecasts, which he based on an analysis of sunspot activity and official meteorological data. Walker's forecasts appeared regularly in the rural press until the early 1980s but it is not clear whether farmers in the southwest heeded Walker's predictions. If they sought further information from Walker at his Crohamhurst Observatory in Queensland, they could subscribe to his service – at a price, of course. It is likely, however, that many farmers in southwest Western Australia considered Walker as reliable a guide to local conditions as the Bureau's forecasters in Melbourne – just another 'wise man' from the east. Most farmers remained dependent on their own local knowledge and the Bureau's short-term forecasts to help them avoid running out.

Many farmers in the southwest's agricultural areas at the end of the decade, therefore, found themselves having to take matters into their own hands. Economic constraints on the expansion of Big Water forced farmers to undertake the measures necessary to improve water and fodder conservation on their farms. Although the government provided some assistance for these projects, the onus was increasingly on farmers to reduce their vulnerability to running out. They could no longer rely on the favour of paternalist governments. But self-reliance came at a cost: technical solutions to water shortage and climate variability, such as cloud seeding, required deep pockets at a time when declining terms of trade and high input costs were crushing many farmers in a cost-price squeeze. After decades of policies promoting the merits of closer settlement, Australian governments were recommending to farmers that they 'get big or get out'. Unless farmers could afford to improve their water supplies, they would remain vulnerable to running out.

Another 'gigantic folk experiment'

Despite the economic difficulties facing the state's agricultural industries and the dry seasons of the late 1970s, the State government announced in 1980 its plan to release 3 million hectares of land in the Ravensthorpe area.[131] Laced with the rhetoric of countrymindedness, this new era of land release echoed the land settlement programs of earlier governments, especially under Premiers Sir John Forrest, Sir James Mitchell and Sir David Brand. Still in the 1980s the government believed that, 'Young aspiring farmers [wanted] a chance to get into primary production without the need for big capital sums to buy an established property'.[132] Moreover, more country shires stood to benefit from a new era of land release. Land releases increased the local population and rating revenues; boosted local industries and businesses; provided better fire and vermin control for neighbouring properties; and enabled young farmers to acquire farms near their parents' properties.

But the expansion of European settlement across the southwest region into areas with little or no meteorological information had been a bitter experience for many farmers, especially during the droughts of 1914 and 1940. Their livelihoods had been 'gigantic folk experiments', characterised by uncertainty, as they struggled to interpret the unfamiliar climatic patterns, soils, flora and fauna of the 'new' lands.[133] By the 1970s, however, some things were certain: soil erosion, salinity, poor seasons and the cost-price squeeze had combined to make life difficult for those on the land. In addition, there were growing environmental anxieties that the earth's climate was changing, which could affect the viability of farming in the southwest. Nevertheless, the government forged ahead and opened the marginal lands in the southeastern wheatbelt for settlement, thrusting another generation of farmers into yet another folk experiment, rendering them vulnerable to running out.

A series of severe climate events in the early 1970s had raised international scientific and political concerns that the earth's climate was changing. During 1972, for instance, drought afflicted the Sahel and the Ukraine, and the Indian monsoon failed, which resulted in crop losses and world shortages of grain. The publication of the Club of Rome's *Limits to Growth* that year had piqued Western anxieties about whether the earth could sustain the burgeoning global population. The international scientific response to these anxieties about the earth's carrying capacity and the added pressures of a changing climate were naturally technocratic, focussing on predicting and monitoring climate variability. In early 1975, the Whitlam government commissioned the Australian Academy of Science to investigate whether the continent's climate was changing and whether such change could be predicted. The Academy organised a group of Australian scientists representing a wide range of disciplines to collaborate on this investigation as a Committee on Climatic Change.[134]

The terms of reference for the Committee were to report on overseas research about changes in global climate and the extent to which these changes were human-caused; whether the climate of Australia was undergoing change; whether future change could be predicted; and to identify the consequences of these changes for agricultural production in Australia. In its report, the Committee highlighted the relationship between human settlement patterns, agricultural production and climate variability. The greater use of lands of marginal rainfall would render these populations and their activities increasingly vulnerable to climate variability, regardless of long-term climate change. For Australian conditions at least, the Committee noted, 'visions of vastly increased agricultural production are unrealistic'. Regardless of climatic change, if this pattern was to continue, warned the Committee, 'the effects of climatic variability are likely to become progressively more serious, frequent and damaging'.[135]

Meanwhile, the Australian Branch of the Royal Meteorological Society had convened a conference titled 'Climatic Change and Variability: a southern perspective' at Monash University in Victoria. Many of the members of the Committee on Climatic Change participated in this conference. One of the presentations assessed the possible implications of climatic change on Mediterranean agriculture in Western Australia.[136] In the paper, Bureau of Meteorology researcher Michael Coughlan speculated on the implications of a regional drying trend in the southwest, which he estimated had commenced prior to World War I.[137] In the higher rainfall areas of the agricultural region, Coughlan expected that less winter rain could benefit farming as waterlogged soils restricted plant growth. In the drier areas, however, lower rainfall would severely affect farming activities. Most of the area that was currently receiving less than 300 mm rainfall 'would go out of agricultural production'.[138] Towns that stood to be affected included Southern Cross, Merredin, Salmon Gums, Kellerberrin, Hyden, Morawa and Mullewa. Over a thousand farms operated in this area, producing over 20 per cent of the state's wheat crop. If these observations were correct and the drying trend persisted, farmers on the eastern fringes of the agricultural areas were at risk of running out of water for cropping.

Geographer Joseph Gentilli, who had been consulted by the Committee on Climatic Change, was also concerned about the consequences of a changing climate for the agricultural production in the southwest. In his 1972 book, *Australian Climate Patterns*, Gentilli had stressed the importance of analysing climates not only spatially, but also temporally in order to assess their variability over time. In light of this attention to climate change, Gentilli also qualified his earlier support for agricultural development in the southwest. He criticised the release of a 'million acres a year' on the margins of the wheatbelt on climatic grounds. He explained:

> These were millions of acres of land with climates precariously balanced between aridity and semi-aridity, released for settlement after a period of increasing rainfall which had just brought their climate into the semi-arid category. Without any great climatic change, a simple return to the conditions of a few decades earlier may now have returned these lands to the margins of the arid region, where land utilisation in any form is more precarious, less effective and more expensive.[139]

This damning assessment of the state's post-war agricultural policies, which Gentilli had once vigorously supported, suggests that he now considered many wheatbelt farmers had been betrayed and rendered vulnerable to running out.

The combination of these findings deeply concerned both the Department of Agriculture and the Water Board in Western Australia.[140] In fact, Coughlan noted, Western Australia was 'the first region that's shown sufficient interest' in the issue of climatic change.[141] Despite Coughlan's findings, however, the Bureau of Meteorology was reluctant to confirm any such change was underway. Their official position was that the 'case is "not proven"'.[142] As Bob Southern, the Regional Director of the Bureau in Western Australia, explained to Noel Fitzpatrick, the Director of the Department of Agriculture in 1976, 'My point is simply that the possible effects of long term climatic change are swamped by the realities of normal seasonal expectancy based on current data'.[143]

Dry conditions alone, however, were not the sole cause of the Department of Agriculture's concerns; there were also growing anxieties about the financial viability of farms in marginal areas of the wheatbelt. Even before scientific and economic concerns over the viability of farming in marginal lands had been voiced, Noel Fitzpatrick had conceded in 1973 that, more generally,

> Recommendations have frequently been made against release of certain areas on grounds of infertility, erosion risk, salinity hazard, economic unviability and flood and waterlogging hazard. Unfortunately it is true that pressure for the release of land for agriculture has in the past resulted in the development of some areas which should have been kept virgin for one or more of the above reasons.

A Commonwealth Inquiry into the New Land Farms scheme had recently concluded that the release of land to farmers in the southeastern wheatbelt in the 1950s and 1960s had been 'poorly conceived and managed'. For instance, the land was marginal in terms of both soil and climate; there had been little experience of farming in the area; and most applicants were inadequately prepared for farming under these circumstances.[144] The worsening economic pressures and poor seasonal conditions of the late 1970s only exacerbated their vulnerable position.

Yet it was lands nearby these struggling farms around Ravensthorpe that the State government planned to release for agricultural development. Despite the financial benefits that might accrue to local shires from such expansion, there was not unanimous support for the government's agenda. In addition to concerns about salinity, wind erosion and local flora and fauna, local and official anxieties about developing these areas centred on the lack of information about the region's climate and the prevailing drought conditions that were affecting farmers in the Esperance, Ravensthorpe and Jerramungup areas. For instance, the Officer in Charge of the Jerramungup Agricultural District Office was reportedly 'worried by the lack of real climatic data for his region'.[145]

So too were members of the Land Release Study Group. A handful of concerned individuals from the Esperance area had come together to put a stop to the government's plans of agricultural expansion. Although there was a diversity of opinions within the group, the members together argued 'for a fair and equitable appraisal of the land'.[146] Among them was Mount Barker farmer Ron Richards, who argued, 'No adequate analysis of effective rainfall has been carried out. Sufficient records do not exist'.[147] Another member, Ongerup botanist Ken Newbey, agreed. He had conducted his own study of the area designated for land release using the daily records of a neighbouring farmer. He also noted the scant nature of the meteorological record as well as the highly variable weather of the region, where Ongerup had recently recorded both its driest (1969) and wettest (1971) years.[148]

In late 1980, Newbey raised his concerns about the release of lands near Ravensthorpe with his local Member of the Legislative Assembly (MLA), the Liberal Party's Geoff Grewar. He reassured Newbey that, 'A government which releases land for settlement in an area that would be extremely marginal would be irresponsible and I do not believe this Government, with all the advices available to it, would release land of doubtful viability'.[149] But Grewar had underestimated the sway that developmentalism continued to hold over the State Liberal government: the land release went ahead. The subsequent Burke Labor government followed suit and provided the infrastructure around Ravensthorpe for settlement to get underway. The expression of environmental anxieties from local farmers and government scientists about climate variability, salinity and the effects of land development on local ecologies, as well as the economic constraints on government expenditure, suggest that the development of the lands near Ravensthorpe put southwest farmers at risk of running out. As George Seddon has suggested, 'A tempting response to a decline in prosperity is to squeeze the environment harder'.[150] But it could only be squeezed so much.

5

Precaution and Prediction:

Economic rationalism, ecologically sustainable development and environmental change (1983 to 2001)

In the final decades of the twentieth century, there was growing concern in Western nations that humankind, through its commitment to industrial development, had fostered the conditions for its own downfall. The corollary of progress was that the world was being rendered vulnerable to natural hazards and environmental problems that threatened to undermine the human race. Urgent action was required to prevent this decline from spiralling out of control. During the 1980s and 1990s, suburban and rural Western Australians became increasingly aware of the toll that unchecked development had taken on their state's natural environment. Logging, land clearing and soil degradation, while significant problems in and of themselves, were also affecting the quality of the region's water supplies, which the dry 1970s had already shown to be limited. Scientists identified a drying trend in the region, which some attributed to the atmospheric effects of global greenhouse gas emissions. As the state's population ticked over the one million mark, this growth and the sprawling suburbs of Perth placed additional pressures on the southwest's water supplies.

These threats to the quality and quantity of the southwest's water resources posed both environmental and economic challenges to the region, and helped to feed Western Australians' environmental anxieties about their future.

Many of the environmental problems facing Western Australians in the 1980s and 1990s spanned space and time; blurred causality, blame and liability; and could not be compensated or insured against.[1] These are what theorist Anthony Giddens terms 'manufactured risks' – risks produced by human progress, particularly science and technology. The scale and complexity of such environmental problems, Giddens has argued, fed a growing disenchantment with modernisation, which posed unprecedented challenges to traditional technocratic decision-making institutions.[2] Such critique, argued sociologists like Ulrich Beck and Giddens in the 1990s, was characteristic of a transition from an industrial society to the local and global 'risk society', whereby the global ecological crisis was perceived as 'a profound institutional crisis of industrial society itself'. These elements of the risk society had already begun to emerge in the southwest, as evidenced in the formation of the Land Release Study Group in the late 1970s to campaign against further agricultural development in the Esperance area. Questioning the established order was, therefore, a result of reaping what previous generations had sown; a product of being rendered vulnerable to disaster.

This reflexivity creates a difficult situation for the technocratic state, not least for its scientific role in disaster prevention. On the one hand, applications of science and technology for economic development are blamed for manufacturing risks; while on the other, scientific research is deemed necessary to identify and address these risks. These tensions strain the relationship between scientific experts and a lay public. Furthermore, these tensions can diminish trust in the very institutions on which societies depend for their protection against harm. This undermining of scientific authority is detrimental to a society increasingly preoccupied with the future and reliant on science and its institutions for information and guidance.[3] Dependent on technocratic solutions but untrusting of experts, citizens are left vulnerable to manufactured risks such as the threats to the quality and quantity of water resources that Western Australians faced in the 1980s and 1990s.

Salt water

By the early 1980s, Western Australian land and water managers in the southwest realised that water scarcity was not only a question of quantity, but also one of quality. The run of dry years in the late 1970s had exposed the vulnerability of the region's water resources as the lack of rain had increased the salinity of rivers and dams.[4] Bans on the further clearing of native vegetation in the catchment areas of the Mundaring Weir, Warren River, Kent River and Denmark River at this time had been the first official acknowledgement of the relationship between land degradation and water quality. But it was too little, too late. By the mid-1980s, national hydrological studies revealed that Western Australia bore the undesirable distinction of having the largest proportion of surface water classified as marginal, brackish and saline in the country.[5] By reducing the availability of the region's potable water supplies, nearly a century of land clearing had diminished the resilience of the southwest's water resources to running out.

The problems of dryland and stream salinity presented quite different challenges to the region's water resources than the more familiar nemesis of drought. Environmental degradation hazards like salinity are, as hazards scholar Douglas Paton argues, 'insidious, incremental, possibly irreversible, have a diffusion pattern across the landscape, and possess a long life expectancy'. As such, salinity represents the kind of 'manufactured risk' that sociologists associated with the risk society in the 1990s. Although primary salinity is a natural feature of the southwest's environment, where salt has accumulated over thousands of years, secondary salinity is a product of the region's agricultural development during the twentieth century. The large-scale clearing of native vegetation across the southwest and its replacement with shallow-rooted crops and pasture dramatically transformed the hydrology of the region. The crops and pasture did not use as much water as the deep-rooted vegetation it had replaced, which allowed water to pool as groundwater across the relatively flat lands of the wheatbelt. As the watertable rose, it brought to the surface the tons of salt that had amassed underground, which was detrimental for many native plants and other salt-intolerant species, including most crops and pastures. In addition to these effects on vegetation, evaporation of the saline groundwater at the surface damaged the soil and, as it drained away over time, degraded the quality of the region's waterways as well as farm water supplies.

Although the State government had taken action to prevent further deterioration of the region's water supplies in the late 1970s, there had been an awareness of the relationship between land clearing and salinity some fifty years earlier. In a paper read before the Royal Society of Western Australia in 1924, W. E. Wood of the Railway Department had argued that, 'It is generally recognised that our streams increase in salinity after the native vegetation is destroyed', which he attributed to a rising watertable.[6] But the allure of agricultural development had muted the repeated calls of government scientists to limit land clearing in the southwest, and thus deepened the vulnerability of Western Australians to water scarcity. The ongoing denial of the theory linking land clearing to salinity was later reinforced by poor equipment, which failed to detect rising salinity in the Wellington catchment in the 1960s.[7] Hydrologist Keith Bartlett recalled nearly fifty years later that, 'The quality of the gauging stations back then was so poor' that the deterioration of the water quality had gone undetected.[8] The degradation of the Wellington catchment exposed the brittle state of the dam's engineered resilience. Furthermore, its deterioration revealed the vulnerability of Big Water to running out.

One of the remedies that the nation's land and water managers prescribed for restoring salt-affected soils and waterways was extensive tree-planting or reforestation.[9] Trees and salt-tolerant shrubs, they hoped, might use some of the excess water and help to lower the watertable. Such programs, however, were beyond the means of many farmers in the salt-affected areas of the southwest, who were in the grip of a cost-price squeeze. Consequently, many were not financially able to implement changes to their farming methods that might reduce land degradation on their properties. Instead they had to continue 'mining' the land to avoid further financial difficulties.[10] As Perenjori farmer Bernie Kuhne rued in the early 1980s, 'I've still got a plough and I can't afford to work my land any other way. I know I'm putting my soil at risk by beating the hell out of it but I wouldn't do it if I didn't have to'.[11]

The process of reforestation also proved challenging for Big Water. In the late 1970s, the Public Works Department had commenced extensive tree-planting in the catchment of Wellington Dam to arrest the deterioration of its water supplies and to rehabilitate the area. Such catchment management strategies were unusual in Australia at this time, where engineers still tended to oversee the management and delivery of water supplies. But it was taking too long for results to materialise and some engineers feared that the water quality might never sufficiently improve to supply potable water to the Great Southern Towns Water Supply Scheme. A new dam, they argued, would produce much quicker results. This aspect of the engineering solution was especially appealing to the new Water Authority of Western Australia, which was more commercially oriented than its predecessor, the Public Works Department (PWD), and placed greater emphasis on processes of cost-benefit analysis.[12] The Water Authority had been the product of the merger of the rural water supply branch of the PWD and the Metropolitan Water Board in 1985, and had taken control of the public water supplies across the state. In contrast to the PWD, the Water Authority was responsible for setting the charges for water to the consumer as well as the management and protection of the state's water resources. After several years of political wrangling over the cost and location of the new dam, the Burke government announced the construction of the Harris Dam north of Collie in June 1987. It would reticulate the Great Southern Towns, while irrigators in the Collie catchment would continue to draw water from the Wellington Dam as scientists considered the saline supplies would not affect the fertility of their pastures. The ongoing use of water from Wellington Dam did little, however, to ameliorate the salinity of their lands, of which over 30 per cent was salt-affected.[13]

Sustainable development?

The dry winters of the mid-1980s brought to the southeastern agricultural areas their lowest rains since the drought of 1969 and reduced Perth's dams to their lowest levels since the parched late 1970s.[14] Winds completely bared some districts as soil erosion took its toll across the wheatbelt, and local water supplies reached critically low levels.[15] Meanwhile, the West Australian reported that residents of the western suburb of Floreat watched in alarm as the 'centrepiece of their green and pleasant suburb, Perry Lakes, dried to a couple of puddles'.[16] Across the southwest, Big Water urged its consumers to reduce their water use. Consumption was restricted in some country towns, while irrigators experimented with new methods to cope with the dry conditions.[17] Farmers in areas that had been declared 'drought affected' and 'water deficient' were provided with financial assistance, transport subsidies and access to emergency water supplies.

But the State government could not sustain this expenditure in the wheatbelt.[18] A large proportion of State government expenditure was on line-haulage – the transport of water to a central place for farmers to access.[19] Already the Federal government had begun to flag to the states that it would reduce its contributions to assistance and that it expected state authorities to foot a larger percentage of the bill.[20] In response, the Western Australian government embarked on a study of farm water supplies in the agricultural areas of the southwest to determine the extent to which farmers were prepared for the effects of dry spells.[21] This study found that across the wheatbelt, 'Farms generally appear to have insufficient capital invested in water supply'. Some of the least adequate water supplies were found in the southern and southeastern wheatbelt – those areas that had only been recently settled in the last phase of land release in the late 1970s. Salinity had also rendered many otherwise satisfactory sites for farm dams unusable.[22]

The State government embarked on a program to remedy these problems of farm water supplies. In the northeastern wheatbelt, where it was difficult to establish supplies due to low rainfall, high evaporation, saline groundwater, and prevailing soil conditions, the government connected towns to the existing Goldfields and Agricultural Water Supply Scheme.[23] This region was an exception to the government's increasingly 'economically rational' outlook because there were no other alternatives to reticulated water.[24] In other areas like the southern districts, the government provided cash incentives to farmers to undertake improvements to their own supplies through the installation of more farm dams and roaded catchments.[25] In line with its emerging neoliberal perspective, the government provided a relatively low level of assistance for farmers to undertake these changes.[26]

The lack of winter rain in the late 1980s was also taking its toll on the dams in the Darling Ranges, which were providing about 70 per cent of the southwest's scheme water supplies.[27] To supplement the dams, Big Water had become increasingly reliant upon the groundwater reserves beneath the Swan Coastal Plain, particularly in the northern suburbs.[28] But if the drying wetlands around Wanneroo were any indication of the health of these sources, their engineered resilience was already under strain.[29] As the population of Perth passed one million, the prevailing dry conditions exposed the vulnerability of the growing metropolis to water scarcity. This heightened significance of groundwater to Big Water in the late 1980s combined with the growing ecological awareness among many Western Australians to spark public debates about the sustainable management of the Swan Coastal Plain's land and water resources.

By the end of the decade, ecologists estimated that up to 80 per cent of the original wetlands of the Swan Coastal Plain had been drained or filled.[30] The remaining wetlands were not only at risk of drying out but also of contamination and pollution, which would have severe consequences for local ecosystems. For instance, in 1984, a large toxic algal bloom in Thomsons and Forrestdale Lakes near Jandakot had poisoned many migratory birds.[31] In response, the Wetlands Conservation Society was formed in early 1985, led by physicist Phil Jennings. Many of its sixty foundation members were 'veterans' of the Farrington Road dispute the previous year, during which they had tried to protect North Lake from development. Their sense of purpose was bolstered by the visit of biologist Paul Ehrlich to Perth in late 1985. The seasoned campaigner and author of *The Population Bomb* (1968), Ehrlich lectured at Murdoch University on the subject of 'Extinction: the implications of the loss of our biological heritage'. The Society aimed to monitor development activities in wetland areas, particularly in the southern suburbs; register wetlands as regional parks; rehabilitate damaged wetlands; and develop recreational and educational facilities. To carry out these aims, the Society developed strong links with the Conservation Council of Western Australia (est. 1967) as well as the Royal Australasian Ornithologists Union (est. 1901).

In response to such public concerns about the effects of private and public groundwater abstraction on the watertable the State government initiated several studies to devise strategies to manage these underground reserves.[32] These studies highlighted the need to ensure water supplies for a growing population, and the protection of all water resources, while noting the high and increasing per capita water consumption of the people of Perth. These studies also revealed that bores in some suburbs were producing increasingly saline water and that environmental constraints on the use of shallow groundwater were necessary.[33]

Using the greater powers of the recently proclaimed *Environmental Protection Act 1986*, the Environmental Protection Authority (EPA) set limits on Big Water's groundwater abstraction to protect significant groundwater-dependent ecosystems, such as wetlands and caves. Furthermore, the government recognised the potential for conflict between land use and groundwater protection, which required greater coordination of catchment planning.[34]

This consideration of water resources in urban planning and of the need for the protection of wetlands and waterways reflected the growing influence of Integrated Catchment Management (ICM) in the southwest. Although ICM was not formally adopted by the State government until 1988, its emphases on the resolution of land and water degradation problems through the coordination of different agencies and greater public involvement were already evident in nascent efforts to address secondary salinity and groundwater protection in the region. The development of ICM in Western Australia reflected international trends towards an 'ecosystem approach' or 'integrated water management' in the 1980s and 1990s.[35] These approaches were later endorsed at the International Conference on Water and Environment in early 1992, which led into the Earth Summit in Rio de Janeiro later that year.

Such strategies relied heavily then on the rise of the 'sustainability sciences', which serviced the notion of 'sustainable development'. The 1987 report of the World Commission on Environment and Development had redefined the very concept of development. Economic development was to be 'sustainable' so as to limit environmental damage, while ensuring environmental and intergenerational justice.[36] The report, argues historian Libby Robin, explicitly linked science to facilitating 'practical outcomes for development'.[37] Among the sciences marshalled for sustainable development would be the so-called crisis disciplines, such as conservation biology, addressing issues where scientists and decision-makers must 'act before knowing all the facts'.[38] Scientific inquiry in these disciplines required constant adaptation in the face of changing circumstances – an experience that local zoologist Bert Main likened to his training as an aircraft navigator in the 1940s: 'The potential for the worst case scenario to eventuate was always present and was only avoided by a continuous series of decisions…[to ensure] arrival at the designated time'.[39]

Meanwhile, local environmentalists were not convinced that Big Water or the state's EPA would adequately protect the groundwater reserves and wetlands of the Swan Coastal Plain. The Conservation Council of Western Australia, for instance, roundly criticised the Hollick Report for its 'narrow perspective dominated by economic rationalism' and failure to guide the management of the 'whole ecosystem on a sustainable basis'.[40] Likewise, the Wetlands Conservation Society argued that the report 'flies in the face of the overwhelming public support for the maintenance of healthy wetlands…and is contrary to the State Conservation Strategy (especially to the principle of sustainable development)'.[41] Furthermore, argued members of the Society, such 'risk analysis is fraught with imperfections as evidenced by the Alaskan oil spill and the Chernobyl disaster'.[42] Such scepticism of scientific authority and expertise reflected the extent to which the characteristics of a 'risk society' were evident in Perth by this time.[43] Critics did not trust the local authorities to protect the wetlands or to manage the city's groundwater reserves sustainably. They feared that the thirst for groundwater would leave the wetlands vulnerable to running out.

Their scepticism proved to be well-founded. In 1989 the State Planning Commission announced its plans to build some 4,000 homes on the Jandakot Mound as part of the East Thomsons Lake development. According to the Banjup Action Group, which formed in response to the announcement, the massive drainage required for the urban development would drain large amounts of water from the Mound, pollute groundwater reserves, and affect local flora and fauna.[44] Amid claims that the government pressured the EPA to approve the housing development, the Conservation Council took legal action to force the Minister for the Environment to release the Authority's report on the project.[45] It then mounted a strong campaign for statutory protection of the Jandakot Mound. Reflecting on the episode in 1991, environmentalist Barbara Churchward mused on the state's financial mismanagement under Labor Premier Brian Burke, 'With the State government trying to recoup millions lost by WA Inc., it is hardly surprising that the prospect of fast-tracking development of non-renewable resources is appealing'.[46] It was not until 1998 that the Court Liberal government (1993–2001) took steps to protect the area from further development.

By the end of the 1980s, concerns about the environment had grown from a special interest of the urban, educated, middle class to a widespread concern of the general public. Australian environmentalism, which had crystallised over wilderness issues such as saving Victoria's Little Desert and Tasmania's Lake Pedder from developers, now appealed to a wider audience, who were concerned about 'ecological risks' to their lifestyles.[47] The *West Australian*, for instance, observed in 1987 that, 'Judging by recent public protests at intrusions into the wetlands, WA's lakes and swamps mean a lot to people – both as sanctuaries for wildlife and as pleasant places for leisure activities. No one wants to have a picnic beside a dried-up mudhole'.[48] This shift in mainstream attitudes, argue sociologists Jan Pakulski and Steve Crook, was consolidated by the end of the decade, in the midst of growing media coverage of pollution and ecological 'disasters', such as the *Exxon Valdez* oil spill.[49] But sustainable development was a complex process. As the *West Australian* continued, 'The trouble is that people want lakes, they want an abundant and cheap public water supply, and a significant number also want green, well-watered gardens fed by private bores. It may, in the end, become a question of the community deciding on its priorities'.[50] The continued support of backyard bores by the State government sustained a disconnect between domestic water consumption and outside 'nature', serving to perpetuate the profligate water culture that the people of Perth enjoyed.

Although the significance of these wetlands sites to local Aboriginal people did not appear to feature in these discussions, greater efforts were being made to undertake heritage studies of these areas. Studies examined the significance of such sites as Lake Claremont or 'Butler's Swamp', Perry Lakes in Floreat, Jolimont Swamp, Lake Monger, Hyde Park, Dogswamp, and Lake Gnangara.[51] Many local Aboriginal people lamented that there would have been a far greater amount of information available had the surveys been conducted earlier. This research suggested a belated realisation that the *Aboriginal Heritage Act 1972* was relevant to the protection of areas in the southwest, not just the more 'traditionally oriented regions' of the state. These studies also reflected the growing movement towards improving social and political justice for Aboriginal people in the 1980s and early 1990s, as demonstrated by such processes as the Seaman Inquiry, the Swan River Brewery dispute, and the recognition of native title. Despite these advances, however, the absence of Aboriginal concerns in debates about wetlands and groundwater during this period reflects the prevailing lack of awareness of Aboriginal heritage issues in the wider community at this time.[52]

Dry horizons

These dry years of the mid- to late-1980s coincided with the emergence of the enhanced greenhouse effect on the Australian political agenda. Local water managers feared these conditions were indicative of a changing climate, which would have severe consequences for Big Water if they were to continue. The well-publicised Villach meetings of the mid-1980s had alerted them to the possibility that decision-makers could no longer rely on 'the assumption that past climatic data without modification are a reliable guide to the future'.[53] These findings prompted local water managers to wonder how long the dry years might continue. When would they abate? Would rainfall return to 'normal'?

The developing climate change agenda of the mid-1980s prompted CSIRO and the Federal Labor government to convene the Greenhouse87 conference at Monash University in late 1987. By this time, the increasing scientific and political concern about anthropogenic climate change and its likely impacts had begun to seriously challenge conventional approaches to environmental and resource management. Greenhouse87 was the first national meeting of scientists and resource managers to discuss the potential socioeconomic and environmental effects of anthropogenic climate change for Australia. The basis of these discussions was a CSIRO climate scenario for the year 2030, by which time the concentration of carbon dioxide in the atmosphere was expected to have doubled.[54] The resulting changes in the atmospheric circulations would, according to the model, cause a decline in the rainfall of the southwest.[55]

With less frequent rainfall and higher temperatures, this scenario depicted a significantly drier and warmer future for the region in the twenty-first century. What made this prospect particularly alarming was that the southwest region had long enjoyed a reputation for the most 'consistent and reliable' rainfall in Australia.[56] According to the CSIRO's scenario, the southwest's future climate might be less suitable for the region's prevailing land practices and water management. Although this was not the first time that the declining rainfall of the southwest had been linked to the enhanced greenhouse effect, Greenhouse87 marked a turning point in the way that Big Water's engineers planned for the future.[57]

The Water Authority suspected that the expected drop in rainfall might have already commenced in about 1970 and that it would continue into the middle of the twenty-first century. Such a climate change would lead to a 20 per cent reduction in rainfall and an even greater decline (over 40 per cent) in the average streamflow of the region's rivers, due to the relationship between the soils, climate and vegetation in catchment areas. With lower rainfall and streamflow, demand for scheme water would exceed supplies more quickly than anticipated. This new line of thinking suggested that water supplies could be insufficient by as early as 2020, rather than lasting until nearly 2040. Other sources for Big Water had to be found and demand for water had to be curtailed as quickly as possible.[58]

Although Western Australian water managers were not the first to consider the challenges that climate change posed to existing water supply networks, they faced a unique situation where the predictions were remarkably similar to the climatic conditions the southwest had actually experienced since the 1970s.[59] In these circumstances, the urgency of preparing a strategy to protect the southwest's water supplies in the face of anthropogenic climate change was far greater than in other regions at the time. Nevertheless, it was not an easy or straightforward decision for Big Water to adjust to this greenhouse scenario. Engineers faced the challenge of recommending significant planning decisions to government ministers under conditions of scientific uncertainty and political scepticism, a state of affairs redolent of Giddens' observation of the risk society, where 'the future becomes ever more absorbing, but at the same time opaque'.[60]

As scientific and political interest in the enhanced greenhouse effect grew in the latter half of the 1980s, so too did doubts over the veracity of global warming claims, particularly in the United States. Some Western Australians shared similar concerns. For the state's resource-based economy, the problem of anthropogenic climate change was (and remains) a double-edged sword. The State Labor government's progressive approaches to tackling the issue, such as committing to a reduction of greenhouse gas emissions by 20 per cent by the year 2000 (based on 1988 figures) and undertaking the first comprehensive greenhouse gas audit in Australia, potentially threatened the fortunes of the mining industry – the foundation of the state's economic prosperity. Furthermore, some sections of the State government were sceptical of CSIRO research on the relationship between the enhanced greenhouse effect and climatic change.[61] Big Water's engineers were faced, therefore, with uncertainty not only in terms of the implications of climate change for the water resources of the southwest, but also in terms of political opinion regarding the state's role in mitigating global warming.

In addition, scientists were themselves uncertain about the accuracy of the predictions of climate models, an uncertainty that remains an issue for climate modellers today. At the Greenhouse87 Conference, for instance, convenor Graeme Pearman, the Chief of CSIRO's Division of Atmospheric Science, was reluctant for resource managers to base their planning decisions on the very tentative Greenhouse87 scenario.[62] The combination of scientific uncertainty and a lack of detail in the climate models combined to leave scientists unable to definitively assess the impact of the enhanced greenhouse effect on regional rainfall patterns and streamflows.[63] These uncertainties were the basis for criticism within the Western Australian policymaking community about the use of general circulation models for the state's water planning.[64] For many critics, the field of climate modelling was simply not at the stage where models could responsibly guide resource managers.

In spite of this scepticism, the lower rainfall levels since the 1970s suggested to water managers that the Greenhouse87 scenario was far from the realm of fantasy. Its coincidence with two winters of below-average rainfall in the southwest fed their anxieties that dry conditions could continue.[65] Furthermore, a failure to act on the prediction of a drier future would have severe consequences if these conditions materialised. If the Water Authority invested in infrastructure for lower winter rainfall but the predictions were not fulfilled, the consequences would be less disastrous than if they had invested for higher winter rainfall or 'business as usual' but received less. Regardless of the scepticism among policymakers, Big Water had to expand to avoid running out. After much deliberation, the Water Authority chose a dam site south of Perth on the North Dandalup river in preference to sites situated further north. This decision took into account the prediction that rain-bearing systems would shift further south under enhanced global warming conditions.[66] In addition, the river had already been 'developed' for Big Water with the construction of a pipehead dam in the 1970s.[67]

Western Australians were invited to learn more about the future of their state at the national Greenhouse88 conference at the Perth Superdrome in November 1988.[68] Several hundred people attended Greenhouse88 in Perth and there was extensive coverage of the meeting in the local media. In addition to the growing ecological awareness among Australians during the 1980s, the close association (in the public eye) of the enhanced greenhouse effect with the problem of ozone depletion might have accounted for this public interest.[69] Earlier that year, the Canadian government had hosted a conference on 'The Changing Atmosphere' in Toronto.[70] Although there had been no official government representation, the conference delegates had declared a 'Call to Action' for developed countries to reduce their emissions of carbon dioxide to 1988 levels by the year 2000. This conference, as well as the discovery of the stratospheric 'ozone hole' and the publication of the Brundtland Report stirred public concern for the global environment.[71] Soon after, the World Meteorological Organisation and the United Nations Environment Program joined forces to establish the Intergovernmental Panel on Climate Change (IPCC).

Local and national conservation groups seized the opportunity to call on the State and Federal governments to reduce fossil fuels and improve energy efficiency to limit climate change.[72] Like its counterparts in New South Wales and Victoria, the Western Australian government publicly adopted the Toronto target for 'planning purposes'.[73] The Commonwealth government followed soon afterwards and established a national climate change program to coordinate research. Despite this early enthusiasm, the Commonwealth signaled its pragmatic approach to the international climate change policy process and warned that attempts to meet such targets would come at a cost to the national economy.[74]

Amidst political and scientific debate about the greenhouse effect, another vision of the future emerged. In the late 1980s, Labor politician Ernie Bridge – the first Aboriginal to become a cabinet minister in Western Australia – began to champion his idea to pipe water from the Fitzroy River in the state's northwest to Perth.[75] The catchment of the Fitzroy River extends from Halls Creek in the East Kimberley to Derby in the West Kimberley, covering some 85,000 square km of ecologically diverse country – Bridge's country.[76] Echoing earlier schemes to water the inland and to make the deserts bloom, Bridge argued that the pipeline would encourage closer settlement and irrigable agriculture north of Geraldton, and that it would drought-proof the southwest well into the twenty-first century.[77] The pipeline could also help to lower greenhouse gas emissions because it would allow trees to grow in the arid inland of Western Australia.[78]

In contrast to a similar proposal that Western Mining Corporation had made to the Court government over a decade earlier, Bridge's idea captured the hearts and minds of many Western Australians and even some Federal Labor politicians.[79] Although critics pilloried the plan, the Premier, Dr Carmen Lawrence, invested in several studies to determine its technical and financial feasibility.[80] These studies concluded that while technically possible, the pipeline was simply too costly to entertain.

Part of the appeal of Bridge's ambitious project was that it allayed long-held anxieties about the 'empty' or 'under-utilised' regions north of the Tropic of Capricorn. According to economist Bruce R. Davidson, who first critiqued these ideas in his 1965 book *The Northern Myth*, the political appeal of developing Australia's north was manifold: it would deter invasion from Asia; it would use the region's 'valuable resources' to provide food for Australians and the world's starving masses; and it would improve the standard of living of the region's Aboriginal people.[81] These northern regions encompass nearly 40 per cent of the Australian continent's area but a mere 1 per cent of its population reside there.[82] Although Bridge's idea was not acted upon, the scheme continued to inspire many Western Australians in the twenty-first century. Its endurance is testament to the appeal of the grand engineering schemes of Big Water with their promises of nation-building, national security and drought-proofing Australia.

Despite the political significance of Aboriginal land rights in the late 1980s and Bridge's own Aboriginal heritage, in the public discussion of the proposal there appears to have been little consideration of the significance of the Fitzroy River to the Indigenous peoples of the Kimberley. One feasibility study conceded that it was unlikely that the pipeline would improve water supplies to remote communities and warned that it might even create health problems due to cultural conflict.[83] Another reported only the economic implications of the pipeline's construction.[84] These reports consistently overlooked Aboriginal relationships to the Fitzroy River and how taking water from this source might affect those connections. The Fitzroy is vital to those Aboriginal peoples who identify and are recognised as 'the river people' – members of the Ngarinyin, the Gooniyandi and the Bunuba groups. The river not only provides food and water resources, but also provides a spiritual and cultural link between the past, present and future.[85] As Margaret Kunjuka said in 2001, 'The river, that's our life. That's the main one for everyone. It's there for our young people. They got to take over'.[86] Taking their water to benefit the southwest would have unimaginable effects on the cultural and socioeconomic resilience of these Aboriginal people. That these possible effects were barely considered demonstrates the political significance of slaking the thirst of Big Water and its customers, as well as the status of Aboriginal interests in Western Australian society.

The (economic) dries

Whether they were serviced by Big Water or lived outside its reach, the responses of Western Australians to the dry seasonal conditions of the early 1990s bore the imprint of the growing influence of economic rationalism among Australian policymakers. Although those outside Big Water were worst affected, most Western Australians in the southwest found that they themselves had to assume an unprecedented level of financial responsibility for overcoming the difficulties posed by climate variability and water scarcity. This shift in responsibility from the state to the individual further diminished the hydroresilience of less affluent sections of the community.

Although the construction of the Harris Dam had assured the continuity of reliable water supplies for the towns and properties already connected to the Great Southern Towns Water Supply Scheme, many areas in the southwest remained self-reliant for their water supplies. This independence, however, did not necessarily mean that these farmers were undertaking measures to ensure their resilience to climate variability. Many had continued to neglect their water supplies because of a false sense of security, a dependence on emergency government supplies, and/or because they could not afford the investment.[87] Some of the worst affected were the recently settled farmers on the south coast in the areas around Esperance, Jerramungup and Ravensthorpe, which had been released for development in the early 1980s.

By the end of the 1980s, as noted earlier, Australian governments were reconsidering the ways that they responded to drought. It had become too expensive to continue to frame droughts as 'natural disasters' or 'Acts of God' in a continent where climate variability was increasingly recognised as the norm. In response, State and Commonwealth governments cooperated to develop a national drought policy (finalised in 1992) that rewarded self-reliance, risk management, and the long-term maintenance of environmental resources such as soil and water.[88] An act of collective amnesia allowed these governments to forget the efforts of their predecessors to encourage agricultural settlement in climatically marginal areas where they would be vulnerable to water scarcity. Under this new regime, as historian Judith Brett has observed, 'Drought-stricken farmers were no longer heroic victims of fickle nature, but merely bad risk managers'.[89]

In the southwest in the early 1990s, this new approach to climate variability was translated into the encouragement of local initiatives to identify and resolve problems in water supplies in order to improve the hydroresilience of farmers. The Department of Agriculture, for instance, developed a suite of computer models that could help farmers to better plan their farm management for the year, including the prediction of crop yields and the design of farm water supplies.[90] Although the design of such models was well-intentioned, many farmers considered them to be too complex and not developed to address the most risky of their management decisions, such as acquiring neighbouring properties.[91] Furthermore, as with responses to salinity, it was the farmers themselves who were expected to fund most of this investment.

This shift to greater self-reliance coincided with great challenges facing the nation's rural sector in the 1980s and 1990s. These challenges were not only economic, but also cultural and political, as Australians collectively lost their sense of 'countrymindedness'. The forces of globalisation were taking their toll on farming communities as pressures mounted for farm amalgamation, greater efficiency and productivity gains, and increased involvement with agribusiness. These changes compounded the persistent problems of the cost of keeping up with technological change, environmental degradation and rising debt, accelerating a drift to the cities, economic hardship and a decline in morale. Historian Graeme Davison has observed that while none of these challenges were unique, 'What was new was the strength of the combined force with which they now acted, and the changed framework of expectations in which their impact was now interpreted'.[92] In the late 1980s, for instance, the *Western Farmer* regularly juxtaposed headlines such as, 'Future rests on efficiency', 'Aim first for conservation' and 'Innovation the key to future development', with the sombre observations of 'Rural communities fighting for survival', 'Fighting to save the future', and 'Farm debt swells'.

Under these unprecedented conditions, many farmers across the nation struggled to improve not only their hydroresilience, but also the economic, social and environmental sustainability of their communities.

In the suburbs, meanwhile, low metropolitan dam storages after the dry winter of 1994 had led the Liberal government to impose the first water restrictions on Perth householders since the late 1970s.[93] The relatively moderate restrictions commenced on November 1 and prohibited the use of garden sprinklers between 8 am and 8 pm (later, 9 am to 6 pm) in the areas serviced by Big Water's Integrated Water Supply Scheme – Perth, Mandurah and the eastern goldfields. Surprisingly, the policy was met with little resistance from the community, particularly when compared to earlier periods. This lack of public dissent indicates that the restrictions did not affect householders to the same extent as they had in the past. The muted response to restrictions reflected a shift in the public perception of responsibility for the restrictions from Big Water to householders themselves.

In addition to the introduction of user pays in the late 1970s, the Water Authority had increasingly encouraged their customers to reduce their scheme water consumption. Mirroring campaigns underway elsewhere around Australia, the objective of reducing scheme water demand reflected the economic and environmental position faced by many water utilities, namely that the cheapest water supplies had been exhausted such that further water source development would be expensive and potentially, environmentally harmful. The success of these campaigns in limiting the growth in per capita demand was influential in the planning of the future sources of the southwest's scheme water supplies in the late 1980s.[94] These efforts to curb scheme water demand reflected the changing identity of Big Water in Australia at the end of the twentieth century. Big Water had once promised Australians endless water supplies and thirsty households had happily watered and flushed away. Now that Big Water was under economic and environmental pressures, it called for its customers to exercise restraint. Blaming water users alone for their unsustainable levels of consumption, argues cultural theorist Zoë Sofoulis, ignores the central role that Big Water has played in delivering the 'sublime illusion' of unlimited water supplies.[95] Big Water, therefore, does not engage in a process of reflection on its role in facilitating unsustainable water use nor is it held accountable for perpetuating consumers' delusions of infinite supplies. As a result, the technologies and infrastructure that have facilitated the supply of seemingly limitless quantities of water go unchallenged and unchanged.

Customers would not have accepted the blame for their high water use had they not been primed to consider themselves at fault and in need of curbing their consumption. Despite the political prominence of economic issues during the 'recession we had to have' in the early 1990s, Australian political scientists Stephen Crook and Jan Pakulski observed in 1994 that 'environmental concerns have entered the public consciousness and are likely to stay there'. Among the myriad environmental problems that were threatening the world at the end of the twentieth century was the growing sense of an impending water crisis, for which humankind was at least partly responsible. The El Niño drought of 1994, which ravaged farmers and pastoralists in New South Wales and Queensland, provided Australians with what some perceived as grim evidence to substantiate these claims. Excessive consumption of limited resources, like water, was no longer (morally) acceptable and needed to be curbed. Strategies of demand management, such as user pays and water restrictions, therefore, were widely and equally regarded as reasonable methods to relieve the pressure on scarce water resources.

The price mechanism had become an especially useful tool for Big Water to influence demand for its product. In the southwest, the experience of user pays since the 1970s had helped condition Big Water's customers to accept water as an 'economic resource', and therefore, a 'precious commodity'. By the early 1990s, the unprecedented national focus on economic efficiency and competitiveness had become 'the most pervasive policy shift of recent decades'.[96] Led by the Council of Australian Governments (comprising the heads of Australian State, Territory and Commonwealth governments), the National Competition Policy, which was based on these ideas, was rolled out across the country. In the area of water reform, Big Water's attentions were focussed on 'productivity, reduction of state subsidies, user-pays, separation of policy and provision, privatisation and corporatisation of functions, break-up to allow competition, use of market and property rights mechanisms and importantly, provisions of flows to the environment'.[97]

The introduction of these reforms in Western Australia led to the split of the Water Authority into three agencies in 1996: the Office of Water Regulation, the Water and Rivers Commission, and the Water Corporation, all of which answered to the Minister for Water Resources and therefore, were subject to political influence. The Office of Water Regulation was responsible for the regulation of the state's water industry through a system of licences that applied to all providers of water supply, sewerage, drainage and irrigation services. The Office also provided advice to the Minister on a wide range of policy matters affecting the industry and monitored the performance of the industry. The Water and Rivers Commission was accountable for the sustainable development of the Western Australia's water resources and the conservation of the environment, and allocated water resources between competing interests to achieve these ends. The Commission was also responsible for the investigation, measurement and assessment of the state's surface and subterranean water resources.[98] The Water Corporation supplied water and wastewater services across the state, including water supplies to irrigation schemes in the southwest.

This restructuring of the state's water sector was met with scepticism from local environmentalists. For the Conservation Council, the changes reflected the insidious influence of 'economic fundamentalism', a 'virus' that was spreading across all levels of Australian government in the 1990s.[99] Although the 'catchcry was more efficiency and competitiveness', a member of the Council wryly observed that 'nobody dared to ask with whom they were to compete'.[100] The Conservation Council later blamed the attendant processes of restructuring and downsizing for the loss of the water sector's 'most experienced staff', which they considered had left Big Water unprepared for dry spells in the late 1990s.[101]

The function of the Water Corporation was to supply water and wastewater services to its customers 'in accordance with prudent commercial principles and endeavour to make a profit, consistent with maximising its long-term value'.[102] This charter explicitly commodified Western Australia's water resources and framed the consumers of these supplies in market terms. This suggests that the price mechanism was set to become an increasingly important to the management of demand for water in the late 1990s. But, in practice, such a move would have been politically imprudent.

Despite the emphasis of the National Competition Policy on the ethos of user pays, the State governments felt politically compelled to hold the hand of the market. The Western Australian government was no exception and sought to cushion the effects of user pays on consumers. By this time, water bills were composed of a fixed charge and a usage charge. Since 1993, this usage charge was determined by a system of five inclining block tariffs, whereby water became increasingly expensive as more was consumed.[103] But the structure of the water bill meant that this usage charge composed less than half of the total cost. As a result, this usage charge could not send a strong price signal or provide a significant incentive to reduce water use.[104] The only incentive it provided was to thirsty households who possessed the financial means to invest in water-saving technology in order to pay lower water rates. Besides, the State government already subsidised lower water prices such that consumers did not foot the bill for source development or the cost of water itself.[105] Thus the short-term electoral goals of the State government served to undermine a community shift towards greater hydroresilience in the 1990s.

Meanwhile, the broader policy shifts towards corporatisation and privatisation across the public sector was taking its toll on the most vulnerable members of the Western Australian community. During the 1990s, the state's provider of public housing, Homeswest, was increasingly emphasising cost efficiency in its rental operations, which contributed to the growing privatisation of its services. Indigenous families, who were particularly dependent on public housing, faced longer waiting times and overcrowding as a result of the limited availability of accommodation. With limited financial resources and cultural obligations to house kin, Indigenous tenants also faced a greater likelihood of eviction. In the late 1990s, the rate of eviction on a per capita basis for Aboriginal families in Homeswest housing was three times higher than for non-Aboriginal tenants.[106] Reporting an episode in Karrinyup, journalist Carmelo Amalfi observed, 'The eviction of the Martin family from Paris Way has solved a problem for Homeswest and some residents. But it has exacerbated the problems of the Martin family, with children condemned to the insecurity of homelessness'.[107]

Such problems were compounded by the redevelopment of low-income suburbs like East Perth, where there had been a high level of public housing, emergency accommodation and social services, and the lack of public assistance to improve the rudimentary housing and sanitation conditions at the Swan Valley Nyoongar Community in Lockridge.[108] Beyond the city, these neoliberal reforms also exacerbated geographical differences in economic development, service provision and social wellbeing, which served to aggravate the spiral of rural decline in parts of the southwest.[109] The changing face of the provision of public services in the 1990s was producing a cascade of challenges for the least fortunate, particularly Aboriginal people, and leaving many beyond the reach of the benefits of Big Water at the end of the twentieth century.

Drought-proofing Perth

With the overhaul of the management of the state's water resources in the mid-1990s came closer scrutiny of the lower levels of rainfall that had prevailed since the 1970s. Less rainfall and less streamflow would have significant consequences for the operation of the new Water Corporation. Drier conditions would necessitate the development of other sources and curbs on water consumption to meet its mandate to provide water services to its customers across the state. For a profit-driven business, these were both costly options and, for the Liberal Government, it was politically unpopular to either enforce tighter water restrictions or to raise water rates to cover expensive infrastructure investments.[110] Furthermore, a less reliable water supply network would increase the risk exposure of the Water Corporation's Board of Management.[111] It was both politically and financially imperative, therefore, to determine the extent of the drying trend and whether it would continue indefinitely. Faced then with the possibility of a drying climate, Big Water implemented the technocratic responses of climate monitoring and prediction in order to help it maintain the illusion that it could indefinitely provide 'endless supplies' to its thirsty customers.

In early 1996 the newly established Water and Rivers Commission convened a seminar and workshop in Perth to address the recent low levels of rainfall; its effects on the hydrology of the southwest region; and the extent to which seasonal climate variability could be predicted.[112] Climate scientists and water managers reviewed the existing state of knowledge of regional climate variability and the impacts of rainfall decline on water supply. According to one of the participants, Brian Sadler, the workshop represented a turning point for scientists and decision-makers as the rainfall conditions were no longer viewed as a prolonged drought.[113] They now identified a 'non-linear jump' to a new regional climate equilibrium: a state of lower winter rainfall.

This new perspective on the region's climate saw the state's water managers further reduce the estimated long-term annual inflow to the southwest water supply system. As Jim Gill, the former head of the Water Corporation later reflected, 'In '96, we decided we were kidding ourselves with the amount of water we expected from the dams, and we de-rated the system…so it came from…280 GL down to about 230 GL'.[114] By this stage, the region's supply capacity was considerably exceeded by expected demand. In order to meet this demand and to avoid imposing tighter water restrictions on its consumers, the Water Corporation brought forward its plans to expand and develop the region's water supplies.[115] The strategy to provide its customers with additional supplies by 2021 was now fast-tracked by a decade to ensure that there would be sufficient supplies by 2010.

The Court government translated this plan to increase water supplies into a political spectacle of 'drought-proofing' Perth, which was reminiscent of the Big Water of the 1950s and 1960s. Although the prospect of completely drought-proofing an area was no longer a credible option for water managers, it remained a potent ideal for politicians seeking to demonstrate their great vision to the electorate. In 2000, Minister for Water Resources Kim Hames announced, 'We're trying to get as close as possible to drought-proofing Perth without the enormous expense of pipelining from the Kimberley'.[116] This position was supported by the Water Corporation, which argued that 'plentiful water sources should be developed, essentially without limit, and provided for those who are prepared to pay for them'.[117] Although these views appeared at odds with the more restrained approach of consumers regarding scheme water use, their persistence attested to the enduring political capital of Big Water, of the vision of endless water supplies.

The government's perception of a thirsty electorate undoubtedly informed its continued promotion of backyard bores to alleviate the pressures on scheme water supplies. In 1997, the government argued that sinking bores not only reduced demand on scheme water but also helped the environment. Drawing on bores that tapped into shallow groundwater reserves helped lower the water-table, which had risen in some areas due to urban development.[118]

The government also published the *Perth Groundwater Atlas* so that householders could determine whether their property was well-situated for accessing groundwater supplies. As backyard bores remained unlicensed, unmetered, and therefore, unmonitored, such a strategy, argued environmentalists, contradicted measures to protect the groundwater reserves of the Swan Coastal Plain. As the Conservation Council wondered, 'How will sustainable groundwater yields be ensured when the drawdown from the thousands of domestic bores in Perth cannot be measured and yet they are depleting the same groundwater sources as those used for water supply'.[119] In some coastal areas, the use of household bores had already led to saltwater intrusion and rendered these backyard investments useless. By supporting the unfettered persistence of a profligate water culture, the government was putting groundwater supplies at risk – the same reserves that might sustain Big Water in the future.

In addition to encouraging residents to invest in private water supplies, the government declared its intentions to build additional dams and draw more water from already strained groundwater sources. Its major project in the late 1990s was the Stirling–Harvey Redevelopment Scheme, which involved replacing the existing Harvey Dam with a larger reservoir to meet irrigators' needs. Water from the Stirling Dam, which would no longer provide water to irrigators, would be piped to Big Water in Perth, Mandurah and the goldfields. The government reassured the electorate that the expansion of Harvey Dam did not represent a new source as such because the river had already been dammed.[120] But some critics questioned the wisdom of investing in dams in the context of a drying climate. Both the Greens and the Labor Opposition observed, 'If it doesn't rain, Harvey won't fill'.[121]

The plans to rebuild Harvey Dam and pipe water to the city also raised concerns among farmers in the Harvey catchment that their water needs were of less importance than those of the city. These tensions revived anxieties that had simmered since at least the 1970s, that water would be transferred away from productive uses in rural areas to meet the needs of 'wasteful' suburban households. For the government and Water Corporation, the Stirling–Harvey Redevelopment Scheme was ideal because it would 'balance' the extraction of groundwater north of Perth; enlarge an existing scheme; and it was a source of good quality water that was located in an area of relatively high and reliable rainfall.[122] Local politicians, however, framed the plan as a blow to country livelihoods, tapping into rural anxieties about the pending deregulation of the local dairy industry and the growing marginalisation of rural (Western) Australians more generally.[123] For instance, the president of the National Party's Collie branch claimed, 'We know the votes are in Perth and...once the pipeline is in place, there will be an irresistible appeal in catering to the masses in Perth to the detriment of rural people'.[124] Such populist rhetoric aside, the wider Harvey community considered that the Water Corporation needed to guarantee water for local irrigators before water was transferred to Perth.[125] In their view, Big Water would divert 'local' water for the benefit of the people of Perth, which would leave Harvey residents and irrigators more vulnerable to climate variability and water scarcity.

Although some of the additional water supplies would come from enlarging the Harvey Dam, most of the extra water would be drawn from the Gnangara Mound. In terms of the amount of water available, the costs of abstracting and piping the water, and the environmental impact of using this source, the Water Corporation considered that groundwater was the best option for increasing water supplies. Furthermore, the prevailing scientific view was that the drying regional climate would have less of an impact on groundwater than on dams. Like its proposal to enlarge the Harvey Dam, the Water Corporation argued that its increased reliance on the Gnangara Mound was cheaper, with fewer ecological consequences than alternative sources, because it was merely extending an existing scheme.

But again this reasoning did not convince local environmentalists. They cited recent episodes during which wetlands and trees were suffering as a result of the exploitation of this shallow groundwater source.[126] The Conservation Council argued that the Water Corporation was prioritising cheap water supplies over environmental protection. A Council spokeswoman noted, 'We could double Perth's total consumption tomorrow using [the deeper] Yaragadee (sic). But the Corporation, which is committed to delivering water at the lowest price, will tell you it is too expensive'.[127] Most importantly, conservationists argued, the government should explore other sources of water, such as recycling wastewater, and curtail the water consumption of Perth households.

Although demand management strategies and the 1994 restrictions had kept per capita demand at bay since the late 1970s, total scheme water consumption in Perth had increased by at least 25 per cent since 1990.[128] Undoubtedly water consumption was far greater in households that had access to unmonitored bore water. Rather than further restrict water use, the State government and the Water Corporation preferred to encourage householders to supplement their supplies through backyard bores. This policy protected the government from voter backlash and the Water Corporation from loss of revenue, whilst maintaining the profligate water culture of the suburbs. Could this approach continue in a drying climate?

Looking to the Indian Ocean

The Water and Rivers Commission workshop in 1996 at which scientists and engineers had reviewed the planning for the southwest's water resources, had taken place just a year before the Kyoto Conference of the Parties to the United Nations Framework Convention on Climate Change (UNFCCC). Despite the Hawke government's initial enthusiasm for the international climate change policy process at the Earth Summit in 1992, both Labor and Coalition governments had since been reluctant to accept legally binding targets and had advocated the merits of a 'differentiated' approach in the pursuit of greenhouse gas emission reduction goals.[129] Meanwhile, in Western Australia, the conservative Court government had not agreed to the terms of the UNFCCC and was proceeding to build a coal-fired power station in Collie. Furthermore, there had been no inventory of greenhouse gas emissions in Western Australia since the 1990 audit and the state's Greenhouse Coordination Council had been in indefinite recess for over two years.

Not long after the workshop had been convened, the Second Assessment Report of the IPCC (1996) concluded that 'the balance of evidence suggests a discernible human influence on global climate'. The workshop participants had found that a decade later, the questions that had been raised in the response of Western Australian engineers to the Greenhouse87 scenario remained unanswered. These were questions seeking to determine the nature of the regional climate change, and its timing, rate and magnitude. The workshop concluded that the answers to those questions remained 'beyond the current limits of science'. Further study of the region's climate was necessary, with an additional question regarding the 'fundamental nature of climate variability in the South West'.[130]

To answer these questions, the Court government established the Indian Ocean Climate Initiative (IOCI) in 1998. By the early 1990s, Australian climate scientists had become increasingly aware of the relationship between the sea surface temperatures of the Indian Ocean and winter rainfall in Australia. A better understanding of this relationship, they believed, could hold the key to improved seasonal forecasting across the country. The recent development of forecasting methods derived from the Southern Oscillation Index, which could indicate the development of El Niño and La Niña events based on temperatures in the Pacific Ocean, had proven especially valuable for the eastern states. With the existing scientific understanding of this relationship between rainfall and the El Niño – Southern Oscillation (ENSO), forecasters struggled to calculate forecasts for the late summer and autumn periods of eastern Australia, and for the western third over most of the year.[131] A closer examination of the Indian Ocean, scientists hoped, would reveal its interactions with the Pacific Ocean and the effects of these on Australian climate conditions.

Scientific interest in the Indian Ocean had increased significantly during the 1950s and 1960s, particularly in the wake of the International Geophysical Year (1957–58) and the creation of the Scientific Committee on Oceanic Research in 1957. Compared to the Atlantic and Pacific Regions, the Indian Ocean was underrepresented in the scientific literature and its exploration, oceanographers believed, was vital to marine science and necessary to build up scientific communities in the region. The resultant network of observations on the Indian Ocean provided data for local geographer Joseph Gentilli to further develop his comparative studies of climate regions. It was the southwest region that particularly interested him, because it differed from the west coast climates of Africa and South America.[132] In the mid-latitudes of those regions, rainfall was relatively low, whereas the southwest of Australia received comparatively high rainfall. Gentilli's analysis of the Indian Ocean data revealed the presence of 'rafts' of warm water that spread along the southwest coast and fostered the conditions for coastal showers.[133] The availability of more sophisticated technology in the late 1970s led oceanographer George Cresswell to characterise these poleward flowing rafts of warm water, which he named the Leeuwin Current in 1980.[134]

Later in the 1980s, Australian climate scientists from CSIRO and the Bureau of Meteorology looked further north, towards the Equator, to examine the interactions of the Indian and Pacific Oceans in the Indonesian region. Meteorologist Neville Nicholls hoped that such studies 'might add to the skill obtainable in seasonal rainfall prediction' for Australia.[135] These inquiries led to two findings that guided the research of IOCI in the late 1990s. Firstly, marine and climate scientists found that the complex interactions of currents in the Indian and Pacific Oceans (a system called the Indonesian Throughflow) caused El Niño events to affect both

170

eastern Australia and the western third, albeit in different ways. Although these events cause drought in the east, similar conditions do not necessarily develop in the west. Complicating the effects of the El Niño in Western Australia was another phenomena, the Indian Ocean Dipole, or the Nicholls Dipole. The Dipole, when it is present, causes westerly winds to direct rains over the continent. Climate and marine scientists concluded that more research on the Indian Ocean was needed to improve the national meteorological community's ability to predict the weather – both in eastern and Western Australia.

It was this promise of better forecasting, rather than the declining rainfall trend per se, that was instrumental in the establishment of IOCI. The ability to predict the nature of the coming season had long proven elusive in Western Australia. Forecasting the weather conditions of the year ahead, or even several years ahead, would be an incredibly valuable service for the rural community and water managers alike. Forecasting seasonal conditions could help Big Water avoid 'financial losses of tens of millions annually and socio-political "fallout"' of introducing harsh water restrictions.[136] If the Water Corporation had sufficient warning of dry conditions, it could implement 'milder forms of water restrictions', accelerate its development of other water sources, and seek approval from the Water and Rivers Commission to draw additional supplies from groundwater reserves.[137] For the agriculture and water sectors alike, there were direct economic benefits to be derived from unravelling the secrets of the southwest's climate.

The State government hoped that IOCI would consolidate the research conducted by the Bureau of Meteorology and CSIRO on the climate processes of the southwest and provide state agencies with much-needed information on the climate variability affecting the region.[138] Its principal purpose was to analyse the possible relationships between sea temperatures in the Indian Ocean; the declining rainfall pattern of the southwest; and the ENSO phenomenon, with the aim of improving the accuracy of weather forecasting and the prediction of climate change. Despite the focus of IOCI's research on the complexities of the Indian Ocean and its implications for climate variability and change in the southwest, its establishment coincided with the closure of CSIRO's Marine Branch laboratories in Perth. Members of its staff were either made redundant or transferred to Hobart, which 'virtually eliminated CSIRO's marine presence in Western Australia'.[139] Marine research for the west coast, therefore, would be chiefly conducted in Brisbane or Hobart, ensuring that scientific understandings of southwest conditions would be developed far from the affected region.

By the end of the 1990s, the issue of the region's drying trend had been absorbed into competing but not exclusive scientific and policymaking positions on climate change, drought, and climatic variability. The water managers of the southwest did not have the luxury of waiting for more definite conclusions on the possible impacts of climate change. In their view, the climate in the southwest had changed, and it was adversely affecting the region's water supplies. Although the collaborative research effort embodied by IOCI reflected a range of concerns for the region, these concerns were all directed at understanding the climate processes that affected the southwest. As a response to agricultural and environmental concerns about the causes and implications of the ongoing dry conditions in the southwest, IOCI represented the latest chapter in the checkered history of state–sponsored scientific investigation into the region's climate for the purposes of economic development and reducing the effects of water scarcity.

6

Watershed:

Climate and water in the early twenty-first century
(2001 to 2014)

On the eve of a new century, Western Australians were poised for another mining boom in the state's north. But this renewed prosperity was not without its difficulties. With the flow of good fortune to Perth came more people to the suburbs, placing further demands on the strained environment of the Swan Coastal Plain, particularly its groundwater reserves. In what would become a watershed for the region's water resources, the onset of dry conditions from 2001 added to the pressures on Big Water to maintain its illusion of endless supplies for its customers. These lean years further burdened the southwest's farmers, who were already beset with environmental and financial challenges. The southwest was not alone, however, in confronting the challenges of drought and water scarcity, as large parts of Queensland, New South Wales, Victoria and South Australia were also running dry. Growing lay and scientific anxieties about the role of anthropogenic climate change in the regional drying trend focussed political attentions on the future of the southwest's water resources in a drier climate.

Despite a lingering mistrust of science and technology, most Western Australians continued to rely on technocratic means to understand and respond to the risk of running out. Although the government's tightening of water restrictions and development of additional sources of supply averted shortages, this approach left Big Water and its customers vulnerable to dry conditions in the future. These technocratic solutions perpetuated consumers' dependency on reticulation and diminished the resilience of the region's groundwater reserves to ecological change. For those beyond Big Water, drought and the prospect of a drying climate added to the swathe of financial and environmental challenges they faced, which shaped the ways in which farmers in particular responded to climate variability and water scarcity in the early twenty-first century.

On the ropes

On the eve of the new millennium, drought crept across the wheatbelt's paddocks once again. As the dry conditions wore on, government officials declared that the agricultural areas faced the region's worst drought on record. The onset of the drought hit some farmers especially hard. Many were still recovering from devastating episodes of frost and locust plagues in the late 1990s. The De Landgrafft family at Lake King, who had acquired their property in the dying days of land release, were up against their fourth 'lean harvest' in a row, as were the Wyatts in Pingaring.[1] Meanwhile, the Browning family at Kondinin were 'trying to be positive' as they adopted 'survival tactics'.[2] Even areas that farmers had long regarded as 'safe' from drought were hit, as the affected area extended from Mullewa in the northeast to Esperance on the south coast.[3] The persistence of dry conditions in 2002 and early 2003 had many farmers against the ropes with crashing waves of dust and emu invasions offering few opportunities to shield themselves from the blows. The dry conditions combined with earlier misfortunes to grind down the resilience of many farmers in the southwest to climate variability and water scarcity.

Although the state's Department of Agriculture had warned farmers in early 2002 that the development of a moderate El Niño would lead to below-average rainfall in the Western Australian wheatbelt, farmers did not necessarily act on this information. Some felt the risk of dry conditions was not significant enough to warrant changing their plans, while others had little confidence in the Department's forecasts, particularly as they differed from those issued by other agencies, such as the Melbourne-based Bureau of Meteorology. Farmers in the central and eastern areas of the wheatbelt who had heeded these forecasts reduced the size of their cropping programs and the amount of fertiliser they applied to their crops, which prevented them suffering financial losses.[4]

Most drought-affected farmers had very few financial resources to shield themselves from the consequences of the climate conditions and prepare themselves for the future. The average farm debt in the dry Lake Grace district had more than doubled since the late 1990s and parts of the eastern wheatbelt, which had been hit hard by the drought, were among the state's lowest-earning areas.[5] For many farmers, the regime of self-reliance and efficiency had exacerbated their troubled financial circumstances. The risk-averse farm planning and management that these policies encouraged left lean margins with which to operate and few financial reserves with which to gamble. In some cases, the implementation of strategies that were less risky in terms of production, to cope with seasonal variability, could make the farming enterprise much more prone to financial risk. For instance,

> Low stocking rates may not allow enough income to be generated in the good seasons to allow a farmer to survive the poor seasons. Stocking according to season may result in stock being purchased at high prices and sold at low prices. Dates of lambing or calving that favour production may not favour marketing. Fodder may be

conserved on the farm to support higher stocking rates, but with the extra stock numbers, less surplus is available to be conserved.[6]

In a market economic context, the political emphasis on drought risk management, therefore, had heightened the financial vulnerability of many southwest farmers to climate variability.

Although the severity of the drought qualified many farmers in affected areas for relief under the provisions for 'exceptional circumstances' in the national drought policy, their financial difficulties flowed through to the wider rural community. The farmer's lighter pockets meant they had less to spend on machinery; slashed property values meant lower council rates and dwindling shire coffers; and a lack of hope was devastating for family wellbeing and mental health. Less spare change also meant there was less room in farmers' budgets to undertake land and water conservation projects that might reduce their vulnerability to further degradation of their properties. Already more than a third of the region's dams were brackish or saline and even more were of marginal quality.[7] One drought-affected Narembeen farmer, for instance, reported that he could no longer afford to construct additional drains on his property to divert saline water, which he feared would lead to the loss of even more of his land to salt.[8] The more precarious financial situations of many farmers also affected their access to government assistance for water supplies. Most government grants to improve dams and construct pipelines, for instance, required farmers to contribute at least half of the cost of this infrastructure, reflecting the prevailing influence of user pays on agricultural policy.[9]

The dry conditions also prompted calls from farming organisations for access to 'multi-peril crop insurance' to serve as another tool of risk management. But a government appointed taskforce found the scheme had 'no future…in the absence of significant government subsidisation of premiums of underwriting of risk'.[10] Even though analysts considered that the relatively reliable climate of the southwest made the region ideal for crop insurance, the concept was out of step with the neoliberal direction of Australian agricultural policy. With a change of government and deteriorating conditions for farmers, this insurance was made available to the state's wheat and barley growers in early 2011.

Although the government had worked hard to shore up supplies for Big Water, those beyond the reticulated network had to bear the brunt of the return of dry conditions in 2005 and 2006. Farmers on the south coast and the northeastern wheatbelt were hit particularly hard once again, with many recording their worst harvests to date. Meanwhile, in the northern wheatbelt over 70 per cent of farmers had changed their management practices 'in response to perceived changes in climate'.[11] The growing trend towards reduced tillage and early sowing since the 1980s, as well as the introduction of new crop varieties, had led to higher yields, despite the run of dry seasons.[12] Whether southwest farmers considered the 'changes in climate' were natural or human-induced, many were certain that 'humans would adapt naturally as the climate changed'.[13]

Big Water marches on

The dry winter of 2001 delivered the lowest streamflows to Perth's dams since the drought of 1914. Although the Court government had promised to 'drought proof' Perth the previous year, Big Water now had to increase its draw on groundwater reserves and tighten water restrictions on its customers to ensure sufficient supplies. In addition to the prohibition of sprinklers during the day, customers were now forbidden from using their sprinklers more than twice a week. Bore owners were also expected to tighten their belts and had their water use restricted to night-time. The government also targeted Perth's thirstiest residents with a price hike for those households who used more than 550 kL of scheme water a year. Although these restrictions and price rises failed to address the inherent vulnerability of Big Water arising from its large and complex technical networks, they achieved a reduction in scheme water use and helped to force a small degree of cultural change surrounding water consumption in the suburbs.

The tightening of water restrictions and higher prices focussed household conservation efforts on their gardens and helped to reduce water consumption in Perth from over 180 kL per head per year in 2000/2001 to about 150 kL the following year.[14] In many households, bore water most likely made up the difference. Although the use of bores was restricted, the government again encouraged residents to invest in these independent supplies to relieve the pressures on Big Water, despite the potential ecological effects of this unmonitored private abstraction on shallow groundwater reserves. The government also relaxed regulations on the use of grey water in suburban gardens and later offered small rebates on less thirsty showerheads, washing machines and toilet cisterns, as well as rainwater tanks. Although fewer than 10 per cent of households invested in a rainwater tank, more than a quarter had a bore to ensure their gardens did not suffer.[15] The obvious benefit of the bore was that it could run all year, while the rainwater tank relied on rains, which was not necessarily helpful during Perth's dry summer months.

As the reduction in consumption suggests, most of Big Water's customers were receptive to the need to conserve scheme water. Many remained concerned, however, about the consequences of such measures for the appearance of their gardens. The people of Perth were just as anxious about maintaining their lawns and gardens as they had been in the late 1970s. After a hiatus during the 1980s and early 1990s, customers had begun to use as much water outside the home as they had before the introduction of user pays in the late 1970s. During this time, observed George Seddon, Perth had 'gone palm', favouring lush and thirsty greenery over more hardy species that could withstand dry spells.[16] Although homes were occupying a larger proportion of the residential block, leaving less space for outdoor areas, these areas had become sites of entertainment, recreation and conspicuous consumption. From elites through to the aspirational working class, front gardens especially were places of spectacle, which required large amounts of water to maintain their verdant appearance to residents and visitors. As a resident from the leafy, riverside suburb of Applecross explained, 'If you drive down the street and everybody has got reasonable lawns and one's got a dead patch, it's like pointing the finger of scorn isn't it?'.[17]

The association of a dry garden with an uncivilised household remained powerful in the suburbs. Faced with the daunting prospect of maintaining the appearance of a large verge area under water restrictions, one resident complained, 'If I left it looking like nature it would look like an Aboriginals' camp wouldn't it? You know I am nearly forced to put a lawn in aren't I?'.[18] This racist turn of phrase underlines the potent legacy of the discriminatory sanitary order that had been forged in the southwest at the turn of the twentieth century and continued to play a part in the marginalisation of the region's Aboriginal people. Despite the greater availability of welfare services for disadvantaged Western Australians, Indigenous people remained overrepresented among the state's homeless population, and many therefore lacked regular access to the benefits of Big Water.[19]

Although Big Water's demand management polices achieved the desired reduction in water consumption, these approaches were not unproblematic. The combination of water restrictions and rebates again pointed the finger solely at consumers for the southwest's water worries, rather than the infrastructure of Big Water itself, which continued to detach water users from the processes of water supply and allowed the persistence of a profligate water culture. The strategy of water restrictions is cheap, quick and effective, but it is an especially blunt instrument because it does not differentiate between users and uses of household water. Moreover, it does not challenge the path dependencies of the technologies and institutional cultures of Big Water. As environmental policy analyst Stephen Dovers has observed, this 'blame-shifting onto the individual…eases need for effective reform of patterns of production and consumption, settlement and governance'.[20] In other words, these strategies did little to question the status quo of Big Water in the suburbs.

The popularity of automatic reticulation systems in Perth's suburbs had a similar effect. About a quarter of Perth households owned such systems, which meant those who could afford them could adjust their watering regime at very little inconvenience.[21] By 2008, over two-thirds of Perth properties had invested in this technology.[22] Although such reticulation systems made it much easier for households to comply with water restrictions, the lack of interruption to their daily routines allowed many to remain divorced from the processes of water supply as they did not have to alter their personal routines to accommodate the restrictions. Culturally and physically remote from the source of their water supplies, the people of Perth remained vulnerable to climate variability and water scarcity in the future.

A water crisis?

Although restrictions had managed to reduce the residential demands on Big Water, the government's anxieties about the persistence of dry conditions in the southwest remained. The idea of a 'water crisis' facing the southwest, particularly Perth, took hold early in the first term of the Gallop Labor government. The state Environment Minister uttered the phrase in Parliament in late August 2001 and the media followed, as the prospect of tighter water restrictions loomed after a dry winter.[23] The state of crisis was seemingly confirmed in October when the Water Corporation declared that the inflows into the dams of Big Water were the worst since 1914.[24] Government-funded scientific research suggested that the declining rainfall trend would continue and that it was more than likely a consequence of anthropogenic climate change. Despite these findings, the head of the Indian Ocean Climate Initiative (IOCI), Brian Sadler, confided to colleagues at the Bureau of Meteorology in August 2002 that 'the water situation is actually being managed pretty well and falls short of being the crisis that it is often labelled to be'.[25] So why had the government declared a 'water crisis'?

The onset of these dry conditions in the southwest coincided with the publication of the first stage of IOCI research in 2002, which appeared to substantiate the government's declaration. IOCI scientists reported that the region had experienced a rainfall decline since the mid-1970s due to a combination of natural climate variability and the enhanced greenhouse effect.[26] For several decades then, the southwest had been experiencing those drier conditions that many scientists predicted would afflict the southern region of Australia as carbon dioxide levels increased into the middle of the twenty-first century. The dry conditions that were affecting the southwest in 2002, therefore, were not merely a passing episode, but were instead evidence of an ongoing drying trend. Scientists identified fewer days where rain fell, and less rain when it did fall.[27] With less rainfall, there was even less runoff or streamflow into the region's dams because dry soils take longer to saturate, which delays the process of water seeping into waterways and aquifers. These forecasts of even drier conditions in the future captured the headlines and conjured a vision of the metropolis deserted for want of water: simply, 'Perth water options dry up'.[28]

The recently elected Labor State government used IOCI's findings to underpin some of its policies, particularly in the areas of the environment, transport, and water resource development. This approach contrasted strikingly with that of the conservative Federal government, which, since its election in 1996, had worked tirelessly to suppress and undermine greenhouse debate within Australia and to stymie attempts to negotiate an international climate change regime. The Federal Coalition government argued that any global agreement on reducing greenhouse emissions would be detrimental to the resource-dependent Australian economy. This position reflected the Coalition's traditional support base, the business, mining, and agriculture sectors. As a result, Commonwealth-funded scientists were pressured to avoid engaging in the public debate on anthropogenic climate change.[29] For the Coalition, the nation's economic development took precedence over the long-term future of the environment.

The State government was arguably more receptive to the research of climate scientists because their findings aligned with both the Labor Party's focus on sustainable economic development and the environmental concerns of its predominantly urban support.[30] The 2001 state election had been largely fought over environmental issues, particularly the logging of old-growth forests in the southwest region. Promising to protect the remaining old-growth forests, Labor had achieved a landslide victory against the conservative Coalition and initiated the process to cease logging in the southwest forests. Labor's election had also coincided with the release of findings from the Intergovernmental Panel on Climate Change (IPCC) that, 'There is new and stronger evidence that most of the [global] warming observed over the last 50 years is attributable to human activities'.[31] A year later, the eastern states experienced a dry spell that the Bureau of Meteorology reportedly described as the nation's 'first climate change drought'.[32]

In late 2002, IOCI published an image of this water situation that became synonymous with the southwest's 'water crisis' and the campaign to invest in another source of water supplies. The image was a graphical representation of the amount of water flowing into Big Water's dams and the steady reduction of these amounts since the 1970s (Figure 6.1). Although dams were no longer the only major source of water supplies for the Integrated Water Supply Scheme, the vivid depiction of the ebbing flows into the region's dams portrayed the water situation as critical. This position would only worsen with a growing population and IOCI's prediction of an ongoing drying trend.

The image was first presented to the public in the State government's State Water Strategy, which emphasised the urgency of addressing the future of water supplies in the southwest. In the 2003 document, Premier Geoff Gallop warned, 'Western Australia has reached a critical point in the way we use and reuse our precious water resources'. This message of urgency prevailed under the Gallop government and it was underscored by the graph of the diminishing amount of water entering Perth's dams. This graph was (and continues to be) used regularly in government reports and scientific papers regarding the southwest's water resources. The nature of the graph, with its bars of water quantities and lines of average inflows, provides its reader with a clear and simple representation of declining water supplies. This interpretation is enhanced by the additional 'step declines' of average inflow that scientists consider to have occurred since 2001 (Figure 6.2). This staircase-like image leads even the most unimaginative reader to expect further step declines to occur until there is zero inflow.

This representation of the region's water position warrants further examination. As these graphs (Figures 6.1 and 6.2) do not indicate the state of the region's groundwater reserves, which were supplying over 50 per cent of scheme water supplies, laypeople in the government and wider community could (and did) interpret them as depicting a supply system perilously close to running out of water. Likewise, the graphs generally accompany discussions of the region's 'drying climate', which reinforces the inevitability of the looming water crisis. To the layperson, the graphs therefore illustrate the declining rainfall trend, rather than the state of the dams. It follows then, that other sources of water must be developed to avert the crisis. The creation and circulation of these graphs, therefore, supported the shared agenda of the State government and Water Corporation to expand Big Water, and earn votes and revenue in the process.

The simplicity of the graphs also presents the situation as detached from their geographical context. Although they infer the diminishing storages of Big Water's dams, they do not show the spatial change of rainfall patterns as rains move southwards towards the Southern Ocean. Nor do they show the toll of Big Water and private bores on the groundwater reserves of the Swan Coastal Plain. Read together, these graphs arguably helped to present the

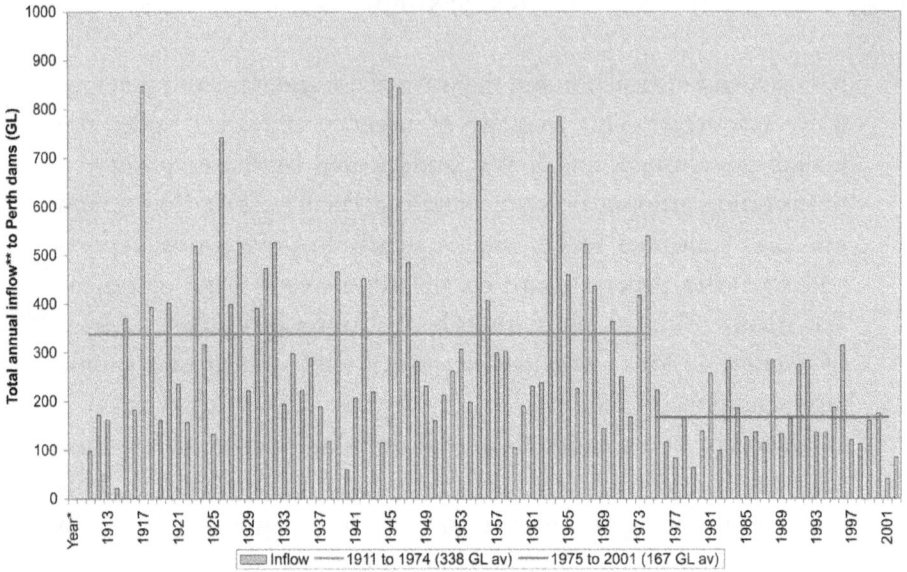

Figure 6.1.
Inflow into dams providing water to the Integrated Water Supply Scheme (1911 to 2001).[33]

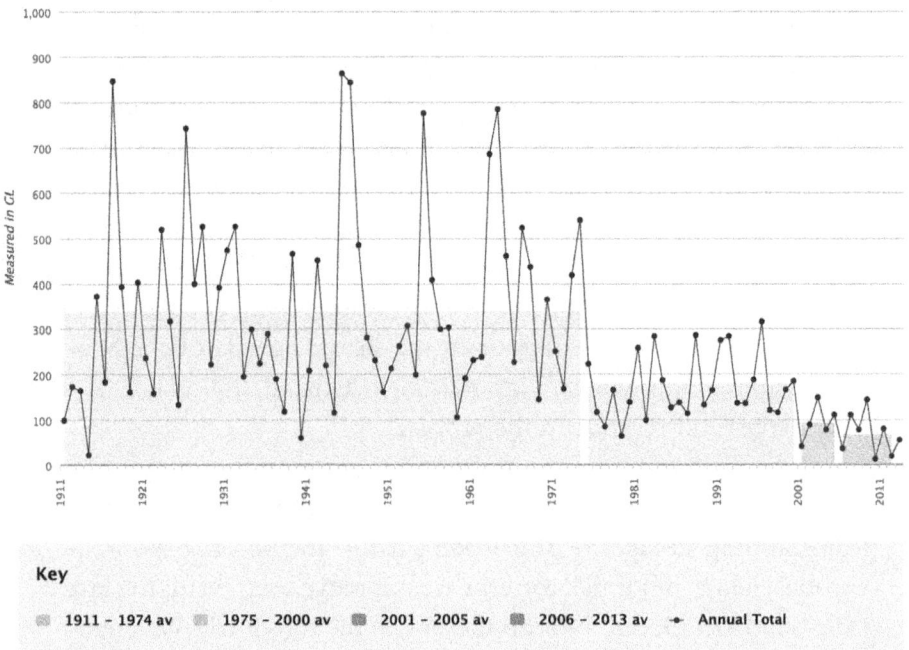

Key

1911 – 1974 av   1975 – 2000 av   2001 – 2005 av   2006 – 2013 av   Annual Total

*In order to provide an accurate historical comparison streamflow from Stirling, Wokalup and Samson Brook Dams are not included in this data as these dams only came online in 2001. Inflow is therefore modelled on Perth dams pre-2001.

Figure 6.2.
Inflow into dams providing water to the Integrated Water Supply Scheme (1911 to 2012).[34]

water supply situation of southwest Western Australia as a product of global climate change, requiring urgent and far-reaching local responses. Accurate as this association with anthropogenic climate change was, it also lent scientific and political legitimacy to the State government's program to develop additional water supplies in the southwest.

Filling the gap

The unusually dry conditions since 2001 had already exposed the vulnerability of the groundwater reserves of the Gnangara and Jandakot Mounds to the effects of drought and Big Water's thirst. With less rain in the future, water managers expected that Big Water's dams would struggle to fill and it would have to draw more heavily on its groundwater reserves. Meanwhile, less rain would also slow the replenishment of these aquifers. The overall effect on these sources would accelerate the depletion of the subterranean reserves with severe repercussions for both horticulture and wetlands. By 2004, the Environmental Protection Authority (EPA) had observed that water levels in the caves in Yanchep National Park had declined to such an extent that 'some loss of species is likely to have occurred'.[35] Some wetlands had experienced fires and greater acidity due to drying out and vegetation had collapsed at Lake Nowergup and declined at Lake Wilgarup. These problems prompted the government to accelerate the thinning of pine plantations on the Gnangara Mound in order to alleviate the pressures on these ecosystems.

Even before the drought of 2001, Big Water had come under fire for its voracious appetite and the toll this had exacted upon the groundwater reserves of the Swan Coastal Plain. And in response to the series of dry years at the turn of the twenty-first century, Big Water drew even more heavily on these reserves to meet the demands of its consumers. The dry conditions exposed the inadequacy of the monitoring procedures, which had failed to ensure the protection of these reserves. The ecological consequences of this failure underlined the inherent fragility of the engineered resilience of these groundwater systems.

The plundering of these reserves reinforced community scepticism about the government's ability to protect the environment from overexploitation by Big Water in the future. The limited scientific understanding of the complex workings of these groundwater systems only heightened this lack of trust. As a CSIRO scientist explained to journalist Åsa Wahlquist in 2008,

> There are still major questions about the recharge under different climate and land-use regimes, what the sustainable yield is, what the relationship between the fluctuations of those water levels and the environmental health is. So even a system like that on the doorstep of Perth, and half of the water supply of Perth, is not as well understood as we would wish it to be.[36]

This uncertainty only served to deepen anxieties about the security of Big Water in a drier future.

The erosion of the ecological resilience of Perth's groundwater reserves and wetlands had cultural implications for many local Aboriginal people. Where Nyoongar had once been able to rely on soaks at swamps and other sources for fresh water, these were now dry. Aboriginal people told anthropologists that the declining watertable was affecting the growth of medicinal plants and that much of the local fauna was no longer present. The ailing health of these wetlands had serious consequences for Aborigines: as one Nyoongar man pointed out, 'without water there wouldn't be any Aboriginal spiritual life'.[37] The careful monitoring of groundwater levels, therefore, was necessary not only to protect these reserves for ecosystems and for the use of Big Water, but also to ensure they continued to meet the spiritual and cultural needs of the region's Aboriginal people.

Securing Big Water's future?

Following the dry conditions of 2001, the State government announced in early 2002 its intentions to use seawater desalination technology to supply water for Perth. Under this plan, a reverse-osmosis desalination plant would be constructed in the vicinity of the southern suburbs of Kwinana or East Rockingham to provide scheme water during periods of 'drought emergency', that is, to avert total sprinkler bans. Of course, a drought emergency in Perth's suburbs is a far cry from the nature of drought in rural Australia, and still more remote from the conditions in less developed regions of the world, such as the Sahel and East Africa. Nevertheless, total sprinkler bans were anathema to the State government. The harsh restrictions of 1978 would not be repeated as Western Australian politicians considered them akin to electoral suicide. The people of Perth, they believed, could not be deprived of water for their gardens.

Reverse-osmosis desalination of seawater had been on Big Water's long-term agenda since the 1980s, when the then Water Authority had concluded that it was preferable to obtaining water from farther afield.[38] But it was too expensive to warrant investment. Seawater desalination re-emerged under the Court government, when the Water Resources Minister Kim Hames asked the Water Corporation to conduct a study into the state of the technology, its use in Western Australia, and the possibilities of its use in the future. The study focussed mainly on the use of desalination plants to supply water for industrial and agricultural purposes.[39] But Hames was unconvinced of the need to invest in the technology. In 2000 he declared: 'The prospect of desalination on a large scale in Perth is still a long way off', because his government had invested in projects that would 'deliver a supply security last enjoyed more than thirty years ago'.[40] During the particularly wet winter that year, Hames and his colleagues had not imagined the onset of the dry conditions in 2001. Nor had they appreciated the effects of the region's drying trend on Big

Water and the deterioration of the Gnangara Mound, Big Water's main source of supplies.

Despite these problems affecting the Gnangara Mound and the evidence of declining rainfall levels, the plan to use desalination technology was met with staunch opposition from environmentalists, rural politicians, and the media. Among their concerns was the expense of the desalination plant, the cost of which consumers would bear. Another problem was the plant's environmental impact, not only on the marine environment but also on the atmosphere, due to the emission of greenhouse gases. After all, if the drying trend was the result of climate change, which is due to increased greenhouse gas emissions, it seemed unwise to resort to solutions that would only increase those emissions. Besides, Western Australian greenhouse gas emissions per capita were already the highest in Australia and among the highest in the developed world.[41] Finally, rural politicians argued that the plan was too focussed on Perth and that it did not provide sufficient benefits for regional Western Australians. In light of these issues, in February 2003 the government turned its attention to tapping the South West Yarragadee aquifer in the southwest Capes region.

The appeal of the South West Yarragadee aquifer was that it could provide the necessary amount of water quickly and cheaply. The borefield's proximity to the Donnelly River was also attractive to Big Water, which had its sights set on damming this river or its tributaries in the future.[42] The South West Yarragadee describes the section of the Yarragadee Formation near the Blackwood River in the southwest corner of the state.[43] The Yarragadee aquifer is a large and complex groundwater system that lies beneath the superficial and Leederville aquifers, and extends roughly from Geraldton to the south coast. According to the Water Corporation's plan, the underground water would be extracted from bores in an area between Margaret River and Nannup, and piped north to the Harvey Dam, from where it would supply Big Water.[44] Conveniently, the Water Corporation had recently negotiated with Harvey irrigators to fund the piping of their irrigation channels in return for the water savings, which would go towards Big Water. Although the irrigators had initially rejected this deal on the grounds that it would affect their businesses, they eventually came to a satisfactory arrangement.

During 2003 and early 2004, the environmental and economic impact of this plan to use the water resources of the South West Yarragadee became the subject of intense public debate. The advocates of tapping this groundwater reserve maintained that it would provide Perth, Mandurah and the goldfields with a cheaper water supply than other options over a long period of time. As such, it would alleviate the need to make further investments in water supplies in the near future. But this economic argument left many unconvinced, particularly those with concerns about its impacts on the environment and the economy of the Capes region. The transfer of water from a rural area to the suburbs came under fierce criticism from local shires, which argued that the plan threatened the region's 'pristine environment and agricultural potential'.[45] Rural politicians deployed agrarian rhetoric in the media, arguing that the groundwater had productive uses in the Capes region. Many Perth residents were also unconvinced about the plan, sharing the concerns of those beyond the suburbs.

Underlying these concerns about the abstraction of water from the South West Yarragadee was the scientific uncertainty surrounding the size of the aquifer and the amount of water that could be sustainably withdrawn. Although government hydrologists had realised the enormity of the aquifer in the late 1980s, there had been limited exploration of its size and features since. A major reason for this lapse was the reorganisation of the state's water sector in the mid-1990s and a subsequent decline in funding for hydrological research.[46] Despite this, government scientists were generally satisfied that the aquifer could sustain further abstraction of groundwater.[47] But their research indicated that the salinity levels and flows of the Blackwood River stood to be affected. Furthermore, the deterioration of the wetlands of the Gnangara Mound had diminished the community's faith in the monitoring of the ecological effects of Big Water's groundwater abstraction activities. Critics argued that similar damage could be caused to the South West Yarragadee if Big Water was permitted access.

In 2004, the mounting criticism of Big Water's plan to tap the South West Yarragadee led the government to reassess the construction of a seawater desalination plant in Kwinana. Although the desalination plant was by no means uncontroversial, the South West Yarragadee proposal was simply proving too contentious in the lead up to the 2005 state election. With electoral redistribution looming, the government sought to protect its hold on the marginal seats in the vicinity of the aquifer.[48] In spite of the myriad political challenges that desalination posed to the government seeking re-election, it had a trump card: seawater desalination offered Perth a 'climate-independent' water supply.[49]

By the 2005 election, the prospect of a 'water crisis' in the southwest had been revived. For instance, in June 2004, the *West Australian* reported, 'Perth will die, says top scientist', referring to paleontologist Tim Flannery's predictions for the future of the southwest region. According to Flannery, 'Perth will become a ghost metropolis over the next few decades unless governments acknowledge that global warming is a reality'.[50] The prevailing dry conditions and water restrictions provided the physical 'evidence' for this prediction, which fed anxieties about the prospect of very scarce water resources in the future. Seawater desalination, however, offered a solution to protect Big Water from the vagaries of the weather. It was simple, as the director of the state water strategy proclaimed: 'We need a water supply which is independent of climate'.[51] To 'green' the proposal, which had come under fire for its potential energy consumption, the government assured voters that renewable energy would power the plant, thus reducing its greenhouse gas emissions and its impact on the global climate.

These ongoing political anxieties about the southwest's water future in the lead up to the 2005 state election revived the prospect of using water from the Kimberley region to slake the southwest's thirst. The idea to bring water from the north had been raised at a community forum on water resources in 2002 but once again, the government and economists deemed the infrastructure too expensive. Undeterred, Ernie Bridge announced the launch of the Watering Australia Foundation's 'National Distribution Program', which involved harnessing the water resources of the rivers of northern Australia, such as the Fitzroy, Daly and Burdekin, for the benefit of the drought-stricken southern states. Meanwhile, a Sydney-based defence and technology firm had made separate approaches to the State government and the Coalition Opposition regarding its own proposal to deliver water from the Fitzroy River to the southwest. Although the government had committed to the seawater desalination plant in late 2004, the popular support for the idea of the Kimberley pipeline forced the government to undertake a more detailed study of the plan. Before this study was completed, however, the Opposition announced on the eve of the 2005 election that a Coalition government would build a canal to bring the vast water resources of the Kimberley to the southwest.[52]

For economists and environmentalists, the costs involved in the 3,700 km Kimberley canal were simply too great to entertain. Several studies had been undertaken into the feasibility of the plan to use water from the Kimberley since Ernie Bridge had proposed it in the late 1980s.[53] These reports shared the same conclusion: bringing water south required an astronomical investment. When the feasibility study commissioned by the government was eventually completed in April 2006, it restated these earlier findings.[54] The energy required to pump water from the north was much higher than the energy required for desalination – after all, the water wouldn't run by gravity. If water was brought from the Kimberley, the average household water bill would increase by 100–400 per cent.[55] These critics had the support of former Premier Sir Charles Court, who maintained his view that the plan compromised the economic development of the state's northwest.[56] There were also concerns from the Kimberley that transferring water south would affect the local ecology, the cultural practices of the traditional owners, and the viability of pastoral and horticultural lands. Yet again, as anthropologist Sandy Toussaint observed, 'Kimberley Indigenous groups were hardly visible throughout the campaign' and 'largely absent from public debate'.[57]

Nevertheless, many Western Australians in the southwest shared Bridge's vision. It offered the opportunity of water supplies for the northern pastoral and agricultural lands near the canal, areas otherwise unconnected to scheme water and some of which had been recently drought-affected. The construction of the project, advocates argued, would also provide jobs to local workers and stimulate the economy of regional Western Australia. Underpinning the project's appeal, the Water Corporation suggested, was that it was a familiar idea for the lay public to grasp. Unlike the other water supply options that had been tabled, water from the Kimberley was perhaps 'popular because it made people feel comfortable because it's not a new technology, it's just a big dam some place with a pipeline' – or canal.[58] But the enduring appeal of these large water projects, which persists in Western Australia and other states, warrants further exploration.

As it had in the 1980s and 1990s, the Kimberley canal project resonated with long-held Australian ideas about the 'empty' North. Underlying political desires to develop and populate the north has been an enduring (non-Indigenous) sense of the region's emptiness and wasted potential. The 2005 plan to divert water from the Fitzroy River to the southwest of the state was one such plan to take advantage of the Kimberley region's underused resources. Tapping the vast resources of the Fitzroy, the project's proponents argued, made good sense – the river has, on average, the greatest volume of annual flow and floods in the state.[59] Furthermore, the region stood to become wetter due to climate change, in contrast to the drying southwest, so even more water would be going to 'waste' if it were not used.[60]

An examination of the debates over the canal also reveals a recurring allusion to the past, the persuasiveness of which cannot be underestimated. References to historical figures and their legacies proved to be politically potent, resurrecting the hope and vision especially associated with Western Australia's gold rush era. Supporters of the plan to transport water from the Kimberley revived the ghosts of Engineer-in-Chief C. Y. O'Connor and Premier Sir John Forrest, associating the new idea with Western Australia's golden age of pioneering development and engineering ascendancy. Like O'Connor's 'golden pipeline', the Kimberley canal would make the desert bloom. Incidentally, the invocation of O'Connor's name in connection with the new project arose shortly after the centenary of his death (2002). The power of this gold rush past not only recalled an earlier phase of 'water dreaming', but also tapped into a seam of disenchantment in the electorate, of discontent with the state of Australian political leadership and society at large at the turn of the twenty-first century.

The rhetorical connection between the Kimberley project and visionary leadership in media and political circles suggests that journalists and politicians perceived a lack of voter confidence in their elected leaders. The Opposition manipulated this sentiment through its evocation of an enduring mythology in Western Australian history, what historian Geoffrey Bolton has described as the 'myth of dynamic entrepreneurship'. 'Bold entrepreneurs', Bolton explains, 'have pushed projects for investment and development...with limitless faith in the West's resources and too little appreciation for the need for assessment and conservation of those resources'.[61] Where, asked the government's critics, was this strong, visionary leadership in Western Australia now?

By this time, there developed a widespread public disaffection, or at least anxiety, regarding the prevailing ethos of economic rationalism. It was this populism that the leader of the conservative Opposition, Colin Barnett (who had been executive director of the state's Chamber of Industry and Commerce in the 1980s), invoked in a reflection on the Kimberley project after the 2005 election. Barnett wondered,

> If you go back in history and do mind-numbing cost-benefit, internal rates of return, all those sorts of analyses, which great

projects in Australia would have been built? Would we have had a trans-Australian railway? I doubt it. We probably wouldn't have had the overland telegraph, we wouldn't have had the Snowy Mountains scheme...In this booming State with its powerful tradition of can-do enterprise, surely the ingenuity, drive and resolve can be found to use Kimberley water to secure future prosperity.[62]

This reference to Australia's grand nation-building engineering projects appealed to a nostalgia for a golden age of the country's economic history. The pace of microeconomic reform since the Hawke and Keating governments of the 1980s had arguably strengthened the economy but for many Australians, this had come at a personal cost. As journalist Michael Gordon reported in 2004, Australia was 'a country with an economic surplus but a confidence deficit'.[63]

The appeal of the Kimberley canal arguably lay both in its visionary scale and its potential to provide tangible benefits for regional Western Australians, such as employment in the construction phase and irrigation for their properties. Indeed, surveys conducted by the *West Australian* newspaper revealed that the project appealed more to country voters than to those in the suburbs.[64] Another aspect of the project's rural appeal lay with its chief exponent: Ernie Bridge. Although Bridge might not have possessed the statesman qualities of figures like Sir John Forrest or Sir David Brand or Sir Charles Court, his enduring passion for the project evidently endeared him to many Western Australian voters. He was an 'everyman', a 'good bloke', a 'battler', especially against the 'pointy heads' who were stifling his vision, and holding back the state's long-awaited northern development. Importantly, Bridge and his Kimberley project contrasted with the elitist, intellectual, urban focus of the Labor government.

In spite of the popular appeal of the Kimberley canal, the project proved to be the undoing of the Coalition during the 2005 electoral campaign. A series of bungled budgets for the project portrayed a poorly prepared Opposition. These errors played a significant role in the Coalition's failure to win the confidence of the electorate at the polls and ushered in the Labor government for a second term. Nevertheless, water from the Kimberley remains a tantalising prospect in the southwest, while the tapping of the South West Yarragadee continues to divide Western Australians.

In November 2006, Big Water's customers in the southwest became the first in Australia to sip desalinated seawater. Other State governments took note and before long, desalination plants were on the drawing board in similarly drought-affected areas, including the Gold Coast, Sydney, Melbourne and Adelaide. Desalination no longer represented 'bottled electricity', as former New South Wales Premier Bob Carr had once quipped; rather, it represented to governments seemingly limitless water and perhaps most importantly, electoral security. The allure of 'climate independent' water supplies was difficult to resist, especially as severe water restrictions bit hard in the eastern states. But desalination in Perth at least was no silver bullet. Although it relieved some of the pressure on groundwater sources, the desalination plant only provided a fraction (17 per cent) of Big Water's supplies.[65] This amount hardly matched the rhetoric of climate independence that deluded politicians and Big Water's customers, and lulled them into a false sense of security about the future reliability of the southwest's water supplies.

Hosing down climate change

'Give the people water and their votes will follow', wrote philosopher Clive Hamilton of the approach of the Howard government to the politics of climate change in Australia in its final year in office. According to Hamilton, the conservative Prime Minister had sought to change the tenor of the climate change debate by turning 'the climate problem into a water problem'. John Howard had pursued this strategy, argued Hamilton, because he was aware that:

For most Australians the most worrying manifestation of climate change was the drought. The two had become joined in the popular understanding, both in the bush where the paddocks were parched and in the cities where water restrictions had turned lawns brown.[66]

Despite their ideological differences, similar observations might be made of the maneuverings of the Gallop Labor government in Western Australia during Perth's water crisis. The State government tapped into the enduring anxieties of Western Australians in the southwest that their verdant city was a fleeting mirage; that due to their isolation and their position between the desert and the sea, they would inevitably run out of water. Addressing water issues in the southwest, therefore, had a broad appeal in the electorate.[67] With the promise of a climate-independent water supply and a limited program of water restrictions, the State government was able to manage the crisis without causing severe hardship for voters. The water crisis also served to mask the government's lack of action on the much more difficult long-term issue of reducing the state's greenhouse gas emissions.

The State government's anxieties about the ongoing drying trend in the southwest and its association with anthropogenic climate change prompted its implementation of technocratic responses to guard against worsening water scarcity for Big Water and its customers. From the outset, the government proclaimed its intent to 'secure' Perth's water future through a program of water restrictions and additional water supplies.[68] Between the droughts of 2001 and 2006, the government had invested twice as much in the development of supplies for Big Water as its counterparts in Sydney, Melbourne, Brisbane and Adelaide.[69] The implication of such promises of water security was that without government investment in additional infrastructure, Big Water and its customers would be *in*secure and at dire risk of water scarcity, which would be detrimental to the economy and consumers' lifestyles. Although such investment has allowed the government to avoid harsh restrictions, these measures have served largely to perpetuate the expectation of relatively unfettered water supplies, thereby weakening the hydroresilience of scheme water users in the southwest to climate variability in the future. Rather than a solution to the southwest's water worries, therefore, Big Water's growing infrastructure is symptomatic of the inherent vulnerability of the southwest's economy and settlement patterns to water scarcity.

The promise of additional supplies served to undermine the government's promotion of residential water conservation because the prospect of water scarcity appeared more remote. A comparison of household scheme water use across Australian cities in 2005 revealed that Perth was third behind Canberra and Adelaide, despite the city's heavy reliance on backyard bores.[70] Even allowing for the year-round rainfall of the other capitals, this statistic is intriguing, given the policy of water restrictions and the spectre of a drying climate in the southwest. This relatively high water consumption of Perth households can be partly attributed to the lack of financial incentive to curtail scheme water use. Although a market mechanism had been introduced in order to manage water scarcity in the late 1970s, the price of water did not adequately reflect the increasing cost of supplies for Big Water. Despite the 'water crisis', successive governments had not allowed the price of water to increase in real terms since 1998. The political sensitivity of price rises, therefore, hampered the function of the price signal to encourage consumers to reduce their demand for water.[71] Already cognitively distanced from the source of scheme water supplies, this lenient pricing of water served to further insulate households from the effects of the southwest's drying climate and the growing difficulty of supplying Big Water.

By 2005, the State government considered that the electorate would not tolerate tighter limits on water consumption and pledged to reduce the likelihood of a total ban on water sprinklers from one year in thirty, to just one year in two hundred, which was an extremely conservative approach to water planning.[72] Australians in other capital cities, meanwhile, were likely to face sprinkler bans once every twenty-five years. In parts of New

South Wales, Victoria, Queensland and South Australia, residents were later prevented from washing their cars and using scheme water on their gardens – a far cry from the twice-a-week watering regime in Perth. The financial losses for Big Water that restrictions had already produced in the southwest were also likely to have influenced this decision to limit restrictions. The possible effects on the plant nursery, turf-growing, lawn-mowing, and swimming-pool industries also played a role.[73] Such a populist policy, however, demanded the development of further supplies for Big Water. As the South West Yarragadee continued to divide the electorate after the 2005 state election, the government committed to the construction of a second desalination plant in 2007 at Binningup, which was completed in 2011 and expanded in 2013.

Premier Gallop and his government had earned praise from around the nation for the way that they had managed the city's water crisis and averted total sprinkler bans. That they had achieved this success as the 'national canary in the climate change coal mine' had made the feat all the more remarkable.[74] But was it? For the most part, the government's strategy appeared to be business as usual – expanding water supplies to meet the demands of consumers. A more remarkable approach for the Gallop government would have been to make more concerted efforts to encourage the development of a water-conserving culture to improve the hydroresilience of Western Australians in the southwest. In light of IOCI findings that the regional drying trend was associated with anthropogenic climate change, the government might also have implemented strategies to reduce the state's greenhouse gas emissions.

The Labor government had teased environmentalists with the announcement in 2005 that IOCI formed the cornerstone of its new state greenhouse strategy. Although this strategy might have 'raised the priority of greenhouse issues and committed departments…to a range of actions aimed at reducing emissions and adapting to climate change', it was more a symbolic gesture than a roadmap for action.[75] Not long after his election in 2001,

Premier Gallop had expressed his opposition to Australia's ratification of the Kyoto Protocol because its implications for Western Australia's resource-based economy. This position put his government at odds not only with local environmentalists, but also with the Labor governments of New South Wales, Victoria and South Australia. Furthermore, his government commissioned another coal-fired power plant in the southwest and promoted greenhouse-intensive industries in Kwinana and the state's northwest. Environmentalists criticised the Gallop government for its contradictory approach. As a campaigner for the Australian Conservation Foundation argued in 2005,

> Western Australia is in the grip of a water crisis, which is consistent with climate change predictions. The Gallop government is on the one hand searching for ways to combat the crisis, and on the other, knowingly contributing to it by allowing inefficient coal-fired power stations to be built.[76]

The government's lip service to climate change mitigation did little to improve the southwest's hydroresilience, leaving Western Australians vulnerable to running out in a drier future.

Boom state

The Federal election of 2007 was arguably the world's first climate change election and the success of the Australian Labor Party brought a greater political will to address the issue. The Commonwealth ratified the Kyoto Protocol, encouraged investment in renewable energy sources, and, much to the chagrin of the Western Australian government, put a price on carbon. Despite the 2008 global financial crisis, Western Australia served as a quarry for the ravenous Chinese and Indian markets. In his provocative study of the future of Perth, *Boom Town*, architect Richard Weller reported in 2008 the city's rate of economic growth had exceeded that of China.[77] The strength of the state's economy has supported further population growth, particularly in the southwest, which has placed additional strain on Big Water and its supplies.[78]

After the humiliation of the 2005 campaign, water issues were noticeably absent in the state election that swept Colin Barnett and his Coalition government to power in September 2008. Nevertheless, the dry seasons have ensured that water remains high on the government's agenda. In 2010, Perth and other parts of the southwest recorded their driest year since records began. With little fanfare, the government imposed total sprinkler bans during the winter months of June, July and August, and restricted bore use to three days per week – a policy that has continued.

In the suburbs, the resort to technocratic strategies to overcome climate variability and water scarcity has continued. A 2008 study showed that some Perth suburbs were sinking at a faster rate – as much as 5 mm a year – than anywhere else in the nation, as a result of the widespread pumping from aquifers beneath the city.[79] In response to the deteriorating condition of the groundwater reserves of the Swan Coastal Plain and the ongoing decline in rainfall, the government commenced a trial to replenish the Gnangara Mound with treated wastewater in 2011.[80] Satisfied with the results, the Water Corporation announced in early 2013 that it would add this recycled water to the Integrated Water Supply Scheme.[81] Mirroring similar schemes in California, wastewater will undergo several stages of treatment before its injection into aquifers, where it mixes with the existing groundwater before returning to scheme water supplies. This process underlines the engineered resilience of these groundwater reserves such that systems of measurement and monitoring ensure constancy, efficiency and predictability to ensure that neither Big Water nor the aquifers run out. In contrast to the experience of Toowoomba in Queensland, where residents rejected a similar proposal in 2006, this plan seems to have caused barely a ripple. Aside from a few concerns about water quality, water users have been remarkably quiet on the matter. On the one hand, their acquiescence might represent the acceptance of a viable water source, while on the other, it might suggest indifference as the policy requires no change to household behaviour.[82]

The Barnett government has also overseen the expansion of the Binningup seawater desalination plant, reflecting the growing importance of this 'climate-independent' source. As the Water Corporation reported in 2013, after the driest June on record, 'Rainfall is no longer relied upon as our primary source of water'.[83] Without the addition of groundwater and desalinated water to metropolitan dam storages, low levels in Big Water's dams would have rendered them unusable. Although seawater desalination appears to be the answer to the government's water woes, this may change in the future. As energy prices continue to increase, the cost of water from desalination will also rise and these costs will inevitably be passed onto consumers. Whether this will reduce demand remains to be seen. In a positive sign of the efficacy of demand management measures and environmental awareness, the Water Corporation reported in 2013 that water consumption across the state had fallen by 8 per cent per person over the past five years.[84] But with the southwest's population expected to reach nearly 2.5 million people by 2031, there will be additional pressures on water resources from urban development.[85] With the likelihood of the drying trend continuing, Big Water will inevitably feel the strain to meet consumer expectations of endless supplies, and the prospect of piping water from the north will continue to inspire many Western Australians in the southwest. Nevertheless, the slow but growing involvement of Aboriginal people in water resource planning and management in both the southwest and northwest of the state, as well as the enormous cost of this plan, may affect the development of such a scheme.

Beyond Big Water, a series of dry seasons since 2010 has hit wheatbelt farmers particularly hard and further whittled away their finances. The media has largely portrayed their plight in Steinbeckian terms, depicting scenes of rural decline and exodus.[86]

The announcement of national reforms to drought assistance in 2014 might come too late for some of them. But many farmers are fighting on: a ten-year study of broadacre farming in Western Australia found that nearly two-thirds of farm businesses are in a growing or strong position.[87] These farms, the study reported, are largely dependent on wheat-growing, and their profitability is the product of improving productivity, training, and technical efficiency – the cornerstones of Australian agricultural policy since at least the 1990s. Even so, with the decline in rainfall expected to continue, Western Australian farmers outside the reticulated reach of Big Water will continue to face the challenges of strengthening their hydroresilience to avoid running out in the twenty-first century.[88]

7

Running Out?

In an updated edition of his 2010 study of the Murray–Darling Basin, *The River*, journalist Chris Hammer described the experience of finding himself 'consigned to history'.[1] Browsing through his local bookshop in November 2010, he had realised that his volume had 'somehow migrated' from the Environment and Ecology section, where it had stood six months ago, to a new place on the History shelves. A significant influence on this move, he observed, had been the dramatic change in the weather affecting the east coast of the continent, from drought to devastating floods in late 2010. These conditions have since led some commentators to pillory climate change activists, particularly Tim Flannery, for predicting that the dams supplying Australia's largest city, Sydney, would never fill again. Similarly, the New South Wales and Victorian governments have been roundly criticised for their investment in desalination technology as metropolitan storages increase. Such are the challenges of planning for both climate variability and climate change on a continent of extremes.

The drying trend examined in this book cannot be relegated to history: it is past, present and, seemingly, the future. Here, the fear of running out prevails: the short-lived Climate Commission (established by the Gillard Labor government in 2010 and abolished by the Coalition government in 2013), confirmed that the region had undergone a drying trend since 1970 and that almost all climate change models project continuing dry conditions there.[2] The 2012 *State of the Climate* report, by CSIRO and the Bureau of Meteorology, restated these observations. The publication of these findings in March coincided with data from the Water Corporation, which revealed that since June 2011, over three thousand households had been fined for violating water restrictions – ten times the number of fines issued during the 2009/10 financial year.[3] In contrast, the Department of Water reported that it had not charged any license holders on the Gnangara Mound since metering of the heaviest users began in 2007, despite reports that a quarter of them had exceeded their allowances during the previous year.[4] This contrast between the regulation of residential and horticultural consumers highlights the persistence of political sensitivities surrounding productive and unproductive water use, as well as the ongoing inadequacy of groundwater protection in the southwest.

The southwest's agricultural areas continue to grapple with significant environmental, economic and social challenges. According to the most recent Western Australian *State of the Environment* report, over 14,000 hectares of land is lost to salinisation every year – the equivalent of nineteen football ovals each day. Similarly, salinity levels continue to rise in many major southwest rivers.[5] Despite Western Australia's farmers recording their largest harvest in 2013–14, winter crop production for 2014–15 is expected to be more modest.[6] Furthermore, in both rural and urban areas of the southwest, many Aboriginal families continue to face challenges in accessing public and private housing, which can contribute to homelessness and family breakdown.

Although climate change appears to be playing a role in creating a drier future for the southwest, these changes do not mean that climate and water histories are not useful for informing our vision for the future. The climatic conditions that we will face might be 'new' to us, but change itself is not new and environmental history can reveal how humans have responded to and understood environmental change in the past. By improving our understanding of the past, we can better assess how we might best adapt to environmental change in the future. Moreover, history is well-positioned to reflect on the structures that support the very cultural aspirations that lie at the root of environmental crises. Put bluntly, if we are running out of water as experts predict, we have to understand how we got here in the first place.

When we look back, we notice that Western Australians in the twenty-first century might have a greater level of hydroresilience had their forebears made different decisions. For instance, had previous state governments heeded scientific and environmental warnings about closer settlement in the southwest's marginal areas, many farmers might have opted for less risky ventures, such as pastoral development and forestry. Likewise, the salinisation of the southwest's land and water resources may not have been so extensive and severe had these same governments also acted on scientific concerns about the consequences of the widespread clearing of native vegetation.

In light of ongoing scientific monitoring of the declining groundwater levels of the Swan Coastal Plain, environmental pro-tection authorities might also have been granted greater power to curb the thirst of Big Water for the precious reserves of the Gnangara and Jandakot Mounds. Similarly, backyard bores could have been licensed, monitored, and even metered so that the amount of water privately abstracted could be measured and better regulated. More recently, state governments might have committed themselves to lowering Western Australia's greenhouse emissions, particularly in light of the association of the southwest drying trend with anthro-pogenic climate change. It is significant that these are not fanciful imaginings – these alternatives were advocated repeatedly over the past century. There is still time for some of them to be acted upon.

Western Australians have reaped great spoils from the southwest but they cannot continue to be its spoilers. Although Western Australians in the present must live with the consequences of this past, there remains the need for discussion and decision-making about the ways in which they reduce their vulnerability to climate variability and water scarcity, now and in the future. These are significant debates that affect current and future generations of Western Australians, as 'debates about water are really debates about the sort of society and the sort of environment we want to live in'.[7] They are debates about the state's sustainable development, to ensure that its economic development 'meets the needs of the present without compromising the ability of future generations to meet their own needs'.[8] These future generations include both Australians and citizens of other nations who stand to be affected by the decisions that are made today.

Central to such discussions about society and the environment will be a consensus on the economic aspirations of the current generation of (Western) Australians. Their aspirations, and the paths taken to achieve them, will shape the distribution of wealth, power and access to resources, as well as affecting the natural resources and biodiversity of the continent. In terms of anxieties about climate variability and water scarcity in the southwest, the 'old' state of mind has historically relied upon technocratic measures to 'tame chance'. The long-held faith in science and technology to predict, protect and provide has allowed many Australians to become detached from the basic environmental processes, which has diminished their hydroresilience. A 'new' state of mind, in contrast, might accept the futility of taming chance in a continent of extremes, and instead seek adaptive and flexible strategies, including cultural change, to reduce the vulnerability of present and future generations of (Western) Australians to running out of water. Furthermore, this mindset would temper economic aspirations with consideration for social equity and the environment. Such a state of mind would go some way to end our long-running battle with the elements and 'live in peace within our ecological limits', as historian Libby Robin suggests.[9]

How might such considerations of society and environment affect the ways that Western Australians understand and use the water resources of the southwest in the future? The development of Western Australia's urban and rural water supplies improved the health of the community, while the rise of Big Water provided the foundation for the state's post-war economic development. Despite the irrefutable benefits of these projects, they have also produced significant drawbacks – 'an inflexible, institutionalised water and waste system based on a large-scale, engineered, "big pipe in, big pipe out" logic'.[10] As only a small proportion of the water now consumed needs to be of a potable quality, Big Water could invest in dual-flow water systems, while industrial, commercial and agricultural needs could be met through recycled wastewater.

In addition, a large proportion of household water could be obtained from what might be called 'Small Water', such as residential rainwater tanks and greywater reuse. To encourage such measures, the state government could reconsider its lenient pricing policies to ensure that water is supplied to households at a minimum guaranteed volume per person each year at an equitable price, to reward low use and to protect low-income consumers. The price charged for consumption above this minimum could be set at a steep inclining rate to ensure that those who used more than this base amount paid significantly more for their water consumption.[11] In terms of the equity of water supply, state governments must work much harder to improve the housing, health and living standards of the southwest's Indigenous peoples, to overturn the insidious discriminatory sanitary order that has persisted in the region for far too long.

Reducing the need for Big Water to provide potable water for all uses and users would help to delay the need to develop new sources of supply and relieve pressure on groundwater reserves. Tighter regulation of all consumers of groundwater, both private and public, would curb the abstraction of these reserves and alleviate the strain on the wetland ecosystems of the Swan Coastal Plain. Better protection of these complex ecologies not only conserves their biodiversity, but also safeguards places that are of cultural significance, particularly to many of the region's Aboriginal people.

In the rural areas of the region, this book has highlighted the significant roles that markets, agricultural policies, and financial security play in shaping the resilience of farmers to climate variability and water scarcity. Further research into seasonal forecasting as well as drought-resistant and salt-tolerant crops is necessary, as well as greater investment in extension services to ensure farmers can better access and interpret the findings of this research. Although countrymindedness may have waned, Australian governments have a responsibility to farmers, having assiduously encouraged agricultural development during the twentieth century. With the support of their urban constituents, governments should increase their efforts to support farmers to reduce their vulnerability to the elements and to encourage restructuring the nation's cropping areas for other forms of development, such as pastoralism and tree-cropping.

The responsibility for fostering a 'new' state of mind for Western Australians should be shared among the present generation and bequeathed to the next. The state's environmental history shows, however, that local visionaries have played central roles in shaping the aspirations of Western Australians and it is vital that their dreams do not create nightmares for the land, water and people of the southwest. Surrounded by the desert and the sea, they cannot afford to think otherwise.

NOTES

Introduction

1   T. Winton, cited in S. Kennedy, 'New Tim Winton play continues the *Dirt Music* story', *ABC Southwest WA*, 18 June 2012, <http://www.abc.net.au/local/stories/2012/06/18/3527814.htm>, (Accessed: 28 September 2013).

2   R. Drewe, 'Place in the heart', *West Weekend*, 13 July 2013, p. 22.

3   T. Winton, *Land's Edge*, Chippendale, Pan Macmillan, 1993, p. 22.

4   G. Seddon, *Sense of Place*, Nedlands, UWA Press, 1972, p. xiv.

5   T. Flannery, *The Weather Makers*, Melbourne, Text Publishing, 2005.

6   W. Steffen and L. Hughes, *The Critical Decade 2013*, Canberra, Climate Commission Secretariat, 2013, p. 4.

7   R. Glennon, 'The grass is greener in Perth: a water-scarce city adjusting to climate change', *National Geographic*, 10 April 2012, <http://newswatch.nationalgeographic.com/2012/04/10/the-grass-is-greener-in-perth-a-water-scarce-city-adjusting-to-climate-change/>, (Accessed: 28 September 2013).

8   W. deBuys, *A Great Aridness: climate change and the future of the American southwest*, New York, Oxford, 2011, pp. 7–8.

9   CSIRO, *Water Yields and Demands in South-West Western Australia*, Canberra, CSIRO, 2009, p. 125.

10   S. D. Hopper and P. Gioia, 'The southwest Australian floristic region: evolution and conservation of a global hot spot of biodiversity', *Annual Review of Ecology, Evolution and Systematics*, vol. 35, 2004, p. 632.

11   A. Brearley, *Ernest Hodgkin's Swanland*, Crawley, UWA Press, 2005, p. 13. In winter, these westerlies usually pass over the southern parts of the continent between 26°S and 34°S. In summer, these winds move further south and pass below the south coast between 35°S and 45°S.

12   See, 'Western Australia – weather and climate drivers', *Climate Kelpie*, Grains Research & Development Corporation, 2008-2010, <http://www.climatekelpie.com.au/understand-climate/weather-and-climate-drivers/

western-australia#IOD>, (Accessed: 28 September 2013); and C. Pattiaratchi, *Variability in the Leeuwin Current*, Indian Ocean Climate Initiative, 2005, <http://www.ioci.org.au/pdf/IOCIclimatenotes_10.pdf>, (Accessed: 28 September 2013).

13   T. J. Hatton, J. Ruprecht and R. J. George, 'Preclearing hydrology of the Western Australian wheatbelt: target for the future?', *Plant and Soil*, vol. 257, 2003, p. 349.

14   Brearley, *Ernest Hodgkin's Swanland*, pp. 13–14, 442.

15   L. Pen, *Managing Our Rivers*, East Perth, Water and Rivers Commission, 1999, p. 33.

16   W. A. Davidson, *Hydrogeology and Groundwater Resources of the Perth Region, Western Australia*, Perth, Geological Survey of WA, 1995, pp. 5, 9–10, 153.

17   Brearley, *Ernest Hodgkin's Swanland*, p. 14.

18   Hopper and Gioia, 'The southwest Australian floristic region', p. 623.

19   N. Myers et al., 'Biodiversity hot spots for conservation priorities', *Nature*, vol. 403, 2000, pp. 803–8.

20   *Wedjela* or *wadjala* is a Nyoongar term to describe non-Nyoongars.

21   C. W. Hassell and J. R. Dodson, 'The fire history of southwest Western Australia prior to European settlement in 1826–1829', in I. Abbott and N. Burrows (eds), *Fire in Ecosystems of Southwest Western Australia: impacts and management*, Leiden, Backhuys, 2003, p. 72. There are variations of the spelling of the 'generic' word that describes the Nyoongar people, including *Nyungar, Noongar,* and *Nyoongah*.

22   R. van den Berg, *Nyoongar People of Australia: perspectives on racism and multiculturalism*, Leiden, Brill, 2002, p. 2. The *Wagyl* Rainbow Serpent is also spelt *Waukal, Waakal, Wakyl* and *Woggal*.

23   L. Collard, 'The cosmology: the creator of the Trilogy Waakal or Nyungar Rainbow Serpent', in Leybourne and Gaynor (eds), *Water*, p. 122.

24   L. Collard, S. Harben and R. van den Berg, *Nidja Beeliar Boodjar Noonookurt Nyininy: a Nyungar interpretative history of the use of* boodjar *(country) in the vicinity of Murdoch University*, Perth, Murdoch University, 2004, p. 24.

25   van den Berg, *Nyoongar People of Australia*, p. 10.

26   R. Jones, 'Firestick farming', *Australian Natural History*, vol. 16, 1969, pp. 224–31.

27   B. Gammage, *The Biggest Estate on Earth*, Melbourne, Allen & Unwin, 2011, p. 3.

28   ibid., pp. 52–5.

29   D. Connell, 'Managing climate for the Murray–Darling Basin (1850–2050)', in T. Sherratt, T. Griffiths and L. Robin (eds), *A Change in the Weather*, Canberra, NMA, 2005, pp. 82–91; D. Garden, *Droughts, Floods and Cyclones*, North Melbourne, Australian Scholarly Publishing, 2009; J. Gergis, D. Garden and C. Fenby, 'The influence of climate on the first European settlement of Australia', *Environmental History*, vol. 15, no. 3, 2010,

pp. 485–507; R. H. Grove, *Ecology, Climate and Empire*, Cambridge, White Horse Press, 1997, pp. 143–6; R. H. Grove, 'Revolutionary weather', in Sherratt, Griffiths and Robin (eds), *A Change in the Weather*, pp. 128–40; E. O'Gorman, *Flood Country*, Collingwood CSIRO Publishing, 2012; D. Anderson, 'Drought, endurance and "the way things were"', *Australian Humanities Review*, no. 45, 2008, pp. 67–81; and D. Anderson, 'Drought, endurance and climate change "pioneers"', *Cultural Studies Review*, vol. 16, no. 1, 2010, pp. 82–101.

30 Powell has studied the historical management of Australia's water resources in several works, including *Watering the Garden State*, 1989; *Plains of Promise, Rivers of Destiny*, Brisbane, Boolarong, 1991; *The Emergence of Bioregionalism in the Murray–Darling Basin*, Canberra, MDB Commission, 1993; and *Watering the Western Third,* Perth, Water and Rivers Commission, 1998. For recent works on water history in Australia, see R. Ballinger, *An Inch of Rain,* North Melbourne, Australian Scholarly Publishing, 2012; M. Cathcart, *The Water Dreamers*, Melbourne, Text Publishing, 2009; D. Connell, *Water Politics in the Murray–Darling Basin*, Annandale, Federation Press, 2007; H. Goodall, 'Main streets and riverbanks: the politics of place in an Australian river town', in S. H. Washington, P. Rosier and H. Goodall (eds), *Echoes From the Poisoned Well*, Lanham, Lexington Books, 2006, pp. 255–70; H. Goodall, 'Riding the tide: Indigenous knowledge, history and water in a changing Australia', *Environment and History*, vol. 14, no. 3, 2008, pp. 355–84; H. Goodall and A. Cadzow, *Rivers and Resilience: Aboriginal people on Sydney's George's River*, Sydney, UNSW Press, 2009; J. Keating, *The Drought Walked Through*, Melbourne, Dept of Water Resources, 1992; C. J. Lloyd, *Either Drought or Plenty*, Sydney, Dept of Water Resources, 1988; M. McKernan, *Drought*, Crows Nest, Allen & Unwin, 2005; and P. Troy (ed.), *Troubled Waters*, Canberra, ANU Press, 2008.

31 G. Bankoff, 'Constructing vulnerability: the historical, natural and social generation of flooding in metropolitan Manila', *Disasters*, vol. 27, no. 3, 2003, pp. 224–38.

32 U. Beck, *Risk Society,* London, Sage, 1992; and A. Giddens and C. Pierson, *Conversations with Anthony Giddens*, Palo Alto, Stanford University Press, 1998.

33 See for instance, R. H. Grove, *Green Imperialism*, Cambridge, Cambridge University Press, 1996.

34 Å. Wahlquist, *Thirsty Country*, Crows Nest, Allen & Unwin, 2008, p. 192.

Chaper 1. Settling the Seasons: Sowing the seeds of vulnerability (1829 to 1901)

1   P. Statham, 'Western Australia becomes British', and G. C. Bolton, 'Perth a foundling city', in P. Statham (ed.), *The Origins of Australia's Capital Cities*, Oakleigh, Cambridge University Press, 1989, pp. 126, 142.

2   J. M. Powell, *Watering the Western Third,* Perth, Water and Rivers Commission, 1998, p. 14.

3   W. A. Davidson, *Hydrogeology and Groundwater Resources of the Perth Region, Western Australia,* Perth, WA Geological Survey, 1995, p. 3.

4   H. E. Hunt, *Perth's Early Water Supplies,* Perth, Institution of Engineers Australia (WA), 1984, pp. 20–1.

5   N. Green, *Broken Spears,* Perth, Focus Education Services, 1984, p. 183.

6   L. Tilbrook, 'A chronology of the Swan River Colony 1829–1840', in S. Hallam and L. Tilbrook (eds), *Aborigines of the Southwest Region 1829–1840,* Nedlands, UWA Press, 1990, p. xiv.

7   F. C. Irwin, 1835, cited in S. Hallam, *Fire and Hearth,* Canberra, AIAS, 1975, p. 65.

8   G. Bolton, *Land of Vision and Mirage: Western Australia since 1826,* Crawley, UWA Press, 2008, p. 11.

9   J. Belich, 'The rise of the Angloworld: settlement in North America and Australasia, 1784–1918', in P. A. Buckner and R. D. Francis (eds), *Rediscovering the British World,* Calgary, University of Calgary Press, 2005, p. 53.

10   J. M. Powell, *An Historical Geography of Modern Australia,* Cambridge, Cambridge University Press, 1988, p. 12.

11   J. M. R. Cameron, 'Learning as a factor in land use: the inevitability of pastoralism in early Western Australia', *Journal of Australian Studies,* no. 3, 1978, pp. 35–41.

12   J. M. R. Cameron, 'Poison plants in Western Australia and coloniser problem solving', *Journal of the Royal Society of Western Australia,* vol. 59, no. 3, 1977, pp. 71–7.

13   T. Griffiths, 'How many trees make a forest? Cultural debates about vegetation change in Australia', *Australian Journal of Botany,* vol. 50, 2002, p. 381.

14   J. M. R. Cameron, *Ambition's Fire,* Nedlands, UWA Press, 1981, pp. 156–7.

15   P. Statham, 'Swan River Colony 1829–1850', in C. T. Stannage (ed.), *A New History of Western Australia,* Nedlands, UWA Press, 1981, p. 189.

16   W. Anderson, *The Cultivation of Whiteness,* Carlton, Melbourne University Publishing, 2005, p. 13.

17   See the works of J. M. R. Cameron, 'The near collapse of Swan River Colony: review and reappraisal', *Social Sciences Forum,* vol. 1, no. 1, 1973, pp. 7–31; 'Poison plants in Western Australia', pp. 71–7; 'Learning as a factor in land use', pp. 30–43; and *Ambition's Fire,* pp. 86–135; as well as F. K. Crowley, *Australia's Western Third,* Melbourne, Heinemann, 1960, pp. 11–31; and P. Statham, 'Swan River Colony 1829–1850', pp. 181–210.

18   F. R. Clause, 31 March 1827, cited in '6. Report to Darling (and the Colonial Office) on Swan River, 1827', in P. Statham-Drew (comp.), The Stirling Reports and Other Key Documents, 2003, MS0109B, Reid Library, The University of Western Australia.

19 Anderson, *The Cultivation of Whiteness*, pp. 13–14.

20 J. Gentilli, 'A history of meteorological and climatological studies in Australia', *University Studies in History*, vol. 5, no. 1, 1967, pp. 55, 63.

21 Captain Stirling to Governor Darling, 8 December 1826, *Historical Records of Australia*, Series 1, vol. 12, 1919, pp. 775–80.

22 W. H. Stone, 'Change of climate as a remedial agent', *Lancet*, 6 August 1864, p. 167.

23 See, G. Bankoff, 'Rendering the world unsafe: "vulnerability" as Western discourse', *Natural Disasters*, vol. 25, no. 1, pp. 20–2.

24 See, R. Morgan, 'Salubrity and the survival of the Swan River Colony: health, climate and settlement in colonial Western Australia', in A. Varnava (ed.), *The El Dorado in Imperialism*, Manchester, Manchester University Press, (forthcoming, 2014).

25 J. Stirling, *Observations on the Climate and Geographical Position of Western Australia and on Its Adaptation to the Purposes of a Sanatorium for the Indian Army*, London, J. C. Bridgewater, 1859.

26 Morgan, 'Salubrity and the survival of the Swan River Colony'.

27 G. F. Moore, cited in E. Braid, 'John Septimus Roe: first explorer of the wheatlands; the search for an inland sea', *Early Days*, vol. 7, 1975, p. 92.

28 Braid, 'John Septimus Roe', pp. 85–6.

29 Hunt, 1866, cited in L. Hunter, 'Climate and landscape', in L. Hunt (ed.), *Yilgarn*, Southern Cross, Shire of Yilgarn, 1988, p. 45.

30 G. F. Moore, cited in I. A. E. Bayly, *Rock of Ages*, Nedlands, Tuart House, 1999, p. 29.

31 B. D. Clarkson, 1864, cited in, J. Maddock, *Westonia*, Westonia, Shire of Westonia, 1998, p. 49.

32 Hunt, 1866, cited in Hunter, 'Climate and landscape', p. 45.

33 Water Authority of Western Australia, *The Wells of Explorer Charles Hunt*, Leederville, WAWA, 1991.

34 N. Green, 'Aborigines: the changing scene', in Hunt (ed.), *Yilgarn*, p. 130.

35 I. Abbott, 'Historical perspectives of the ecology of some conspicuous vertebrate species in south-west Western Australia', *Conservation Science WA*, vol. 6, no. 3, 2008, pp. 1–214.

36 J. Wollaston, 'An influenza epidemic (Dec, 1841)', in M. Aveling (ed.), *Westralian Voices*, Nedlands, UWA Press, 1979, p. 206.

37 Green, *Broken Spears*, pp. 235–6.

38 A. R. Waylen, 'Report by the Colonial Surgeon on the Public Health of the Colony for the Year 1877', in *Western Australian Votes and Proceedings of the Legislative Council (WALCV&P)*, Perth, Govt Printer, 1878, pp. 3–4.

39 S-J. Hunt and G. C. Bolton, 'Cleansing the dunghill: water supply and sanitation in Perth 1878–1912', *Studies in WA History*, vol. 2, 1978, p. 2.

40 Waylen, 'Report', pp. 3–4.

41 Hunt and Bolton, 'Cleansing the dunghill', pp. 2–3.

42 F. Morel-EdnieBrown, 'Tethered Antipodes: imperial impress in central Perth, Western Australia', in P. Limb (ed.), *Orb and Sceptre,* Clayton, Monash University ePress, 2008, pp. 4.1–4.43.

43 Diogenes, 'Wanted – "medica manus"', *Inquirer,* 22 January 1879, p. 3.

44 'Colonial Surgeon's Report', *Inquirer,* 20 December 1862, p. 4.

45 A. R. Waylen, 'Report by the Colonial Surgeon on the Public Health of the Colony for the Year 1881', in *WALCV&P,* Perth, Govt Printer, 1882, p. 4.

46 Hunt and Bolton, 'Cleansing the dunghill', p. 4.

47 *West Australian,* 24 July 1885, p. 3.

48 Cited in Hunt, *Perth's Early Water Supplies,* p. 9.

49 R. MacLeod, 'Colonial engineers and the cult of practicality: themes and dimensions in the history of Australian engineering', *History and Technology,* vol. 12, no. 2, 1995, p. 148.

50 'The Perth Water Works: visit of inspection', *West Australian,* 3 December 1889, p. 3.

51 Davidson, *Hydrogeology and Groundwater Resources,* p. 3.

52 Bolton, *Land of Vision and Mirage,* p. 32.

53 G. H. Burvill, *Agriculture in Western Australia,* Nedlands, UWA Press, 1979, pp. 12–13.

54 'Meteorology', *Perth Gazette,* 19 June 1868, p. 3.

55 D. Day, *The Weather Watchers,* Melbourne, Bureau of Meteorology, pp. 9–10.

56 D. Garden, *Droughts, Floods and Cyclones,* North Melbourne, Australian Scholarly Publishing, 2009, pp. 147, 240.

57 Waylen, 'Report by the Colonial Surgeon', p. 3.

58 'When will it rain?', *Western Australian Times,* 22 March 1878, p. 2.

59 M. Fraser, 1881, cited in Day, *The Weather Watchers,* p. 10.

60 M. A. C. Fraser, 'Meteorological Report for the Year 1880', in *WALCV&P,* Perth, Govt Printer, 1881, p. 4.

61 'The weather', *West Australian,* 1 February 1886, p. 3.

62 M. A. C. Fraser, 'Meteorological Report for the Year 1882', in *WALCV&P,* Perth, Govt Printer, 1883, p. 4.

63 Bureau of Meteorology, *Results of Rainfall Observations Made in Western Australia,* Melbourne, H. J. Green, 1929, p. 3.

64 'Victoria Plains', *Perth Gazette,* 25 May 1870, p. 3.

65 J. Beattie, 'Rethinking science, religion and nature in environmental history: drought in early twentieth-century New Zealand', *Historical Social Research,* vol. 29, 2004, pp. 95–6.

66 J. Moorhouse, cited in ibid., p. 96.

67 H. E. V., 'Water famine and its prevention', *West Australian,* 17 March 1882, p. 4.

68 'Western Australia: its present and future', *West Australian,* 20 March 1889, p. 3; and 'A distinguished visitor to West Australia', *Western Mail,* 3 September 1892, p. 7.

69 P. Mendell, cited in 'The outlook in Australasia', *Daily News*, 2 November 1891, p. 3.

70 J. Forrest, 'President's address, Section E (Geography)', *Report of the First Meeting of the Australasian Association for the Advancement of Science*, Sydney, Australasian Association for the Advancement of Science, 1888, p. 354.

71 J. Forrest, *West Australian*, 30 September 1896, p. 2.

72 D. Hutchison, 'William Ernest Cooke, Astronomer 1863–1947', *Historical Records of Australian Science*, vol. 5, 1981, p. 62.

73 T. Stannage, *The People of Perth*, Perth, Perth City Council, 1979, p. 274.

74 Hunt and Bolton, 'Cleansing the dunghill', p. 11.

75 'The water supply question', *West Australian*, 13 January 1897, p. 5.

76 Hunt, *Perth's Early Water Supplies*, p. 21.

77 Parched, 'To the Editor', *West Australian*, 17 November 1896, p. 10.

78 Hunt and Bolton, 'Cleansing the dunghill', p. 11.

79 South Australian, 'To the editor', *West Australian*, 13 January 1897, p. 5.

80 'The Perth Waterworks', *Western Mail*, 12 September 1891, p. 24.

81 'Our only garden', *West Australian*, 22 December 1887, p. 3.

82 Stannage, *People of Perth*, p. 278.

83 K. Webber, 'Romancing the machine: the enchantment of domestic technology in the Australian home, 1850–1914', PhD Thesis, University of Sydney, 1997, pp. 150–1.

84 J. Matthews, *Good and Mad Women*, Sydney, George Allen & Unwin, 1984, pp. 86–7.

85 Decent Cleanliness, 'To the editor', *West Australian*, 13 January 1897, p. 5.

86 'Highgate Hill', *West Australian*, 13 January 1897, p. 5.

87 Stannage, *People of Perth*, p. 277.

88 Green, 'Aborigines: the changing scene', p. 125.

89 A. Gaynor, '"Like a good deed in a naughty world": gardens on the eastern goldfields of Western Australia', *Australian Humanities Review*, no. 36, 2005, <http://www.australianhumanitiesreview.org/archive/Issue-July-2005/11Gaynor.html>, (Accessed: 28 September 2013).

90 Maddock, *Westonia*, p. 35.

91 J. Forrest, 1896, cited in J. Stephens, 'Karalee Rock: the formation of place and identity', *Urban Policy and Research*, vol. 20, no. 1, 2002, p. 95.

92 G. Blainey, *The Golden Mile*, St. Leonards, Allen & Unwin, 1993, p. 59.

93 Blainey, *Golden Mile*, p. 75.

94 *Western Australian Parliamentary Debates*, 21 July 1896, p. 151.

95 Gaynor, 'Like a good deed'.

Chapter 2. Thirst in the Golden West: Suburban and agricultural expansion (1901 to 1945)

1   'The closing year of the century', *Western Mail*, 6 January 1900, p. 43.

2   L. Layman, 'Development ideology in Western Australia, 1933–1965', *Historical Studies*, vol. 20, no. 79, 1982, p. 234.

3   J. M. Hodge, *Triumph of the Expert*, Athens, Ohio University Press, 2007, pp. 28–9.

4   G. C. Bolton, *Land of Vision and Mirage*, Crawley, UWA Press, 2008, p. 60.

5   Dept of Public Works and Water Supply, *Comprehensive Agricultural Areas and Goldfields Water Supply Scheme*, Perth, Govt Printer, 1946, p. 6.

6   M. Tonts, 'State policy and the yeoman ideal: agricultural development in Western Australia, 1890–1914', *Landscape Research*, vol. 27, no. 1, 2002, pp. 105-12.

7   J. Forrest cited in 'The celebrations at Kalgoorlie', *West Australian*, 26 January 1903, p. 5. My emphasis.

8   R. G. Hartley, *River of Steel*, Bassendean, Access Press, 2007, p. 220.

9   See for instance, W. H. Shields, 'Water-supply on the Yilgarn railway, Western Australia', *Minutes of the Proceedings of the Institution of Civil Engineers*, vol. 146, 1901, pp. 242–57.

10   J. Powell, *Watering the Western Third: water, land and community in Western Australia, 1826–1998*, Leederville, Water and Rivers Commission, 1998, p. 27.

11   'Water and Sewerage Works Department's Annual Report', *West Australian*, 29 December 1913, p. 3.

12   Bureau of Meteorology, *Results of Rainfall Observations in Western Australia*, Melbourne, H. J. Green, 1929, pp. 53-87.

13   Powell, *Watering the Western Third*, pp. 27–9.

14   G. L. Sutton, cited in, 'Wheatgrowing: the state's resources', *West Australian*, 8 September 1913, pp. 7–8.

15   A. Haebich, 'European farmers and Aboriginal farmers in south Western Australia', *Studies in WA History*, vol. 8, 1984, p. 61.

16   A. Haebich, *For Their Own Good*, Nedlands, UWA Press, 1992, p. 14.

17   A. Haebich, '"Clearing the wheat belt": erasing the Indigenous presence in the southwest of Western Australia', in A. Dirk Moses (ed.), *Genocide and Settler Society*, New York, Berghahn Books, 2004, pp. 271–4.

18   Haebich, *For Their Own Good*, p. 46.

19   'Drainage in the south-west', *Western Mail*, 13 August 1897, p. 41.

20   A. C. Staples, *They Made Their Destiny*, Harvey, Shire of Harvey, 1979, pp. 427–8.

21   W. S. Cooper, 'Drainage and irrigation', in J. Gentilli (ed.), *Western Landscapes*, Nedlands, UWA Press, 1979, p. 248.

22   '1914: the State', *West Australian*, 1 January 1915, p. 4.

23   S. Glynn, *Government Policy and Agricultural Development*, Nedlands, UWA Press, 1975, p. 111.

24 Powell, *Watering the Western Third,* p. 9.

25 J. M. Payne, interviewed by G. O'Hanlon, 1996, Battye Library, OH2738, p. 13.

26 P. Biskup, *Not Slaves, Not Citizens,* St Lucia, University of QLD Press, 1973, p. 147.

27 G. C. Bolton, *A Fine Country to Starve In,* Nedlands, UWA Press, 1994, p. 102.

28 Royal Commission on the Agricultural Industries of Western Australia, p. vii.

29 Ibid., pp. 58, 109, 167, 369, 395, 433.

30 J. Dahlke, 'Evolution of the wheatbelt in Western Australia: thoughts on the nature of pioneering along the dry margin', *Australian Geographer,* vol. 13, 1975, p. 4.

31 K. Hewitt, 'The idea of calamity in a technocratic age', in K. Hewitt (ed.), *Interpretations of Calamity,* Boston, Allen & Unwin, 1983, pp. 9–12.

32 A. Gaynor, 'Looking forward, looking back: towards an environmental history of salinity and erosion in the eastern wheatbelt of Western Australia', in A. Gaynor, M. Trinca and A. Haebich (eds), *Country,* Perth, WA Museum, 2002, p. 108.

33 Royal Commission on the Agricultural Industries of Western Australia, p. xi.

34 J. M. Powell, *An Historical Geography of Modern Australia,* Cambridge, Cambridge University Press, 1988, p. 117.

35 Royal Commission on the Agricultural Industries of Western Australia, p. xi.

36 Burvill, *Agriculture in Western Australia,* p. 23.

37 W. F. McClure, 'Dry farming', *Journal of the Department of Agriculture of Western Australia,* vol. 18, 1909, pp. 134–5.

38 Gaynor, 'Looking forward', p. 110. This attention to American practice reflected a broader trend across agriculture, mining and education, whereby the scientific gaze was looking beyond the British example. See, R. MacLeod, 'Science, progressivism and "practical idealism": reflections on efficient imperialism and federal science in Australia, 1895–1915', *Scientia Canadensis,* vol. 17, 1993, pp. 7–25.

39 See, Gaynor, 'Looking forward', pp. 110–11.

40 Royal Commission on the Agricultural Industries of Western Australia, *Second Progress Report of the Royal Commission on the Agricultural Industries of Western Australia on the Selected Portions of the South-West Coastal Districts,* Perth, Govt. Printers Office, 1918, , pp. xiii-iv.

41 H. E. Hunt, 'Address', in *Seminar H2O,* Nedlands, UWA, 1975, p. 2.

42 G. D. Snooks, 'Development in adversity 1913–1946', in C. T. Stannage (ed.), *A New History of Western Australia,* Nedlands, UWA Press, 1981, p. 257.

43 Hunt, 'Address', p. 2.

44 Hartley, *River of Steel,* p. 170.

45 'Water for the metropolitan area', *Daily News,* 17 May 1923, p. 8.

46 'The city beautiful', *Daily News*, 3 December 1919, p. 4.

47 'Water restriction', *Sunday Times*, 24 December 1933, p. 11.

48 Hunt, 'Address', p. 2.

49 'A waterless city: gross negligence somewhere', *Daily News*, 14 March 1920, p. 8.

50 V. Taylor and F. Trentmann, 'Liquid politics: water and the politics of everyday life in the modern city', *Past and Present*, no. 211, 2011, pp. 203–14.

51 J. A. Gregory, 'Protecting middle-class suburbia: an ideal space for the citizens of interwar Perth', *Studies in WA History*, vol. 17, 1997, p. 77.

52 L. Nash, *Inescapable Ecologies*, Berkeley, University of California Press, 2003, p. 113.

53 J. A. Gregory, '"Let our watchword be 'order' and our beacon 'beauty'": achieving town planning legislation in Western Australia', in R. Freestone (ed.), *Cities, Citizens and Environmental Reform*, Sydney, Sydney University Press, 2009, pp. 173–99.

54 'Shortage of water: the Minister for Water Supply', *West Australian*, 27 November 1920, p. 8.

55 'The city beautiful', *Daily News*, 3 January 1919, p. 4.

56 Gregory, '"Let our watchword be 'order' and our beacon 'beauty'"', pp. 181–2.

57 W. A. Saw, 'Some aspects of town planning', *Journal and Proceedings of the Royal Society of WA*, vol. 5, 1918–19, p. 41.

58 R. Freestone, 'Planning, housing, gardening: home as a garden suburb', in P. Troy (ed.), *A History of European Housing in Australia*, Oakleigh, Cambridge University Press, 2000, p. 133.

59 G. Seddon, *Landprints*, Melbourne, Cambridge University Press, 1997, p. 153.

60 Gregory, 'Protecting middle-class suburbia', p. 77.

61 Malloch Bros, 'Advertisement', *West Australian*, 22 January 1921, p. 9.

62 Wilson and Johns, *Western Australian Gardening Guide*, Perth, Beer's Union Print, 1924.

63 'A waterless city', *Daily News*, 14 March 1920, p. 8.

64 D. R. Williamson, 'Statistics of water use', in *Seminar H2O*, pp. 6–7.

65 R. Evans and K. Saunders, 'No place like home: the evolution of the Australian housewife', in K. Saunders and R. Evans (eds), *Gender Relations in Australia*, Sydney, Harcourt Brace Jovanovich, 1992, pp. 176–90.

66 *Western Homes*, Nov. 1929, p. 7, cited in Gregory, 'Protecting middle-class suburbia', p. 88. Emphasis in text.

67 R. Barton, 'Household technology in Western Australia, 1900–1950', *Oral History Association of Australia Journal*, vol. 7, 1985, p. 109.

68 K. Reiger, 'All but the kitchen sink: on the significance of domestic science and the silence of social theory', *Theory and Society*, vol. 16, 1987, p. 507.

69 Editorial, 'Give us water', *Daily News*, 14 March 1920, p. 4; 'Topics of the day: water for the metropolitan area', *Daily News*, 17 March 1923, p. 8.

70 A. E. Mason, 'Letter to the Editor', *West Australian*, 21 January 1922, p. 8; and A. Victim, 'Letter to the Editor', *West Australian*, 21 January 1922, p. 8.

71 J. Mitchell, cited in 'Water supply', *West Australian*, 14 March 1923, p. 7.

72 Barton, 'Household technology', p. 109.

73 Glynn, *Government Policy and Agricultural Development*, pp. 119–30.

74 Powell, *An Historical Geography*, pp. 121–49.

75 See, G. C. Bolton, *Spoils and Spoilers,* North Sydney, Allen & Unwin, 1992, pp. 138.

76 Bureau of Meteorology, *Results of Rainfall Observations,* p. iii.

77 E. B. Curlewis and M. E. W. O'Dowd, 'Wheat-growing in Western Australia: a review and a forecast', in ibid., p. 65. In the same year, the WA Department of Agriculture opened files on soil erosion, to which dry farming was found to be a significant contributing factor. See, Gaynor, 'Looking forward', p. 111.

78 Curlewis and O'Dowd, 'Wheat-growing', pp. 64–7. This '7.5 wheat period isohyet' appears to generally coincide with what is now the 300 mm line of average annual rainfall, the eastern frontier of the WA wheatbelt.

79 Department of Agriculture, *Annual Report,* 1929 cited in Glynn, *Government Policy and Agricultural Development*, p. 131.

80 G. C. Bolton, *A Fine Country to Starve In*, Nedlands, UWA Press, 1994, p. 24.

81 G. C. Bolton, 'Mitchell, Sir James (1866–1951)', *Australian Dictionary of Biography*, National Centre of Biography, ANU, <http://adb.anu.edu.au/biography/mitchell-sir-james-733>, (Accessed: 28 September 2013).

82 Haebich, *For Their Own Good*, p. 223.

83 Bolton, *A Fine Country to Starve In*, p. 2.

84 G. Prakash, *Another Reason,* Princeton, Princeton University Press, 1999, p. 132.

85 Haebich, *For Their Own Good,* pp. 185, 225-9, 233–4.

86 A. Bashford, '"Is White Australia possible?" Race, colonialism and tropical medicine', *Ethnic and Racial Studies*, vol. 23, no. 2, 2000, p. 149.

87 R. Bropho, *Fringedweller*, Chippendale, Alternative Publishing Co-operative, 1980, pp. 27, 30.

88 P. Hasluck, *Our Southern Half-caste Natives and Their Conditions*, 1936, cited in Biskup, p. 163.

89 Nash, *Inescapable Ecologies*, p. 102. Emphasis in text.

90 Prakash, *Another Reason*, pp. 132–3.

91 Haebich, *For Their Own Good*, pp. 140–2, 237.

92 Haebich, *For Their Own Good*, pp. 144, 236.

93 Haebich, '"Clearing the wheatbelt"', pp. 272–4.

94 Bolton, *A Fine Country to Starve In*, pp. 25–6.

95   J. Maddock, 'Marginal areas', in J. Gregory and J. Gothard (eds), *Historical Encyclopedia of Western Australia*, Crawley, UWA Press, 2009, pp. 552–3.

96   *Western Australian Parliamentary Debates*, vol. 2, 27 October 1938, p. 1,670.

97   Bolton, *A Fine Country to Starve In*, pp. 263–4.

98   Cooper, 'Drainage and irrigation', p. 248.

Chapter 3. A Million Acres a Year: Engineering post-war prosperity (1945 to 1969)

1   L. Layman, 'Development ideology in Western Australia 1933–1965', *Historical Studies*, vol. 20, no. 79, 1982, p. 235.

2   J. C. Foley, *Droughts in Australia*, Melbourne, Commonwealth Bureau of Meteorology, 1957, pp. 1, 223.

3   F. Allon and Z. Sofoulis, 'Everyday water: cultures in transition', *Australian Geographer*, vol. 37, no. 1, 2006, p. 48.

4   David Brand interviewed by Jean Teasdale, 1976, Battye Library, OH 150, p. 45.

5   B. S. Crimp and E. Tindale cited in J. S. H. Le Page, *Building a State*, Leederville, Water Authority of WA, 1986, p. 474.

6   Dept of Public Works and Water Supply, *Comprehensive Agricultural Areas and Goldfields Water Supply Scheme*, Perth, Govt Printer, 1946, p. 6.

7   K. J. Kelsall, 'The Comprehensive Water Supply Scheme', *Journal of Agriculture (Western Australia)*, vol. 18, no. 3, 1977, p. 69.

8   T. Langford-Smith, 'Water supply in the agricultural areas of Western Australia', *Australian Geographer*, vol. 5, no. 6, 1947, p. 121.

9   Langford-Smith, 'Water supply', p. 155.

10   Dept of Public Works and Water Supply, *Comprehensive Agricultural Areas*, pp. 6, 18.

11   Cited in J. Phillips, 'The Rocky Gully exodus', in G. Davison and M. Brodie (eds), *Struggle Country*, Melbourne, Monash University ePress, 2008, p. 8.1.

12   Le Page, *Building a State,* p. 478.

13   Dept of Public Works and Water Supply, *Comprehensive Agricultural Areas*, p. 23.

14   Kelsall, 'The Comprehensive Water Supply Scheme', p. 69.

15   G. C. Bolton, *Spoils and Spoilers*, Sydney, George Allen & Unwin, 1981, p. 138.

16   Q. Beresford et al., *The Salinity Crisis*, 2nd ed., Crawley, UWA Press, 2004, pp. 77-78.

17   L. Higgins, 'State President's Address: 35th State Conference', *Countrywoman of Western Australia*, August, 1959, p. 4.

18   'Problem of milk supply in summer months', *West Australian*, 6 May 1950, p. 3.

19   'W.A. is short of water', *Western Mail*, 14 July 1949, p. 40.

20   W. S. Cooper, 'Drainage and irrigation', in J. Gentilli (ed.), *Western Landscapes*, Nedlands, UWA Press, 1979, p. 250.

21   A. Brearley, *Ernest Hodgkin's Swanland*, Crawley, UWA Press, 2005, pp. 166–7.

22   J. Gregory, *City of Light,* Perth, City of Perth, 2003, p. 38.

23   G. C. Bolton and J. A. Gregory, *Claremont*, Nedlands, UWA Press, 1999, p. 198.

24   F. K. Crowley, *Westralian Suburb*, Perth, Rigby, 1962, p. 111.

25   D. R. Williamson, 'Statistics of water use', in *Seminar H2O*, Perth, University of Western Australia, 1975, np.

26   S-J. Hunt, *Water, the Abiding Challenge*, Perth, Metropolitan Water Board, 1980, pp. 83–4.

27   Layman, 'Development ideology', p. 247.

28   'High water consumption creates storage problem', *West Australian*, 23 July 1953, p. 2.

29   M. Kaïka, 'Interrogating the geographies of the familiar: domesticating nature and constructing the autonomy of the modern home', *International Journal of Urban and Regional Research*, vol. 28, no. 2, 2004, p. 270.

30   G. Davison, 'Australia – the first suburban nation?', *Journal of Urban History*, vol. 22, no. 1, 1995, pp. 49–50.

31   Williamson, p. 6.

32   P. Ritter with E. Pagram, *Faces of Perth*, Kelmscott, Ritter Press, 1967, p. 13.

33   G. Seddon, *Swan River Landscapes*, 1970, cited in G. Seddon, *Swan Song*, Nedlands, UWA, 1995, p. 30.

34   W. Grono, 'The way we live now', in W. Grono and N. Hasluck (eds), *On the Edge*, Claremont, Freshwater Bay Press, 1980, pp. 7–8.

35   S. L. Kessell, 1940, cited in Gaynor, 'Looking forward, looking back', p. 111.

36   V. C. Munt, cited in Public Works Department (PWD), 'Roaded catchments for farm water supplies', *Journal of the Department of Agriculture of WA*, vol. 5, no. 6, 1956, p. 667.

37   J. Lawson, 'Roaded catchments end water shortages', *Countryman*, 25 May 1961, p. 7.

38   I. A. F. Laing, 'Farm dams in the wheatbelt', in *Wheatbelt Water Supply Seminar,* p. 5.

39   B. G. Jennings, 'Farm water supply loans scheme', in *Wheatbelt Water Supply Seminar,* p. 2.

40   Farm Water Supply Advisory Committee, *First Annual Report, 30th May 1966*, Perth, Govt Printer, 1966, pp. 2–3.

41   J. P. Reynolds, Letter to the Commissioners of the Rural & Industries Bank, 4 June 1957, Fodder Conservation Competition, Cons 7204, 1958/017v1, SROWA.

42   A. Haebich, *Spinning the Dream*, North Fremantle, Fremantle Press, 2008, p. 224.

43 A. Haebich, 'Nuclear, suburban and black', in T. Rowse, *Contesting Assimilation*, Perth, API Network, 2005, p. 202.

44 Haebich, *Spinning the Dream*, p. 227.

45 Ibid., p. 243.

46 Ibid., *Spinning the Dream*, p. 255.

47 B. A. McLarty, 'Department of Native Welfare Lectures, Perth Technical College', 1966, Lecture 3, cited in, B. T. Haynes et al., *WA Aborigines 1622–1972*, Fremantle, History Association of Western Australia, 1972, p. 69.

48 S. Toussaint, 'Nyungars in the city: a study of policy, power and identity', MA Thesis, University of Western Australia, 1987, p. 117.

49 Haebich, 'Nuclear, suburban and black', pp. 215, 259.

50 Haebich, *Spinning the Dream*, p. 255.

51 Cited in Aboriginal Legal Service of Western Australia, *Telling Our Story*, Perth, ALSWA, 1995, p. 76.

52 R. Bropho, *Fringedweller*, Chippendale, Alternative Publishing Co-operative, 1980, p. 57.

53 L. Robin, 'Battling the land and global anxiety: science, environment and identity in settler Australia', *Philosophy, Activism, Nature*, vol. 7, 2010, p. 8.

54 D. Day, *The Weather Watchers*, Melbourne, Bureau of Meteorology, p. 265.

55 P. Armstrong, 'Obituary: Joseph Gentilli (1912–2000)', *Australian Geographical Studies*, vol. 39, no. 2, 2001, p. 250.

56 J. Gentilli, *Atlas of Western Australian Agriculture*, Crawley, UWA Text Books Board, 1941, p. 49.

57 J. Gentilli, *Australian Climates and Resources*, Perth, Whitcombe & Tombs, 1946, p. 124.

58 J. Mitchell, 'Preface', in Gentilli, *Atlas of Western Australian Agriculture*, np.

59 D. Serventy, 'The birds of the Swan River District, Western Australia', *Emu*, vol. 47, 1948, p. 254.

60 Gentilli, 'Present climatic fluctuations', pp. 157–8.

61 Serventy, 'The birds of the Swan River District', p. 254.

62 J. Gentilli, 'Bioclimatic changes in Western Australia', *West Australian Naturalist*, vol. 2, no. 8, 1951, p. 184.

63 J. McEwen, Letter to D. Brand, 11 July 1966, Public Works Department, Cons 1109, 1955/0019, SROWA.

64 See, W. J. Gibbs and J. V. Maher, *Rainfall Deciles as Drought Indicators*, Melbourne, Bureau of Meteorology, 1967, pp. iii., 2.

65 D. B. Collett, Letter to K. O'Hara, 6 April 1967, Public Works Department, Cons 1109, 1955/0019, SROWA.

66 Cited in Q. Beresford, 'Developmentalism and its environmental legacy: the Western Australian wheatbelt, 1900–1990s', *Australian Journal of Politics and History*, vol. 47, no. 3, 2001, pp. 406–7.

67 Beresford et al., *The Salinity Crisis*, p. 62.

68 B. Moore, *From the Ground Up*, Nedlands, UWA Press, 1987, p. 198.

4. The 'Age of Anxiety': Reaching the limits of settlement (1969 to 1983)

1   B. Head, 'From the deserts the profits come: state and capital in Western Australia', *Australian Quarterly*, vol. 57, no. 4, 1985, p. 375.

2   G. Seddon, *Swan Song*, Nedlands, UWA Press, 1995, pp. 76, 78.

3   R. D. Rock, 'Rain wanted', *West Australian*, 25 April 1969, p. 6.

4   See, 'Copy of notice appearing in Commonwealth Gazette 6/11/1969', Declared Drought Areas 1969, Cons 2780, 1969/1281 v5, SROWA.

5   J. P. Gabbedy, 'Drought water exercise 1969–1971', 2 August 1971, Farm Water Supply Committee, Cons 7203, V097V2, SROWA.

6   G. Gare, 'Have we under-estimated drought in WA?', *Countryman*, 2 April 1970, p. 5. My emphasis.

7   Meeting Minutes, 'Advisory Committee on adverse seasonal conditions', 12 August 1969, Drought Advisory Committee, Cons 1609, 1969/0801, SROWA.

8   D. Altheer, 'Pastoralists seek drought committee', *Countryman*, 31 July 1969, p. 14.

9   *Western Australian Parliamentary Debates (WAPD)*, vol. 183, 6 August 1969, p. 88.

10   E. C. House cited in, 'False pride prevents drought declarations', *Countryman*, 21 August 1969, p. 9.

11   J. P. Gabbedy, 'Drought water exercise 1969–1971', 2 August 1971, Farm Water Supply Committee, Cons 7203, V097V2, SROWA.

12   K. J. Kelsall, 'The Comprehensive Water Supply Scheme', in *Wheatbelt Water Supply Seminar,* Perth, Water Research Foundation of Australia, WA State Committee, 1977, p. 5.

13   'Water schemes', *West Australian*, 8 October 1969, p. 6.

14   R. L. Southern, 'The Atmosphere', in B. J. O'Brien (ed.), *Environment and Science*, Crawley, UWA Press, 1979, p. 224.

15   'The Perth RO since 1929', *Federation and Meteorology*, Australian Science and Technology Heritage Centre, 2001, <http://www.austehc.unimelb.edu.au/fam/1305.html>, (Accessed: 28 September 2013).

16   R. L. Heathcote, 'Managing the droughts? Perception of resource management in the face of the drought hazard in Australia', *Vegetatio*, vol. 91, 1991, pp. 220–1.

17   W. J. Gibbs, 'Drought amelioration', in *Report of the ANZAAS Symposium on Drought*, Melbourne, Bureau of Meteorology, 1967 cited in Day, p. 338.

18   See, Southern, 'Atmosphere', p. 210.

19   'Farm costs rise, says professor', *West Australian*, 22 September 1969, p. 9.

20   W. R. Stern, 'Trends and prospects' in G. H. Burvill (ed.), *Agriculture in Western Australia, 1829–1979*, Nedlands, UWA Press, 1979, p. 385.

21   G. H. Burvill cited in 'Wheatgrowers may have to change farming pattern', *Countryman*, 22 January 1970, p. 6.

22 I. A. F. Laing, 'Farm dams in the wheatbelt', in *Wheatbelt Water Supply Seminar*, pp. 2–6.

23 G. H. Burvill, Letter to C. Nalder, 18 March 1970, Drought Advisory Committee, Cons 1609, 1969/0801, SROWA.

24 Advisory Committee on Agricultural Education, *Agricultural Education in Western Australia*, Perth, WA Education Dept, 1971, p. 30.

25 G. Davison, 'Down the gurgler: historical influences on Australian domestic water consumption', in P. Troy (ed.), *Troubled Waters*, Canberra, ANU Epress, 2008, p. 56.

26 S-J. Hunt, *Water, the Abiding Challenge*, Perth, Metropolitan Water Board, 1981, p. 96.

27 Head, 'From the deserts', p. 376.

28 'North Dandalup', *Western Mail*, 20 October 1949, p. 26.

29 Cited in Hunt, *Water,* p. 91.

30 'S. W. warning over water', *West Australian*, 23 March 1972, p. 22.

31 I. J. O'Hara, 'Utilization of water resources with particular reference to lawn and garden watering', Metropolitan Water Supply, Sewerage and Drainage Board, Cons 6733, 1967/880672, SROWA.

32 See, B. S. Sadler and C. A. R. Field, *South West Regional Water Planning Study: working report*, Perth, PWD, 1973.

33 See R. Morgan, 'A thirsty city: an environmental history of water supply and demand in 1970s Perth', *Studies in WA History*, vol. 27, 2011, pp. 83–4.

34 D. I. Smith, *Water in Australia*, Melbourne, Oxford University Press, 1998, pp. 191–2.

35 J. W. Offer, 'Viewpoint of an irrigation farmer', in *A Seminar on Irrigated Agriculture on the Coastal Plain*, Crawley, UWA Extension Service, 1977, pp. 83–4.

36 G. D. Oliver, 'Policy and local food sources'; G. M. Cann, 'Agricultural water use: the dairy industry economic aspects'; and B. R. Davidson, 'Economic aspects of Perth's water supply', in *Water Requirements for Agriculture, Industry and Urban Supply for a Metropolis of Two Million in the Southwest of Western Australia*, Perth, AIAS, 1975, pp. 11–12, 13–22; 44–51.

37 J. S. Abbott, 'Water requirements for agriculture, industry and urban supply in the southwest of Western Australia', in ibid, p. 56.

38 Le Page, *Building a State*, pp. 617–8.

39 G. M. Ralph, *Pipe dreams and realities,* Perth, Western Mining Corporation, 1974, p. 16.

40 D. B. Collett, *The usable surface water resources of Western Australia*, Perth, PWD, 1970.

41 C. Court, 'Official opening of the EPA and CSIRO Symposium on groundwater resources of the Swan Coastal Plain', in B. A. Carbon (ed.), *Groundwater Resources of the Swan Coastal Plain*, Perth, CSIRO, 1975, p. 1.

42   B. Sadler, 'Water supply and alternate sources', in Carbon (ed.), *Groundwater Resources of the Swan Coastal Plain*, p. 56.

43   'No plans yet for dam on Fitzroy', *Western Farmer*, 31 March 1977, p. 2; and 'The Ord under scrutiny', *Western Farmer*, 1 September 1977, p. 14.

44   W. Boughton, 'Hydrology and water resources in Australia – the past', in *Proceedings of the 30th Hydrology and Water Resources Symposium*, Sandy Bay, Conference Design, 2006, np.

45   G. C. Cargeg et al., *Perth Urban Water Balance Study*, vol. 1, Leederville, WAWA, 1987, p. 38.

46   After nearly a decade of campaigning, the Star Swamp Bushland was gazetted as an A-Class Reserve in 1985.

47   J. J. Havel, 'The effects of water supply for the city Perth, Western Australia, on other forms of land use', *Landscape Planning*, vol. 2, 1975, pp. 75–132.

48   C. Muir, D. Rose and P. Sullivan, 'From the other side of the knowledge frontier: Indigenous knowledge, social-ecological relationships and new perspectives', *Rangeland Journal*, vol. 32, 2010, p. 262.

49   C. R. Allen, L. H. Gunderson and C. S. Holling, 'Commentary of Part One articles', in L. H. Gunderson, C. R. Allen and C. S. Holling, (eds), *Foundations of Ecological Resilience*, Washington, D. C., Island Press, 2010, pp. 6–7.

50   D. Bennett and D. K. Macpherson, 'Groundwater management – must there be a conflict?', in Whelan (ed.), *Groundwater Resources of the Swan Coastal Plain*, pp. 440–3.

51   See, D. Ritter, 'Trashing heritage: dilemmas of rights and power in the operation of Western Australia's Aboriginal heritage legislation', *Studies in WA History*, vol. 23, 2003, pp. 195–208.

52   S. Toussaint, 'Aboriginal resistance and the maintenance of identity: Nyungars and the state', *Social Analysis*, no. 32, 1992, p. 16.

53   M. Langton, 'Urbanising Aborigines: the social scientists' great deception', *Social Alternatives*, vol. 2, no. 2, 1981, p. 16.

54   R. M. Berndt (ed.), *Aboriginal Sites, Rights and Resource Development*, Nedlands, UWA Press, 1982.

55   S. Toussaint, 'Nyungars in the city: a study of policy, power and identity', Masters Thesis, UWA, p. 104.

56   E. McDonald, B. Coldrick and L. Villiers, *Study of Groundwater-Related Aboriginal Cultural Values on the Gnangara Mound, Western Australia*, 2005, <http://www.water.wa.gov.au/PublicationStore/first/82492.pdf>, (Accessed: 28 September 2013), p. 74.

57   A. D. Allen, 'The Swan Coastal Plain: hydrogeology of superficial formation', in Carbon (ed.), *Groundwater Resources of the Swan Coastal Plain*, p. 14.

58   D. Hewett, *Sandgropers*, 1973, cited in B. Bennett (ed.), *The Literature of Western Australia*, Nedlands, UWA Press, 1979, p. 145.

59   Toussaint, 'Nyungars in the city', p. 113.

60 L. C. Furnell, *Report of the Royal Commission Upon All Matters Affecting the Wellbeing of Persons of Aboriginal Descent in Western Australia*, Perth, Govt Printer, 1974, p. 221.

61 M. Gevers, 'Aboriginal housing – some facts', *Shelter Newsletter*, vol. 2, no. 2, 1983, pp. 6–7.

62 P. Hollingworth, *Australians in Poverty*, West Melbourne, Nelson, 1979, p. 112.

63 M. Heppell, *A Black Reality*, Canberra, AIAS, 1979, pp. 17–19.

64 Toussaint, 'Nyungars in the city', pp. 118–20.

65 M. V. Robinson et al., *An Accommodation Service for Aboriginal Families in Perth*, Perth, Dept for Community Welfare, 1978, p. 17.

66 K. Colbung, in C. Tatz (ed.), *Black Viewpoints*, Sydney, Australia and New Zealand Book Co., 1974, p. 29.

67 Toussaint, 'Nyungars in the city', pp. 22, 151.

68 Seddon, *Swan Song*, p. 54.

69 'Final water gauge', *West Australian*, 4 April 1977, p. 4.

70 Morgan, 'A thirsty city', p. 36.

71 'Final water gauge', *West Australian*, 4 April 1977, p. 4.

72 S. H. Hancke and R. K. Davis, 'Demand management through responsive pricing', *Journal of the American Water Works Association*, 1971, pp. 555, 559.

73 K. Smith, 'Trends in water resource management', *Progress in Physical Geography*, vol. 3, 1979, p. 243.

74 J. J. Pigram, *Issues in the Management of Australia's Water Resources*, Melbourne, Longman Cheshire, 1986, pp. 300–1.

75 T. Moore, 'Life is not meant to be easy', in J. Walter and T. Moore (eds), *What Were They Thinking? The politics of ideas in Australia*, Sydney, UNSW Press, 2010, pp. 250, 255.

76 L. Sharp, 'Water demand management in England and Wales: constructions of the domestic water user', *Journal of Environmental Planning and Management*, vol. 49, no. 6, 2006, p. 872.

77 K. Bakker, 'Paying for water: water pricing and equity in England and Wales', *Transactions of the Institute of British Geographers*, vol. 26, no. 2, 2001, p. 2.

78 Metropolitan Water Authority (MWA), *Domestic Water Use in Perth, Western Australia*, Perth, Metropolitan Water Centre, 1985, p. 52

79 Editorial, 'Think again', *West Australian*, 30 August 1978, p. 6.

80 For instance, 'ALP Attacks Increase in Water Charges', *Daily News*, 1 June 1978, p. 4.

81 V. L. McAulley, 'Charges on water', *West Australian*, 13 September 1978, p. 6; and A. N. Mather, 'Charges on water', *West Australian*, 30 May 1978, p. 6.

82 Correspondents complained of increases of 37, 55.4, and 60 per cent on the previous year's water rates. For example, G. W. Dymond, 'Cost of water comparisons', *West Australian*, 15 August 1978, p. 6; G. M. Easton, 'Rises

in price for water', *West Australian*, 26 August 1978, p. 6; and R. Matthews, 'Call for a review', *West Australian*, 25 August 1978, p. 6.

83 D. Phillips, 'Water charges', *West Australian*, 25 August 1978, p. 6.

84 B. Reid, 'The water charges called a "slug"', *West Australian*, 10 May 1978, p. 6.

85 B. McCartney, 'Quota of water', *West Australian*, 29 August 1978, p. 6.

86 B. J. Alford, 'Query on water', *West Australian*, 31 August 1978, p. 6; R. L. Down, 'Rights on water', *West Australian*, 22 August 1978, p. 6; and G. O'Brien, 'Base water allowance', *West Australian*, 12 May 1978, p. 6.

87 See, Morgan, 'A thirsty city', pp. 81–97.

88 MWA, *Domestic Water Use*, pp. 2, 13, 59, 66.

89 J. Duruz, 'Suburban gardens', in S. Ferber, C. Healy and C. McAuliffe (eds), *Beasts of Suburbia*, Melbourne, Melbourne University Press, 1994, p. 204.

90 See, 'Move to avert water crisis', *Sunday Times*, 24 October 1976, p. 14.

91 K. Holmes, 'In her master's house and garden', in P. Troy (ed.), *A History of European Housing in Australia*, Oakleigh, Cambridge University Press, 2000, p. 175.

92 MWA, *Domestic Water Use*, p. 34.

93 G. Seddon, *Landprints*, Melbourne, Cambridge University Press, 1998, pp. 113–18; and Holmes, 'Growing Australian landscapes', pp. 127–8.

94 G. Lullfitz, *Grow the West's Best Native Plants*, Perth, West Australian Newspapers, 1978, p. 8.

95 MWA, *Domestic Water Use*, pp. 49, 66.

96 G. J. Syme and S. J. Kantola, 'Investment in Private Bores: Underground Water Usage from a Household Perspective', in Whelan (ed.), *Groundwater Resources of the Swan Coastal Plain*, p. 454.

97 MWA, *Domestic Water Use*, pp. 49, 51.

98 I. Hoskins, 'Constructing time and space in the garden suburb', in Ferber, Healy and McAuliffe (eds), *Beasts of Suburbia*, pp. 1–18.

99 Holmes, 'In her master's house and garden', p. 164; and K. Holmes, '"In spite of it all, the garden still stands": gardens, landscape and cultural history', in H-M. Teo and R. White (eds), *Cultural History in Australia*, Sydney, University of New South Wales Press, 2003, p. 184.

100 MWA, *Domestic Water Use,* pp. 40, 63.

101 P. Armanasco, 'State position paper: Western Australia', in *Proceedings of the National Workshop on Urban Water Demand Management*, p. 78.

102 A. J. Peck, 'Water-bore levels', *West Australian*, 25 October 1977, p. 6.

103 C. Burton, 'Water balance of the coastal plain: future', and D. R. Williamson and K. Cole, 'Management aspects in relation to groundwater supplies: urban, garden and sewerage needs', in Carbon (ed.), *Groundwater Resources of the Swan Coastal Plain*, pp. 100, 211.

104 See, K. Webster, 'Profile of Australian water use with reference to domestic water use in Perth', in *Proceedings of the National Workshop on Urban Water Demand Management*, p. 85.

105 M. Kaïka, 'Interrogating the geographies of the familiar: domesticating nature and constructing the autonomy of the modern home', *International Journal of Urban and Regional Research*, vol. 28, 2004, p. 265.

106 M. Peel, 'Between the houses: neighbouring and privacy', in Troy (ed.), *A History of European Housing in Australia*, p. 277.

107 Kaïka, 'Interrogating the geographies', pp. 266, 280.

108 'Towing icebergs to South Australia', *Financial Review*, 3 October 1979, pp. 13–14.

109 G. Mougin, Letter to P. Schwerdtfeger, 20 February 1978, Iceberg Utilization, CSIRO WA State Committee, K637, 40, National Archives of Australia (WA) – hereafter NAA(WA).

110 Report of a Meeting, 1 May 1978, Iceberg Utilization, CSIRO WA State Committee, K637, 40, NAA(WA).

111 M. J. Caldwell, 'Perth water supply – the role of groundwater resources', in Whelan (ed.), *Groundwater Resources of the Swan Coastal Plain*, p. 10.

112 E. Heddle, 'Native vegetation on the northern Swan Coastal Plain, Western Australia', in Whelan (ed.), *Groundwater Resources of the Swan Coastal Plain*, pp. 189, 195.

113 B. J. O'Brien, 'Land use: competitive and compatible', in B. J. O'Brien, *Environment and Science*, Nedlands, UWA Press, 1979, p. 264.

114 B. Collis, 'Jandakot water row', *Western Farmer*, 5 May 1977, p. 25.

115 M. J. Hollick, *The Management of Water Supplies in Western Australia*, Nedlands, UWA Press, 1983, p. 41. The case finally concluded in mid-1978, with the courts ruling in favour of the Metropolitan Water Board.

116 W. S. Cooper, 'Drainage and irrigation', in J. Gentilli (ed.), *Western Landscapes*, Nedlands, UWA Press, 1979, p. 239.

117 'We're living on watered down time', *Western Farmer*, 20 April 1978, p. 4.

118 B. Collis, 'Jandakot chokes on its troubled waters', *Western Farmer*, 15 June 1978, p. 47.

119 B. Collis, 'Jandakot scheme "to fill off coast"', *Western Farmer*, 13 October 1977, pp. 1–2.

120 B. Collis, 'Jandakot chokes on its troubled waters', *Western Farmer*, 15 June 1978, p. 47.

121 Beresford et al., *Salinity Crisis*, pp. 77–8, 91–3.

122 Clearing control legislation was introduced under the *Country Areas Water Supply Act 1947*.

123 B. Collis, 'Urban thirsts pour salt in the wounds', *Western Farmer*, 25 October 1979, pp. 49–50.

124 N. Higgs, 'Rain in a week – that's the limit', *Western Farmer*, 15 July 1976, p. 1.

125 William Peter Bestry, interviewed by John Bannister, 30 March 1998, Battye Library, OH2885.

126 'Drought in WA 1980/81', 14 May 1981, Drought Consultative Committee, Cons 7203, V126, SROWA.

127 Department of Agriculture (WA), *Annual Report 1981*, Perth, Dept of Agriculture (WA), 1981, p. 29.

128 'Morawa farmers chase the rain', *Western Farmer*, 14 July 1977, p. 1.

129 Day, *Weather Watchers*, p. 383.

130 B. F. Ryan and W. D. King, 'A critical review of the Australian experience of cloud seeding', *Bulletin of the American Meteorological Society*, vol. 78, no. 2, 1997, pp. 245–6.

131 K. Newbey, *Land Use Planning of the North Fitzgerald Area*, Perth, Author, 1982, p. 3.

132 Cited in Beresford et al., *The Salinity Crisis*, p. 95.

133 J. M. Powell, *An Historical Geography of Modern Australia*, Cambridge, Cambridge University Press, 1988, p. 12.

134 R. A. Morgan, 'Diagnosing the dry', *Osiris*, vol. 26, 2011, pp. 89–108.

135 Australian Academy of Science Committee on Climatic Change, pp. 10, 23, 78.

136 M. J. Coughlan, 'Changes in Australian rainfall and temperatures', in A. B. Pittock et al. (eds), *Climatic Change and Variability*, Melbourne, Cambridge University Press, 1978, p. 195.

137 According to local ornithologist Dominic Serventy, his friend and colleague Joe Gentilli had observed a similar drying trend in the semi-arid fringe of the southwest. See, D. L. Serventy, 'The use of data on the distribution of birds to monitor climatic changes', *Emu*, vol. 77, 1977, pp. 163–4.

138 G. W. Arnold and K. A. Galbraith, 'Case study one: climatic change and agriculture in Western Australia', in Pittock et al. (eds), *Climatic Change and Variability*, pp. 297–8.

139 Gentilli, *Australian Climate Patterns*, pp. 264–5.

140 E. N. Fitzpatrick, Letter to Regional Director, Bureau of Meteorology (WA), 3 February 1976, Climatic Change, PP956/1, 30/69, NAA(WA); MWSSD Board, *Annual Report for the Year Ended 30th June 1977*, Perth, MWSSD Board, 1977, p. 4.

141 M. Coughlan, Letter to Perth Regional Office, Bureau of Meteorology, 30 May 1975, Climatic Change, PP956/1, 30/69, NAA(WA).

142 Minutes, Climatic change discussion meeting, 13 February 1975, Climatic Change, SI4G-960, vol. 1, Basser Library, Australian Academy of Science.

143 R. Southern, Letter to E. N. Fitzpatrick, 17 February 1976, Climatic Change, PP956/1, 30/69, NAA(WA).

144 Q. Beresford, 'Developmentalism and its environmental legacy: the Western Australia wheatbelt, 1900–1990s', *Australian Journal of Politics and History*, vol. 47, no. 3, 2001, pp. 407, 413–4.

145 R. A. Morgan, 'Farming on the Fringe', in J. Beattie, M. Henry and E. O'Gorman, *Climate, Science and History in Australasia*, Basingstoke, Palgrave Macmillan (forthcoming, 2015).

146 K. Bradby, 'Diversity or dust', in P. Newman, S. Neville and L. Duxbury (eds), *Case Studies in Environmental Hope*, Perth, EPA, 1988, p. 101.

147 C. Bolt, 'Land release policy "dangerous"', *Western Farmer*, 21 May 1981, p. 12.

148 Newbey, *Land Use Planning*, pp. 6–7, 16.

149 G. Grewar, Letter to K. Newbey, 29 December 1980, Ken Newbey Collection, Correspondence, MN 2253, Acc. 6062A/15, Battye Library.

150 Seddon, *Swan Song*, p. 55.

5. Precaution and Prediction: Economic rationalism, ecologically sustainable development and environmental change (1983 to 2001)

1   U. Beck, 'Risk society and the provident state', in S. Lash, B. Szerzyzniski and B. Wynne (eds), *Risk, Environment and Modernity*, London, Sage Publications, 1996, p. 31.

2   A. Giddens and C. Pierson, *Conversations with Anthony Giddens*, Palo Alto, Stanford University Press, 1998, p. 210.

3   F. Fisher, *Citizens, Experts and the Environment*, Durham, Duke University Press, 2000, p. 53.

4   Select Committee on Salinity, *Report on Salinity in Western Australia*, Perth, The Committee, 1988, pp. 20.

5   K. Webster, 'Water resources', in R. T. Appleyard (ed.), *Western Australia into the Twenty-first Century*, Perth, St George Books, 1991, pp. 330–1.

6   W. E. Wood, 'Increase of salt in soil and streams following the destruction of the native vegetation', *Journal of the Royal Society of WA*, vol. 10, no. 7, 1924, pp. 39, 41.

7   B. Sadler and W. Cox, *Water Resources Management*, Paris, UNESCO, 1986, p. 18.

8   K. Bartlett, cited in B. Bunbury, *Till the Stream Runs Dry*, Perth, Dept of Water, 2010, p. 71.

9   N. Barr and J. Cary, *Greening a Brown Land*, South Melbourne, Macmillan, 1992, pp. 65–73.

10 Gaynor, 'Looking forward, looking back', p. 119.

11 B. Kuhne, cited in 'Drought means more than just water losses', *Western Farmer*, 23 February 1984, p. 47.

12 I. C. Loh, 'Appendix 1: the History of Catchment and Reservoir Management on Wellington Reservoir Catchment W.A.', in P. Laut and B. J. Taplin (eds), *Catchment Management in Australia in the 1980s*, Canberra, CSIRO Division of Water Resources, 1989, pp. 218–9.

13 R. George, 'Environmental effects of past and possible future public irrigated agriculture in the region', in G. J. Luke et al. (eds), *Background Papers to Water Authority of Western Australia's South-West Irrigation District Strategy Study*, South Perth, Dept of Agriculture, 1991, p. 41.

14 'Nine shires declared in drought', *Western Farmer*, 2 February 1984, p. 6; WAWA, *Annual Report 1986*, Perth, WAWA, 1986, np; and WAWA *Annual Report 1988*, Perth, WAWA, 1988, np.

15 J. Kronborg, 'Dustbowl danger in south', *Western Farmer*, 18 February 1988, p. 3; L. Schofield, '$20m blown away as drought intensifies', *Western Farmer*, 17 March 1988; and J. Kronborg, 'Dry slashes crops in Great Southern', *Western Farmer*, 9 July 1988, p. 5.

16 D. Britton, 'Wetlands under threat', *West Australian*, 14 February 1987, p. 31.

17 WAWA, *Annual Report*, 1986, np; WAWA, *Annual Report for the Year Ended 30th June 1987*, Perth, WAWA, 1987, np; and WAWA, *Annual Report*, 1988, p. 29.

18 D. A. Wilhite, 'Drought policy in the US and Australia: a comparative analysis', *Water Resources Bulletin: American Water Resources Association*, vol. 22, no. 3, 1986, p. 432.

19 Farm Water Strategy Group, *Western Australian Farm Water Plan Interim Report, March 1994*, Perth, Farm Water Strategy Group. 1994, p. 12.

20 See, N. Coles et al., 'Farm water planning strategies for dryland agricultural areas: local and regional perspectives', in *10th World Water Congress*, Melbourne, International Water Resources Association, 2000, p. 390.

21 I. A. F. Laing, R. G. Pepper and A. F. McCrea, *Problem Districts for On-Farm Water Supply in South Western Australia*, Perth, Dept of Agriculture, 1988.

22 Ibid., pp. 3, 20.

23 See, S. Murphy-White, *Farm Water for the North-Eastern and Eastern Wheatbelt of Western Australia*, Merredin, Dept of Agriculture, 2007, p. 38.

24 S. T. Smith, 'A logical approach to water resource utilisation in the wheatbelt', in *Wheatbelt Water Supply Seminar*, Perth, Water Research Foundation of Australia (WA), 1977, p. 2.

25 'Cash incentives to boost farm water', *Western Farmer*, 17 November 1988, p. 2.

26 Farm Water Strategy Group, *Western Australian Farm Water Plan*, p. 45.

27 G. Mauger, *Planning Future Sources for Perth's Water Supply, 1989 Revision*, Perth, Water Authority of WA, 1989, p. 16.

28 B. J. Fleay, 'Land planning: the water utility viewpoint', in G. Lowe (ed.), *Swan Coastal Plain Groundwater Management Conference Proceedings*, Leederville, WA Water Resources Council, 1989, p. 69.

29 B. Marwick, 'Lakes dry up as you draw water', *Wanneroo Times*, 20 May 1986, p. 11; B. Marwick, 'Where have all the lakes gone?', *Wanneroo Times*, 20 May 1986, p. 9.

30 Government of Western Australia, *State of the Environment Report*, Perth, Government of WA, 1992, p. 107.

31 P. Jennings, 'A decade of wetland conservation in Western Australia', in R. Giblett and H. Webb (eds), *Western Australian Wetlands*, Perth, Black Swan Press, 1996, p. 154.

32 See, J. Singleton, 'The Metropolitan Region Planning Review and groundwater resource considerations', in Lowe (ed.), *Swan Coastal Plain Groundwater Management Conference Proceedings*, p. 41; and K. C. Webster, 'Groundwater management on the Swan Coastal Plain: an overview', in Lowe (ed.), *Swan Coastal Plain Groundwater Management Conference Proceedings*, p. 26.

33 S. J. Appleyard, W. A. Davidson and D. P. Commander, 'The effects of urban development on the utilisation of groundwater resources in Perth, Western Australia', in J. Chilton (ed.), *Groundwater in the Urban Environment*, Rotterdam, A. A. Balkema, 1999, p. 100.

34 Webster, 'Groundwater management', p. 26.

35 B. Mitchell and M. Hollick, 'Integrated Catchment Management in Western Australia: transition from concept to implementation', *Environmental Management*, vol. 17, no. 6, 1993, pp. 735–6.

36 L. Robin, *How a Continent Created a Nation*, Sydney, UNSW Press, 2007, p. 152.

37 L. Robin, 'New science for sustainability in an ancient land', in S. Soerlin and P. Warde (eds), *Nature's End*, New York, Palgrave Macmillan, 2009, p. 192.

38 M. Soulé, 1985, cited in Robin, *How a Continent Created a Nation*, p. 152. Crisis disciplines share the characteristics of 'post-normal' science. In contrast to other strains of scientific inquiry such as applied or pure research, post-normal science 'encompasses the management of irreducible uncertainties in knowledge and its ethics, and the recognition of different legitimate perspectives and ways of knowing'. See, S. O. Funtowicz and J. R. Ravetz, 'Science for the post-normal age', *Futures*, vol. 25, no. 7, 1993, p. 754.

39 A. R. Main, 'How much biodiversity is enough?', *Agroforestry Systems*, vol. 45, 1999, p. 23.

40 R. Siewert, Letter to G. Lowe, WAWRC Water Management and Use Committee, 22 June 1989, WA Water Resources Council, Cons 6197, 1986/048 v3, SROWA.

41 N. Godfrey, Letter to G. Lowe, WAWRC Water Management and Use Committee, 25 July 1989, WA Water Resources Council, Cons 6197, 1986/048 v3, SROWA.

42 Wetlands Preservation Society, Report, 'Hollick Report Proposes Wholesale Destruction of Wetlands', 1989, WAWRC Water Management and Use Committee, Cons 6197, 1986/048 v3, SROWA.

43 A. Giddens, 'Living in a post-traditional society', in Beck, Giddens and Lash (eds), *Reflexive Modernisation*, pp. 87–8.

44 'The fight is on to save rural retreat', *Canning/Melville Times*, 11 April 1989, p. 7; and C. Manly, 'Experts warn on Jandakot', *Sunday Times*, 9 April 1989, p. 23.

45 *Wetlands Conservation Society Newsletter*, June, 1989, np.

46 B. Churchward, 'A conservationist's view', in R. Hughes (ed.), *Reflections on 20 Years*, Perth, EPA, 1991, p. 41.

47 J. Pakulski and B. Tranter, 'Environmentalism and social differentiation: a paper in memory of Steve Crook', *Journal of Sociology*, vol. 40, no. 2, 2004, p. 225.

48 D. Britton, 'Wetlands under threat', *West Australian*, 14 February 1987, p. 31.

49 J. Pakulski and S. Crook, 'Introduction: the end of the green cultural revolution?' in J. Pakulski and S. Crook (eds), *Ebbing of the Green Tide?*, Hobart, University of Tasmania, 1998, p. 9.

50 D. Britton, 'Wetlands under threat', *West Australian*, 14 February 1987, p. 31.

51 R. O'Connor, C. Bodney and L. Little, *Preliminary Report on the Survey of Aboriginal Areas of Significance in the Perth Metropolitan and Murray River Regions*, East Perth, Heritage Council of WA, 1985, pp. 13–20, 25–35, 38–9.

52 D. Ritter, 'Trashing heritage: dilemmas of rights and power in the operation of Western Australia's Aboriginal heritage legislation', *Studies in WA History*, vol. 23, 2003, p. 208.

53 See, World Meteorological Organization, *Report of the International Conference on the Assessment of the Role of Carbon Dioxide and of Other Greenhouse Gases in Climate Variations and Associated Impacts*, Villach, Austria, 9–15 October 1985, <http://www.scopenvironment.org/downloadpubs/scope29/statement.html>, (Accessed: 28 September 2013).

54 G. Pearman, 'Preface', in G. Pearman (ed.), *Greenhouse, Planning for Climate Change*, Collingwood, CSIRO Publications, 1988, p. x.

55 A. B. Pittock, 'Actual and anticipated changes in Australia's climate', in ibid., pp. 42–3.

56 B. C. Bates and G. Hughes, 'Adaptation measures for metropolitan water supply for Perth, WA', in F. Ludwig et al. (eds), *Climate Change Adaptation in the Water Sector*, London, Earthscan, 2009, p. 197.

57 For example, Australian Academy of Science, *Report of a Committee on Climatic Change*, Canberra, Australian Academy of Science, 1976; A. B. Pittock, 'Recent climatic change in Australia, implications for a CO2-warmed Earth', *Climatic Change*, vol. 5, 1983, pp. 321–40; and R. G. Chittleborough, *Planning to Meet Climatic Change*, Perth, Department of Conservation and Environment, 1986.

58 B. Sadler, R. Stokes and G. Mauger, 'The water resource implications of a drying climate in southwest Western Australia', in Pearman (ed.), *Greenhouse*, p. 299–305.

59 R. A. Morgan, 'Dry horizons: the responses of Western Australian water managers to the enhanced greenhouse effect in the late 1980s', *History Australia*, vol. 8, no. 3, 2011, pp. 158–76.

60 Giddens and Pierson, *Conversations*, p. 211.

61 Office of Minister for Resources, Note to W. Carr, Department of Industrial Development, 12 December 1989, Cons 6639, 1989/153 vo1, SROWA.

62   Pearman, 'Preface', p. x.

63   N. Matalas, 'Stochastic hydrology in the context of climate change', *Climatic Change*, vol. 37, 1997, p. 98.

64   B. J. O'Brien, *The Greenhouse Effect and the Death of Mark Twain*, Perth, Eco Ethics, 1994, p. 9.

65   WAWA, *Annual Report*, 1987, p. 27.

66   G. Hughes, 'Meeting the challenge of climate variability in a major water supply system', *Water Science and Technology: Water Supply*, vol. 3, no. 3, 2003, p. 202.

67   L. Schofield, 'North Dandalup's river runs dry', *Western Farmer*, 10 March 1988, p. 26.

68   'WA part of atmosphere seminar', *South Western Times*, 20 October 1988, p. 37.

69   A. Henderson-Sellers, 'Australian public perception of the greenhouse issue', *Climatic Change*, vol. 17, no. 1, 1990, pp. 78, 91.

70   H. Bulkeley, 'The formation of Australian climate change policy: 1985–1995', in A. Gillespie and W. C. G. Burns (eds), *Climate Change in the South Pacific*, Boston, Kluwer, 2000, p. 37.

71   D. Bodansky, 'The history of the global climate change regime', in U. Luterbacher and F. Sprinz (eds), *International Relations and Global Climate Change*, Boston, MIT Press, 2001, p. 23.

72   A. Harris, 'Greenies unite on climate threat', *West Australian*, 3 November 1988, p. 32; and K. Acott, 'Groups join on greenhouse effect', *West Australian*, 7 November 1988, p. 12. These groups included the Australian Conservation Foundation, the Conservation Council of Western Australia, The People for Nuclear Disarmament, Community Aid Abroad, and the Australian Federation of Consumer Organisations.

73   C. Hamilton, *Running from the Storm*, Sydney, UNSW Press, 2001, pp. 31–2.

74   Bulkeley, 'The formation of Australian climate change policy', p. 38.

75   'Two options for water next century', *Great Southern Herald*, 11 January 1989, p. 6; and 'Pipeline a realistic option: Bridge', *Geraldton Guardian*, 5 January 1989, p. 3.

76   S. Toussaint, 'For whom the Fitzroy River flows: a fluctuating analysis of social and environmental sustainability and incremental sovereignty', in D. Ghosh, H. Goodall and S. H. Donald (eds), *Water, Sovereignty and Borders in Asia*, Hoboken, Routledge, 2008, p. 176.

77   See, T. Griffiths and T. Sherratt, 'What if the northern rivers had been turned inland?', in S. Macintyre and S. Scalmer (eds), *What If? Australian history as it might have been*, Carlton, Melbourne University Press, 2006, pp. 234–54.

78   E. Bridge, 'Bridge pipeline for people of 2088', *West Australian*, 7 November 1988, p. 28; P. Walsh, 'A theory that just doesn't hold water', *Australian Financial Review*, 28 January 1992, p. 11; and P. Walsh, 'Pouring cold water

on a pipedream', *Australian Financial Review*, 17 April 1992, p. 13.

79 N. Way, 'In the pipeline', *Business Review Weekly*, 29 November 1991, p. 14.

80 See for example, 'Water scheme a joke – Beahan', *Albany Advertiser*, 29 August 1989, p. 7; and G. B. Davis, 'Kimberley water pipe plan a folly', *West Australian*, 26 March 1992, p. 10. The studies included Kimberley Regional Development Advisory Committee, *Water from the Kimberleys*, Perth, Binnie & Partners, 1988; Infrastructure Development Corporation, *Development of a Water Pipeline, Kimberleys to Perth*, Sydney, The Corporation, 1990; Chase Manhattan Bank, *Kimberleys to Perth Water Pipeline*, Perth, The Bank, 1991; and Kimberley Water Resources Development Advisory Board, *Report of the Kimberley Water Resources Development Advisory Board*, Perth, Kimberley Water Resources Development Office, 1993.

81 B. R. Davidson, *The Northern Myth*, Melbourne, Melbourne University Press, 1972, p. 2.

82 Robin, *How a Continent Created a Nation*, p. 124.

83 Kimberley Regional Development Advisory Committee, p. 90.

84 Chase Manhattan Bank.

85 S. Toussaint, P. Sullivan and S. Yu, 'Water ways in Aboriginal Australia: an interconnected analysis', *Anthropological Forum*, vol. 15, no. 1, 2006, pp. 62, 65–6.

86 M. Kunjuka cited in ibid., p. 65.

87 Farm Water Strategy Group, *Western Australian Farm Water Plan*, pp. 72, 89.

88 L. C. Botterill, 'Uncertain climate: the recent history of drought policy in Australia', *Australian Journal of Politics and History*, vol. 49, no. 1, 2003, p. 72; and D. H. White and L. Karsseis, 'Australia's National Drought Policy: aims, analyses and implementation', *Water International*, vol. 24, no. 1, 1999, p. 3.

89 J. Brett, 'Fair share: country and city in Australia', *Quarterly Essay*, no. 42, 2011, p. 49.

90 See, R. S. Kingwell, D. J. Pannell and S. D. Robinson, 'Tactical responses to seasonal conditions in whole-farm planning in Western Australia', *Agricultural Economics*, vol. 8, 1993, pp. 214–15.

91 P. Hayman, 'Decision support systems in Australian dryland farming', in R. A. Fischer et al. (eds), *New directions for a diverse planet*, Regional Institute, 2004, <http://regional.org.au/au/asa/2004/symposia/4/1/1778_haymanp.htm#TopOfPage>, (Accessed: 28 September 2013).

92 G. Davison, 'Rural sustainability in historical perspective', in ibid., p. 53.

93 The North Dandalup Dam had only been completed in October 1994.

94 WAWA, *Sources Development Plan 1988 Review*, Leederville, WAWA, 1988, np.

95 Z. Sofoulis, 'Big Water, Everyday Water: a sociotechnical perspective', *Continuum*, vol. 19, no. 4, 2005, p. 460.

96 K. Hussey and S. Dovers, 'Trajectories in Australian water policy', *Journal of Contemporary Water Research and Education*, no. 135, 2006, p. 39.

97   Ibid.

98   Laws, 'Restructuring the water industry', pp. 18–19. The responsibilities of the Office of Water Regulation were subsumed by the creation of the Economic Regulation Authority in 2004, which also regulates the gas, electricity and rail industries in Western Australia.

99   J. Payne, 'Streamlining the Water Authority', *Greener Times*, September, 1995, p. 4.

100 Conservation Council of WA, *Annual Report 1995/96*, Perth, Conservation Council of WA, 1996, np.

101 R. Siewert, 'Perth's water crisis', *Greener Times*, September 1998, p. 2.

102 Water Corporation, *Annual Report 1997*, Leederville, Water Corporation, 1997, p. 1.

103 This system replaced the 'free allowance' of 150 kL that had been introduced in the late 1970s.

104 Economic Regulation Authority (ERA), *Inquiry on Urban Water and Wastewater Pricing*, Perth, ERA, 2004, pp. 5, 50.

105 ERA, *Inquiry on Urban Water and Wastewater Pricing: Final Report*, Perth, ERA, 2005, pp. 23, 97.

106 Equal Opportunity Commission, *Finding a Place*, Perth, Equal Opportunity Commission, 2004, pp. 67–8, 159–77, 199.

107 C. Amalfi, 'Privation behind anger in suburb', *West Australian*, 18 June 1997, p. 12.

108 E. Crawford, 'Equity and the city: the case of the East Perth redevelopment', *Urban Policy and Research*, vol. 21, no. 1, 2003, pp. 81–92; and S. Delmege, 'The fringedweller's struggle: cultural politics and the force of history', PhD Thesis, Murdoch University, 2000, pp. 251–68.

109 M. Tonts, 'Spatially uneven development: government policy and rural reform in the wheatbelt of Western Australia', *Anthropological Forum*, vol. 14, no. 3, 2004, pp. 237–40.

110 See, R. A. Stokes et al., *Perth's Water Future: a vision for the water supply of Perth and Mandurah to 2050*, Leederville, Water Authority of WA, 1995, p. v; and J. K. Ruprecht, B. C. Bates and R. A. Stokes (eds), *Climate Variability and Water Resources Workshop*, East Perth, Water and Rivers Commission, 1996, p. 10.

111 Hughes, 'Meeting the challenge of climate variability', p. 203.

112 Ruprecht, Bates and Stokes (eds), *Climate Variability*, 1996.

113 B. Sadler, 'Informed adaptation to a changed climate state, is southwestern Australia a national canary?', *Indian Ocean Climate Initiative*, 2001, <http://www. ioci.org.au/pdf/IOCI_PaperJan6.pdf>, (Accessed: 28 September 2013), p. 3.

114 J. Gill, 'Perth's water future: security through diversity', in *2004 Australian National Plumbing Forum*, Institute of Plumbing, September 2004, p. 3.

115 Bates and Hughes, 'Adaptation measures', p. 198.

116 S. Butler, '$52m dam will quench Perth's raging thirst', *West Australian*, 11 October 2000, p. 34.

117 Water Corporation, *Annual Report*, pp. 3–5.

118 K. Hames, 'Preface', in Water and Rivers Commission, *Perth Groundwater Atlas*, East Perth, Water and Rivers Commission, 1997, np.

119 S. Robinson, 'Accountability problems in the water industry restructure', *Greener Times*, February, 1996, p. 10.

120 Stokes et al., *Perth's Water Future*, p. 3–11.

121 C. Amalfi, 'Summer threat to water ebbs', *West Australian*, 12 August 2000, p. 13; and C. Amalfi, 'Dry city turns to bores', *West Australian*, 20 August 1998, p. 9.

122 Welker Environmental Consultancy, *Stirling–Harvey Redevelopment Scheme*, Perth, EPA, 1999, pp. i, 1.

123 In June 2000, the Western Australian Parliament passed legislation to repeal the regulation of the dairy industry.

124 V. Rechichi, 'Fears new Harris link to city will drain supplies', *West Australian*, 25 August 1999, p. 39.

125 Beckwith & Associates Environmental Planning, *Harvey–Stirling Dam Options*, South Perth, Beckwith & Associates, 1998, p. 64.

126 See for instance, T. Mendez, 'Perth faces water curbs next year', *West Australian*, 9 March 1998, p. 5; and M. Quekkett, 'Water crisis menaces WA', *West Australian*, 29 November 1999, p. 7.

127 C. Amalfi, 'Reservoir of hope lies under Perth', *West Australian*, 31 August 1998, p. 10.

128 Water Corporation, *Annual Report 2000*, Leederville, Water Corporation, 2000, p. 27.

129 Bulkeley, pp. 33, 39. In December 1992, Australia was the eighth nation to ratify the UNFCCC.

130 Ruprecht, Bates and Stokes (eds), *Climate Variability*, p. 11.

131 W. Drosdowsky, 'Potential predictability of winter rainfall over southern and eastern Australia using Indian Ocean sea-surface temperature anomalies', *Australian Meteorological Magazine*, vol. 42, 1993, p. 1.

132 J. Gentilli, 'Homologous peri-oceanic west coast climates in the southern hemisphere', in A. F. Pearce and D. I. Walker (eds), *The Leeuwin Current*, Perth, Royal Society of Western Australia, 1991, pp. 15–33.

133 J. Gentilli, 'Differentiating the rainfall pattern of rain-bearing systems in Western Australia', *Western Geographer*, vol. 7, 1983, pp. 31–34.

134 G. R. Cresswell and T. J. Golding, 'Observations of a south-flowing current in the southeastern Indian Ocean', *Deep-Sea Research*, vol. 27A, 1980, pp. 449–66.

135 N. Nicholls, 'Sea surface temperatures and Australian winter rainfall', *Journal of Climate*, vol. 2, 1989, p. 973.

136 R. Stokes, 'Water Corporation interest in climate variability and seasonal forecasting', 21 February 1997, Indian Ocean Climate Initiative, 65/0008, Bureau of Meteorology, WA Regional Office.

137   R. Stokes, 'Water Corporation interest in climate variability and seasonal forecasting', 21 February 1997, Indian Ocean Climate Initiative, 65/0008, Bureau of Meteorology, WA Regional Office.

138   S. Power, B. Sadler and N. Nicholls, 'The influence of climate science on water management in Western Australia: lessons for climate scientists', *Bulletin of the American Meteorological Society*, vol. 86, 2005, pp. 839–44.

139   E. Davies Ward, 'WA loses CSIRO Marine Branch', *Greener Times*, June, 1998, p. 4.

Chapter 6. Watershed: Climate and water in the early twenty-first century (2001 to 2014)

1   J. Pratley, 'A grim harvest for family', *West Australian*, 2 December 2000, p. 4; and N. Lee, 'Desperate wait for rain and feed', *Countryman*, 7 June 2001, p. 3.

2   N. Lee, 'Family in survival mode', *Countryman*, 28 June 2001, p. 3.

3   L. Tickner, 'Time to act on drought crisis: MP', *West Australian*, 29 June 2001, p. 12; and L. Tickner, 'Drought cost put at $2.5b', *West Australian*, 3 July 2001, p. 5.

4   D. Stephens et al., 'Experiences in the use of climate information, and its communication in 2002/03, from the perspective of the Department of Agriculture, WA', in N. Plummer et al. (eds), *DroughtCom Workshop*, Vol. 2, 2003, Melbourne, Bureau of Meteorology, pp. 42–4.

5   B. Ruse, 'Country-city gap widens', *West Australian*, 18 January 2003, np. These areas were Pingelly, Trayning and Wickepin.

6   D. H. White, D. Collins and M. Howden, 'Drought in Australia: prediction, monitoring, management and policy', in D. A. Wilhite (ed.), *Drought Assessment, Management, and Planning: Theory and Case Studies*, New York, Kluwer, 1993, p. 227.

7   Environmental Protection Authority (EPA), *State of the Environment Report*, EPA, 2007, <http://www.epa.wa.gov.au/AbouttheEPA/SOE/2007/Pages/default.aspx>, (Accessed: 28 September 2013), p. 85.

8   M. Zekulich, 'Farmers going down the drain', *West Australian*, 28 December 2000, p. 13.

9   Department of Water, *Rural Water Plan Implementation 1995–2010*, Perth, Dept of Water, 2011, pp. 10, 16.

10   Cited in G. Hertzler, 'Prospects for insuring against drought in Australia', in L. C. Botterill and D. A. Wilhite (eds), *From Disaster Response to Risk Management*, Dordrecht, Springer, 2005, p. 127.

11   Australian Bureau of Statistics (ABS), *Farm management and climate, 2006–2007*, no. 4625.0, Canberra, ABS, p. 11. These changing practices reflected the findings of L. Head et al., 'A fine-grained study of the experience of drought, risk and climate change among Australian wheat farming

households', *Annals of the Association of American Geographers*, vol. 101, no. 5, 2011, pp. 1,089–1,108.

12 L. Morgan et al., *Climate Change, Vulnerability and Adaptation for South West Western Australia, 1970 to 2006*, South Perth, Dept of Agriculture and Food, 2008, p. 55.

13 C. Evans, C. Storer and A. Wardell-Johnson, 'Rural farming community climate change acceptance', *International Journal of the Society of Agriculture and Food*, vol. 18, no. 3, 2011, p. 228.

14 Australian Academy of Technological Sciences and Engineering (ATSE), *Perth's Water Balance: the way forward*, Melbourne, ATSE, 2002, p. II.

15 See, ABS, 'Water choices of Perth households', *Western Australian Statistical Indicators, 2010*, no. 1367.5, Canberra, ABS, 12 February 2010, <http://www.abs.gov.au/ausstats/abs@.nsf/Latestproducts/1367.5Feature%20Article82010?opendocument&tabname=Summary&prodno=1367.5&issue=2010&num=&view=>, (Accessed: 28 September 2013).

16 G. Seddon, *Landprints*, Oakleigh, Cambridge University Press, 1997, p. 105.

17 Cited in T. Kurz et al., 'The ways that people talk about natural resources: discursive strategies as barriers to environmentally sustainable practices', *British Journal of Social Psychology*, vol. 44, 2005, p. 609.

18 Cited in ibid., p. 609. Note that roadside verge areas in Perth are the property of local governments, although they do not pay for their maintenance. In addition, many local governments prevent residents from planting the verge with anything other than lawn.

19 C. Chamberlain and D. MacKenzie, *Counting the Homeless*, Canberra, ABS, 2008, pp. 45–6.

20 S. Dovers, 'Urban water: policy, institutions and government', in ibid., p. 83.

21 M. Loh and P. Coghlan, *Domestic Water Use Study in Perth, Western Australia 1998–2001*, Leederville, Water Corporation, 2003, p. 6.

22 Water Corporation, *Perth Residential Water Use Study 2008/2009*, Perth, Water Corporation, 2010, p. 17.

23 *Western Australian Parliamentary Debates*, vol. 369, 22 August 2001, p. 2,748.

24 C. Amalfi, 'Water crisis deepens', *West Australian*, 19 October 2001, np.

25 B. Sadler, Email to William Wright and John Cramb, 'Re: brief question or two', 20 August 2002, Bureau of Meteorology, Indian Ocean Climate Initiative, 65/0008–09, Bureau of Meteorology, WA Regional Office.

26 IOCI, *Climate Variability and Change in South West Western Australia*, Perth, IOCI, 2002, np.

27 B. C. Bates et al., 'Key findings from the Indian Ocean Climate Initiative and their impact on policy development in Australia', *Climatic Change*, vol. 89, no. 3–4, 2008, p. 342.

28 P. Trott, 'Perth water options dry up', *West Australian*, 7 March 2002, np.

29 N. Khadem, 'Scientists free to talk, says CSIRO', *Age*, 14 February 2006, <http://www.theage.com.au/news/national/scientists-free-to-talk-says-csiro/2006/02/13/1139679536438.html>, (Accessed: 28 September 2013).

30 J. Pakulski and B. Tranter, 'Environmentalism and social differentiation: a paper in memory of Steve Crook', *Journal of Sociology*, vol. 40, no. 3, 2004, p. 227.

31 J. T. Houghton et al., 'Preface', *Climate Change 2001: the scientific basis*, IPCC Third Assessment Report, Cambridge, Cambridge University Press, 2001, p. ix.

32 M. Coughlan, cited in Å. Wahlquist, *Thirsty Country*, Crows Nest, Allen & Unwin, 2008, p. 41.

33 Ibid., p. 3.

34 Water Corporation, *Historical Streamflow*, 2012, <http://www.watercorporation.com.au/water-supply-and-services/rainfall-and-dams/streamflow/streamflowhistorical>, (Accessed: 28 September 2013).

35 Water and Rivers Commission, *Environmental Management of Groundwater Abstraction from the Gnangara Mound 2000–2003*, East Perth, Water and Rivers Commission, 2004, p. 6.

36 T. Hatton, cited in Wahlquist, *Thirsty Country*, pp. 101–2.

37 Cited in E. McDonald, B. Coldrick and W. Christensen, 'The green frog and desalination: a Nyungar metaphor for the (mis-)management of water resources, Swan Coastal Plain, Western Australia', *Oceania*, vol. 78, 2008, pp. 66.

38 G. Mauger, *Planning Future Sources for Perth's Water Supply*, Leederville, Water Authority of WA, 1987, p. 14.

39 Water Corporation, *Desalination – creating new water sources*, Leederville, Water Corporation, 2000.

40 K. Hames, 'Foreword', in Water Corporation, *Desalination*, p. 1.

41 EPA, *State of the Environment Report*, p. 29.

42 D. McFarlane, *Context Report on Southwest Water Resources for: expert panel examining Kimberley water supply options*, Canberra, Water for a Health Country National Research Flagship, CSIRO, 2005, pp. 25, 63, 102–3. The possibility of damming the Donnelly River for public water supplies emerged in the mid-1970s and by the turn of the twenty-first century, it was the 'largest undeveloped fresh surface water resource in the south of the State' (p. 102). In 2004, the Gallop government created the Greater Beedelup National Park, which included the preferred reservoir site on the river, as part of its Old Growth Forests Policy.

43 See, P. Whincup (Chair), *South-West Yarragadee Aquifer*, Perth, Dept of Environment (WA), 2004, p. 1.

44 Water Corporation, *Water Forever*, Leederville, Water Corporation, 2008, p. 58.

45 P. Trott, 'Big water project on way', *West Australian*, 12 December, 2002, np.

46 D. D. R. Pearson, *Second Public Sector Performance Report*, Perth, Auditor General of Western Australia, 2003, pp. 4–5.

47 P. Trott and E. Dortch, 'Bores to solve water problem', *West Australian*, 10 December 2003; and E. Dortch and S. Jerrard, 'SW aquifer store raised 50pc', *West Australian*, 20 September 2005, p. 12.

48 Dortch and Pryor, 'Now the truth emerges', p. 1.

49 W. Pryer, 'Garrett lends hand as Gallop changes tack on greenhouse', *West Australian*, 15 September 2004, p. 19.

50 Cited in C. Amalfi, 'Perth will die, says top scientist', *West Australian*, 25 June 2004, np.

51 C. Amalfi, 'Desalination plant involves private sector', *West Australian*, 28 April 2004, p. 14.

52 P. van Onselen, 'The Western Australian election of 26 February 2005: a canal too far for the Coalition', *Australian Journal of Political Science*, vol. 40, no. 3, 2005, p. 454.

53 Kimberley Regional Development Advisory Committee, *Water from the Kimberleys*, Perth, Binnie & Partners, 1988; Infrastructure Development Corporation, *Development of a Water Pipeline, Kimberleys to Perth*, Sydney, The Corporation, 1990; Chase Manhattan Bank, *Kimberleys to Perth Water Pipeline*, Perth, The Bank, 1991; and Kimberley Water Resources Development Advisory Board, *Report of the Kimberley Water Resources Development Advisory Board*, Perth, Kimberley Water Resources Development Office, 1993.

54 R. T. Appleyard (chair), *Options for Bringing Water to Perth from the Kimberley: an independent review*, Perth, Dept of Premier and Cabinet, 2006.

55 Wahlquist, *Thirsty Country*, p. 77.

56 G. Parker, 'The challenge of a generation', *West Australian*, 13 January 2007, p. 1.

57 S. Toussaint, 'For whom the Fitzroy River flows: a fluctuating analysis of social and environmental sustainability and incremental sovereignty', in D. Ghosh, H. Goodall, and S. H. Donald (eds), *Water, Sovereignty and Borders in Asia*, Hoboken, Routledge, 2008, p. 181.

58 K. MacDonald, 'Water pipe from north "too costly"', *West Australian*, 11 November 2004, p. 48.

59 Toussaint, 'For whom the Fitzroy River flows', pp. 175–6.

60 J. Strutt, 'Kimberley canal plan unveiled', *Sunday Times*, 21 November 2004, p. 31. Radio broadcaster Alan Jones employed similar rhetoric in his promotion of drought-proofing initiatives in the Murray–Darling Basin in 2002. See, S. Bell, 'Concerned scientists, pragmatic politics and Australia's green drought', *Science and Public Policy*, vol. 33, no. 8, 2006, p. 562.

61 G. Bolton, *Land of Vision and Mirage: Western Australia since 1826*, Crawley, UWA Publishing, 2008, pp. 1–2.

62 G. Parker, 'Keep an eye on water in north: Appleyard', *West Australian*, 13 January 2007, p. 9.

63 M. Gordon, 'Howard's Australias', *Age*, 7 August 2004, <http://www.theage.com.au/articles/2004/08/06/1091732092416.html>, (Accessed: 28 September 2013).

64 R. Taylor, 'Poll gives new desal plan a big tick', *West Australian*, 22 May 2007, p. 10.

65 Banks, 'Tap turned on', p. 1.

66 Cited in C. Hamilton, *Scorcher*, Collingwood, Black Inc., 2007, p. 219.

67 L. van Schoubroeck, *The Lure of Politics: Geoff Gallop's Government 2001–2006*, Crawley, UWA Publishing, 2010, pp. 232, 235.

68 W. A. Water Symposium, *Our Water Future*, Perth, W. A. Water Symposium, 2002.

69 J. Marsden, and P. Pickering, *Securing Australia's Urban Water Supplies*, Camberwell, Marsden Jacob Associates, 2006, p. ES ii.

70 McFarlane, *Context Report*, p. 69.

71 Economic Regulation Authority (ERA), *Inquiry on Urban Water and Wastewater Pricing*, Perth, ERA, 2005, pp. 23, 25–30, 30–8.

72 Marsden and Pickering, *Securing Australia's Urban Water Supplies*, p. 16; and Water Corporation, *Source Development Plan 2005–2050: an overview*, p. 3.

73 McFarlane, *Context Report*, p. 68.

74 M. Turnbull, 'Malcolm Turnbull speaks to National Press Club in Adelaide', Parliament of Australia, 22 November 2006, <http://parlinfo.aph.gov.au/parlInfo/download/media/pressrel/4VLL6/upload_binary/4VLL6.pdf;fileType=application%2Fpdf#search=%22PRIME%20MINISTER%20turnbull,%20malcolm,%20mp%22>, (Accessed: 28 September 2013).

75 Morgan et al., *Climate Change*, p. 56.

76 T. Fairfield, cited in 'WA government ignores global warming', *Greener Times*, June 2005, p. 3.

77 R. Weller, *Boom Town*, Crawley, UWA Publishing, 2009, p. 419.

78 Australian Bureau of Statistics, *Regional Population Growth 2011–12: Western Australia*, 30 April 2013, <http://www.abs.gov.au/ausstats/abs@.nsf/Products/3218.0~2011-12~Main+Features~Western+Australia>, (Accessed: 28 September 2013).

79 D. Hatch, 'Suburbs sinking as water use gets blame', *West Australian*, 17 March 2008, p. 9.

80 D. Mercer, 'Sharp fall in Gnangara water levels', *West Australian*, 10 June 2011, <http://au.news.yahoo.com/thewest/a/-/newshome/9615870/sharp-fall-in-gnangara-water-levels/>, (Accessed: 28 September 2013).

81 M. Hopkin, 'Recycled waste water gets go-ahead for Perth', *WA Today*, 1 August 2013, <http://www.watoday.com.au/wa-news/recycled-waste-water-gets-goahead-for-perth-20130801-2r10k.html>, (Accessed: 28 September 2013).

82 Letters of support featured in *West Australian*, 21 June 2013, p. 22.

83 Cited in D. Mercer, 'Desal water props up dams', *West Australian*, 3 July 2013, p. 5.

84   Water Corporation, *Water Forever, Whatever the Weather*, Leederville, Water Corporation, 2013, p. 1.

85   Government of Western Australia, *Strategic Directions to 2030: Perth–Peel regional water plan discussion paper*, Perth, Dept of Water, 2009, p. 6.

86   S. Neales, 'Farm exodus as drought sows seeds of despair', *Australian*, 5 March 2013, pp. 1, 6; B. Thompson, 'Wheatbelt farmers need rain to avoid a crop crisis', *West Australian*, 4 July 2013, p. 9; B. Thompson, 'Farmers sell off sheep as winter rains vanish', *West Australian*, 10 July 2013, p. 11; and M. Rigoll, Cartoon, *West Australian*, 10 July 2013, p. 20.

87   R. Kingwell, et al., *Broadacre Farmers Adapting to a Changing Climate*, Gold Coast, NCCARF, 2013.

88   W. Steffen and L. Hughes, *Critical Decade 2013*, Canberra, Climate Commission Secretariat, 2013, p. 66.

Chapter 7. Running Out?

1   C. Hammer, *The River*, Carlton, Melbourne University Press, 2011, p. ix.

2   Climate Commission, *The Critical Decade*, Canberra, Dept of Climate Change and Energy Efficiency, 2011, p. 32.

3   D. Mercer, 'Bore users let off amid record fines', *West Australian*, 13 March 2012, <http://au.news.yahoo.com/thewest/a/-/wa/13149057/bore-users-let-off-amid-record-fines/>, (Accessed: 28 September 2013).

4   Ibid. The Department of Water was formed in 2008 to replace the Water and Rivers Commission and the Office of Water Regulation. Its function is to manage the state's water resources in a sustainable manner.

5   Environmental Protection Authority (EPA), *State of the Environment Report*, EPA, 2007, <http://www.epa.wa.gov.au/AbouttheEPA/SOE/2007/Pages/default.aspx>, (Accessed: 10 May 2012), pp. 56, 81.

6   Australian Bureau of Agricultural and Resource Economics and Sciences (ABARES), *Australian Crop Report*, no. 169, Canberra, ABARES, 2014; ABARES, *Australian Crop Report*, no. 170, Canberra, ABARES, 2014.

7   Å. Wahlquist, *Thirsty Country*, Crows Nest, Allen & Unwin, 2008, p. 11.

8   World Commission on Environment and Development, *Our Common Future*, Oxford, OUP, 1987, p. 43.

9   L. Robin, 'Battling the land and global anxiety: science, environment and identity in settler Australia', *Philosophy, Activism, Nature*, no. 7, 2010, p. 8.

10   S. Dovers, 'Urban water: policy, institutions and government', in Troy (ed.), *Troubled Waters*, p. 91.

11   P. Troy, 'Conclusion', in P. Troy (ed.), *Troubled Waters: confronting the water crisis in Australia's cities*, Canberra, ANU Press, 2008, pp. 198–9.

SELECT BIBLIOGRAPHY

This bibliography contains a selection of the sources most often referred to in the chapter endnotes.

Unpublished Government and Non-Government papers

Basser Library, Australian Academy of Science; Committee on Climatic Change, 1975, SI4G-960.

JS Battye Library of Western Australia, Ken Newbey Collection; Correspondence, MN 2253, Acc. 6062A/15.

JS Battye Library of Western Australia, Russell Dumas Papers, MN 156, 1295A/O.

Bureau of Meteorology, Regional Office WA, Indian Ocean Climate Initiative, 65/0008.

Bureau of Meteorology, Regional Office WA, Indian Ocean Climate Initiative, 65/0008-pt 1, 1997–98.

Bureau of Meteorology, Regional Office WA, Indian Ocean Climate Initiative, 65/0008-09, 2002.

National Archives Australia (WA), Climatic Change, PP956/1, 30/69.

National Archives Australia (WA), CSIRO, WA State Committee, K637, 40.

State Records Office of Western Australia (SROWA), Bores – Other – Private Bores, General, Cons 6756, 1972/375533.

SROWA, Drought Advisory Committee, Agriculture, Cons 1609, 1969/0801.

SROWA, Drought Areas 1969, Agriculture, Cons 2780, 1969/1281 v5.

SROWA, Drought Consultative Committee, Correspondence Files, Cons 7203, V126.

SROWA, Environment Policy Formultn Greenhouse Effect, Industrial Development, Cons 6639, 1989/153 vo1.

SROWA, Farm Water Supply Committee, Correspondence Files, Cons 7203, Vo97V2.

SROWA, Fodder Conservation Competition, Correspondence Files, Cons 7204, 1958/017vi.

SROWA, Metropolitan Water Supply, Sewerage and Drainage Board, Water – Overall – Utilization of Water Resources with Particular References to Lawn and Garden Watering, General, Cons 6733, 1967/880672.

SROWA, WAWRC Water Management and Use Committee, Environmental Assessment, Cons 6197, 1986/048 v3.

University of Western Australia, Reid Library; '6. Report to Darling (and the Colonial Office) on Swan River, 1827', in P. Statham-Drew (comp.), The Stirling Reports and Other Key Documents, 2003, MS0109B.

Interviews

Bestry, W. P., interviewed by John Bannister, 30 March 1998, Battye Library, OH2885.

Brand, D., interviewed by Jean Teasdale, 1976, Battye Library, OH 150.

Payne, J. M., interviewed by G. O'Hanlon, 1996, Battye Library, OH2738.

Williamson, J. and B., interviewed by Bill Bunbury, 2008, National Library of Australia, TRC 5945/6.

Newspapers and periodicals

Age, 2004–06.

Augusta–Margaret River Times, 2007.

Australian Broadcasting Corporation (online), 2002–11.

Australian Financial Review, 1979–92.

Chronicle, 1987–91.

Countryman, 1955–87.

Daily News, 1882–1990.

Fremantle Gazette, 1977–94.

Geraldton Guardian, 1948–2012.

Great Southern Herald, 1901–2012.

Greener Times, 1990–2007.

Inquirer, 1840–55.

Kalgoorlie Western Argus, 1896–1916.

Midland Reporter, 1986–94.

Perth Gazette and Independent Journal of Politics and News, 1848–64.

Perth Gazette and Western Australian Journal, 1833–47.

PerthNow, 2010–13.

Southern Gazette, 1983–94.

Sunday Times, 1897–2013.

WA Business News, 1992–2013.

West Australian, 1879–2013.

Western Australian Times, 1874–1979.

Western Farmer, 1977–92.

Western Mail, 1855–1955.

Wetlands Conservation Society Newsletter, 1985–2006.

Books, chapters and articles

Abbott, I., 'Aborigines, settlers and native animals: a zoological history of the south-west', *Early Days*, vol. 12, 2004, pp. 231–49.

Abbott, I., 'Historical perspectives of the ecology of some conspicuous vertebrate species in south-west Western Australia', *Conservation Science Western Australia*, vol. 6, no. 3, 2008, pp. 1–214.

Abbott, J. S., 'Water requirements for agriculture, industry and urban supply in the southwest of Western Australia', in *Water Requirements for Agriculture, Industry and Urban Supply for a Metropolis of Two Million in the Southwest of Western Australia*, Perth, AIAS, 1975, pp. 52–6.

Aboriginal Legal Service of Western Australia, *Telling Our Story: a report by the Aboriginal Legal Service of WA (Inc) on the removal of Aboriginal children from their families in Western Australia*, Perth, ALSWA, 1995.

Aitkin, D., '"Countrymindedness" – the spread of an idea', *Australian Cultural History*, vol. 4, 1985, pp. 34–41.

Aitkin, D., 'Return to "countrymindedness"', in G. Davison and M. Brodie (eds), *Struggle Country*, Melbourne, Monash University ePress, 2008, pp. 11.1–11.6.

Allen, A. D., 'The Swan Coastal Plain: hydrogeology of superficial formation', in B. A. Carbon (ed.), *Groundwater Resources of the Swan Coastal Plain*, Perth, CSIRO, 1975, pp. 12–33.

Allen, C. R., Gunderson, L. H. and Holling, C. S., 'Commentary of Part One articles', in L. H. Gunderson, C. R. Allen and C. S. Holling, (eds), *Foundations of Ecological Resilience*, Washington, D. C., Island Press, 2010, pp. 3–18.

Allon, F. and Sofoulis, Z., 'Everyday water: cultures in transition', *Australian Geographer*, vol. 37, no. 1, 2006, pp. 45–55.

Allon, F., 'The nuclear dream: everyday life in the atomic age', in S. Ferber, C. Healey and C. McAuliffe (eds), *Beasts of Suburbia,* Melbourne, Melbourne University Press, 1994, pp. 35–52.

Alston, M., 'Drought policy in Australia: gender mainstreaming or gender blindness?', *Gender, Place and Culture*, vol. 16, no. 2, 2009, pp. 139–54.

Anderson, L., *Windows on the Wheatbelt*, Bassendean, Access Press, 1999.

Anderson, W. K. et al., 'The role of management in yield improvement of wheat crop – with special emphasis on Western Australia', *Australian Journal of Agricultural Research*, vol. 56, 2005, pp. 1137–49.

Anderson, W., *The Cultivation of Whiteness*, Carlton, Melbourne University Publishing, 2005.

Aplin, T. E. H., 'Consequences of variations of the water table level: vegetation and flora', in B. A. Carbon (ed.), *Groundwater Resources of the Swan Coastal Plain*, Perth, CSIRO, 1975, pp. 126–39.

Appleyard, R. T., 'Western Australia: economic and demographic growth 1850–1914', in C. T. Stannage (ed.), *A New History of Western Australia*, Nedlands, UWA Press, 1981, pp. 211–36.

Appleyard, S. J., Davidson, W. A. and Commander, D. P., 'The effects of urban development on the utilisation of groundwater resources in Perth, Western Australia', in J. Chilton (ed.), *Groundwater in the Urban Environment*, Rotterdam, A. A. Balkema, 1999, pp. 97–104.

Armanasco, P., 'State position paper: Western Australia', in *Proceedings of the National Workshop on Urban Water Demand Management*, Perth, WA Water Resources Council, 1986, pp. 71–94.

Armstrong, P., 'Obituary: Joseph Gentilli (1912–2000)', *Australian Geographical Studies*, vol. 39, no. 2, 2001, pp. 249–52.

Arnold, G. W. and Galbraith, K. A., 'Case study one: climatic change and agriculture in Western Australia', in A. B. Pittock et al. (eds), *Climatic change and variability*, Melbourne, Cambridge University Press, 1978, pp. 297–300.

Arnold, J. M. and Sanders, C. S., 'Wetlands of the Swan Coastal Plain', in B. R. Whelan (ed.), *Groundwater resources of the Swan Coastal Plain*, Perth, CSIRO, 1981, pp. 81–98.

Australian Academy of Science, *Report of a Committee on Climatic Change*, Canberra, Australian Academy of Science, 1976.

Australian Academy of Technological Sciences and Engineering (ATSE), *Perth's Water Balance*, Melbourne, ATSE, 2002.

Bankoff, G., 'Constructing vulnerability: the historical, natural and social generation of flooding in metropolitan Manila', *Disasters*, vol. 27, no. 3, 2003, pp. 224–38.

Bankoff, G., 'Rendering the world unsafe: "vulnerability" as Western discourse', *Disasters*, vol. 25, no. 1, 2001, pp. 19–35.

Barr, N. and Cary, J., *Greening a Brown Land*, South Melbourne, Macmillan, 1992.

Barton, R., 'Household technology in Western Australia, 1900–1950', *Oral History Association of Australia Journal*, vol. 7, 1985, pp. 108–29.

Bates, B. C. and Hughes, G., 'Adaptation measures for metropolitan water supply for Perth, Western Australia', in F. Ludwig et al. (eds), *Climate Change Adaptation in the Water Sector*, London, Earthscan, 2009, pp. 187–204.

Bates, B., Hope, P., Ryan, B., Smith, I. and Charles, S., 'Key findings from the Indian Ocean Climate Initiative and their impact on policy development in Australia', *Climatic Change*, vol. 89, no. 3–4, 2008, pp. 339–54.

Bayly, I. A. E., 'Review of how Indigenous people managed for water in desert regions of Australia', *Journal of the Royal Society of WA*, vol. 82, 1999, pp. 17–25.

Beattie, J., 'Rethinking science, religion and nature in environmental history: drought in early twentieth-century New Zealand', *Historical Social Research*, vol. 29, no. 3, 2004, pp. 82–103.

Beattie, J., *Empire and Environmental Anxiety*, New York, Palgrave Macmillan, 2011.

Beck, U., *Risk Society*, London, Sage, 1992.

Bennett, D. and Macpherson, D. K., 'Groundwater management – must there be a conflict?', in B. R. Whelan (ed.), *Groundwater Resources of the Swan Coastal Plain*, Perth, CSIRO, 1981, pp. 437–52.

Beresford, Q. et al., *The Salinity Crisis*, Crawley, UWA Press, 2004.

Beresford, Q., 'Developmentalism and its environmental legacy: the Western Australia wheatbelt, 1900–1990s', *Australian Journal of Politics and History*, vol. 47, no. 3, 2001, pp. 403–14.

Binnie International (Australia), *Development Study*, Perth, MWSSD Board, 1977.

Biskup, P., *Not Slaves, Not Citizens: the Aboriginal problem in Western Australia 1898–1954*, St Lucia, University of QLD Press, 1973.

Black, D., 'Liberals triumphant: the politics of development, 1947–1980', in C. T. Stannage (ed.), *A New History of Western Australia*, Nedlands, UWA Press, 1981, p. 441–70.

Blainey, G., *The Golden Mile*, St. Leonards, Allen & Unwin, 1993.

Blake, N. and Stocker, L., 'Greenhouse gas audit for Western Australia', *Sustainable Development*, vol. 2, no. 2, 1994, pp. 20–8.

Bolton, G. C., 'Black and white after 1897', in C. T. Stannage (ed.), *A New History of Western Australia*, Nedlands, UWA Press, 1981, pp. 124–78.

Bolton, G. C., *A Fine Country to Starve In*, Nedlands, UWA Press, 1972.

Bolton, G. C., *Land of Vision and Mirage*, Crawley, UWA Press, 2008.

Bolton, G. C., *Spoils and Spoilers*, North Sydney, George Allen & Unwin, 1981.

Bolton, G. C. and Hutchison, D. E., 'The beginning', in B. J. O'Brien (ed.), *Environment and Science*, Nedlands, UWA Press, 1979, pp. 1–21.

Botterill, L. C., 'Uncertain climate: the recent history of drought policy in Australia', *Australian Journal of Politics and History*, vol. 49, no. 1, 2003, pp. 61–74.

Bradby, K., 'Diversity or dust', in P. Newman, S. Neville and L. Duxbury (eds), *Case Studies in Environmental Hope*, Perth, EPA, 1988, pp. 97–104.

Braid, E., '"Explorer surveyors" classification work', *Journal of the Royal Historical Association of WA*, vol. 8, no. 4, 1980, pp. 22–40.

Braid, E., 'John Septimus Roe: first explorer of the wheatlands; the search for an inland sea', *Early Days*, vol. 7, 1975, pp. 81–97.

Brayshay, M. and Selwood, J., 'Dreams, propaganda and harsh realities: landscapes of group settlement in the forest districts of Western Australia in the 1920s', *Landscape Research*, vol. 27, no. 1, 2002, pp. 81–101.

Brearley, A., *Ernest Hodgkin's Swanland: estuaries and coastal lagoons of southwestern Australia*, Crawley, UWA Press, 2005.

Brett, J., *Robert Menzies' Forgotten People*, Carlton, Melbourne University Press, 2007.

Bropho, R., *Fringedweller*, Chippendale, Alternative Publishing Co-operative, 1980.

Bulkeley, H., 'The formation of Australian climate change policy: 1985–1995', in A. Gillespie and W. C. G. Burns (eds), *Climate Change in the South Pacific*, Boston, Kluwer, 2000, pp. 33–50.

Bunbury, B., *Till the Stream Runs Dry*, Perth, Dept of Water, 2010.

Bureau of Meteorology, *Results of Rainfall Observations Made in Western Australia*, Melbourne, H. J. Green, 1929.

Burvill, G. H. (ed.), *Agriculture in Western Australia,* Nedlands, UWA Press, 1979, pp. 4–17.

Caldwell, M. J., 'Perth water supply – the role of groundwater resources', in B. R. Whelan (ed.), *Groundwater Resources of the Swan Coastal Plain*, Perth, CSIRO, 1981, pp. 1–28.

Cameron, J. M. R., 'Learning as a factor in land use: the inevitability of pastoralism in early Western Australia', *Journal of Australian Studies*, no. 3, 1978, pp. 30–43.

Cameron, J. M. R., 'The near collapse of Swan River Colony: review and reappraisal', *Social Sciences Forum*, vol. 1, no. 1, 1973, pp. 7–31.

Cameron, J. M. R., 'Poison plants in Western Australia and coloniser problem solving', *Journal of the Royal Society of WA*, vol. 59, no. 3, 1977, pp. 71–7.

Cameron, J. M. R., *Ambition's Fire,* Nedlands, UWA Press, 1981.

Cameron, J. M. R. and Jaggard, E. K. G. (eds), *Western Australian Readings*, Perth, Churchlands College, 1977.

Carbon, B. A., 'Introduction', in B. A. Carbon (ed.), *Groundwater Resources of the Swan Coastal Plain*, Perth, CSIRO, 1975, pp. 3–6.

Cargeeg, G. C. et al., *Perth Urban Water Balance Study*, Leederville, Water Authority of Western Australia, 1987.

Casey, M. H. M. and Laing, I. A. F., *A Review of Four On-farm Water Supply Demonstration Farms*, Perth, Dept of Agriculture (WA), 1993.

Climate Commission, *The Critical Decade: climate science, risks and responses*, Canberra, Dept of Climate Change and Energy Efficiency, 2011.

Coles, N. et al., 'Farm water planning strategies for dryland agricultural areas: local and regional perspectives', in *10th World Water Congress*, Melbourne, International Water Resources Association, 2000, pp. 388–96.

Collard, L. and Harben, S., '*Nartj katitj bidi ngulluckiny koorl?* (Which knowledge path will we travel?)', *Studies in Western Australian History*, vol. 26, 2010, pp. 75–95.

Collard, L., 'The cosmology: the creator of the Trilogy Waakal or Nyungar Rainbow Serpent', in M. Leybourne and A. Gaynor (eds), *Water*, Crawley, UWA Press, 2006, pp. 121–30.

Collard, L., Harben, S., and van den Berg, R., *Nidja Beeliar Boodjar Noonookurt Nyininy: a Nyungar interpretative history of the use of* boodjar *(country) in the vicinity of Murdoch University*, Perth, Murdoch University, 2004.

Collis, B., *Fields of Discovery: Australia's CSIRO*, Crows Nest, Allen & Unwin, 2002.

Cooper, W. S., 'Drainage and irrigation', in J. Gentilli (ed.), *Western Landscapes*, Nedlands, UWA Press, 1979, pp. 235–53.

Coughlan, M. J., 'Changes in Australian rainfall and temperatures', in A. B. Pittock et al. (eds), *Climatic Change and Variability*, Melbourne, Cambridge University Press, 1978, pp. 194–9.

Crook, S. and J. Pakulski, 'Shades of green: public opinion on environmental issues in Australia', *Australian Journal of Political Science*, vol. 30, 1995, pp. 39–55.

Crowley, F. K., *Australia's Western Third*, Melbourne, Heinemann, 1970.

CSIRO, *Groundwater Yields in South-West Western Australia*, Canberra, CSIRO, 2009.

CSIRO, *Water Yields and Demands in South-West Western Australia*, Canberra, CSIRO, 2009.

Dahlke, J., 'Evolution of the wheat belt in Western Australia: thoughts on the nature of pioneering along the dry margin', *Australian Geographer*, vol. 13, 1975, pp. 3–14.

Davidson, B. R., *Australia: wet or dry?*, Carlton, Melbourne University Press, 1969.

Davidson, W. A., *Hydrogeology and Groundwater Resources of the Perth Region, Western Australia*, Perth, Geological Survey of WA, 1995.

Davis, J. E., 'Supplementary public water supply schemes constructed by the Public Works Department', in *Wheatbelt Water Supply Seminar,* Perth, Water Research Foundation of Australia, WA State Committee, 1977, pp. 1–12.

Davison, G., 'Country life: the rise and decline of an Australia ideal', in G. Davison and M. Brodie (eds), *Struggle Country*, Melbourne, Monash University ePress, 2008, pp. 1.1–1.15.

Davison, G., 'Down the gurgler: historical influences on Australian domestic water consumption', in P. Troy (ed.), *Troubled Waters*, Canberra, ANU Press, 2008, pp. 37–66.

Davison, G., 'Introduction', in G. Davison and M. Brodie (eds), *Struggle Country*, Melbourne, Monash University ePress, 2005, pp. ix–xvi.

Davison, G., 'Rural sustainability in historical perspective', in C. Cocklin and J. Dibden (eds), *Sustainability and Change in Rural Australia*, Sydney, UNSW Press, 2005, pp. 38–55.

Day, D., *The Weather Watchers: 100 years of the Bureau of Meteorology*, Carlton, Melbourne University Publishing, 2007.

Dempsey, R. (ed.), *The Politics of Finding Out*, Melbourne, Cheshire, 1974.

Dept of Agriculture, *Agricultural regions of Western Australia, a regional classification of the agricultural areas of the South West of the State according to physiography, climate and soils*, Perth, Dept of Agriculture (WA), 1947.

Dept of Public Works and Water Supply, *Comprehensive Agricultural Areas and Goldfields Water Supply Scheme: a comprehensive scheme for reticulating water for towns, stock and domestic purposes to certain areas of the mixed farming (cereals and sheep) districts of Western Australia; a request for aid from the Commonwealth government*, Perth, Govt Printer, 1946.

Department of Water, *Rural Water Plan Implementation 1995–2010*, Perth, Dept of Water, 2011.

Dibden, J. and Cheshire, L., 'Community development', in C. Cocklin and J. Dibden (eds), *Sustainability and Change in Rural Australia*, Sydney, UNSW Press, 2005, pp. 212–29.

Dingle, T., 'The life and times of the Chadwickian solution', in P. Troy (ed.), *Troubled Waters*, Canberra, ANU Press, pp. 7–18.

Douglas, K., 'Under such sunny skies': understanding weather in colonial Australia, 1860–1901, Metarch Papers no. 17, Melbourne, Bureau of Meteorology, 2007.

Dovers, S. R., 'Urban water: policy, institutions and government', in P. Troy (ed.), Troubled Waters, Canberra, ANU Press, 2008, pp. 81–98.

Duruz, J., 'Suburban gardens', in S. Ferber, C. Healy and C. McAuliffe (eds), Beasts of Suburbia, Melbourne, Melbourne University Press, 1994, pp. 198–213.

Economic Regulation Authority (ERA), Inquiry on Urban Water and Wastewater Pricing: Final Report, Perth, ERA, 2005.

Ehrlich, P. R., Extinction: the implications of the loss of our biological heritage, Perth, Murdoch University, 1985.

Environmental Protection Authority (EPA), Next Major Public Water Supply for Perth (post 1992): Water Authority of Western Australia, report and recommendations of the Environmental Protection Authority, Perth, EPA, 1988.

EPA, Perth Metropolitan Desalination Proposal: Water Corporation of Australia – report and recommendations of the Environmental Protection Authority, 2002, <http://www.watercorporation.com.au/_files/Desalination_Bulletin_1070.pdf>, (Accessed: 1 February 2012).

EPA, State of the Environment Report 2007, EPA, <http://www.epa.wa.gov.au/AbouttheEPA/SOE/2007/Pages/default.aspx>, (Accessed: 10 May 2012).

ERA, Inquiry on Urban Water and Wastewater Pricing: Issues Paper, Perth, ERA, 2004.

Evans, C., Storer, C. and Wardell-Johnson, A., 'Rural farming community climate change acceptance', International Journal of the Society of Agriculture and Food, vol. 18, no. 3, 2011, pp. 217–35.

Evans, R., 'A passion for white elephants: some lessons from Australia's experience of nation building', in J. Butcher (ed.), Australia Under Construction, Canberra, ANU Press, 2008, pp. 49–56.

Facey, A. B., A Fortunate Life, Ringwood, Penguin, 1985.

Farm Water Supply Advisory Committee, First Annual Report, 30th May 1966, Perth, Govt Printer, 1966.

Farm Water Supply Advisory Committee, Supplementary Report, 2nd March 1967, Perth, Govt Printer, 1967.

Fiske, J., Hodge, B. and Turner, G., Myths of Oz, Sydney, Allen & Unwin, 1987.

Flannery, T., The Weather Makers, Melbourne, Text Publishing, 2005.

Foley, J. C., Droughts in Australia: review of records from the earliest years of settlement to 1955, Melbourne, Commonwealth Bureau of Meteorology, 1957.

Freestone, R., 'Planning, housing, gardening: home as a garden suburb', in P. Troy (ed.), A History of European Housing in Australia, Oakleigh, Cambridge University Press, 2000, pp. 125–41.

Gammage, B., The Biggest Estate on Earth, Sydney, Allen & Unwin, 2011.

Gaynor, A., '"Like a good deed in a naughty world": gardens on the eastern goldfields of Western Australia', Australian Humanities Review, no. 36, 2005, <http://www.australianhumanitiesreview.org/archive/Issue-July-2005/11Gaynor.html>, (Accessed: 28 September 2013).

Gaynor, A., 'Looking forward, looking back: toward an environmental history of salinity and erosion in the eastern wheatbelt of Western Australia', in A. Gaynor, M. Trinca, and A. Haebich (eds), *Country*, Perth, WA Museum, 2002, pp. 105–23.

Gaynor, A. and Davis, J. 'People, place, and the pipeline: visions and impacts of the Goldfields Water Supply Scheme, 1896–1906', in M. Leybourne and A. Gaynor (eds), *Water*, Crawley, UWA Press, 2006, pp. 15–27.

Gaynor, A., *Harvest of the Suburbs*, Crawley, UWA Press, 2006.

Gentilli, J., 'A history of meteorological and climatological studies in Australia', *University Studies in History*, vol. 5, no. 1, 1967, pp. 55-88.

Gentilli, J., 'Climatic fluctuations', in J. Gentilli (ed.), *Climates of Australia and New Zealand*, Amsterdam, Elsevier Publishing Co., 1971, pp. 189–212.

Gentilli, J., 'Climatological score: climatological research in Australian and New Zealand universities, 1968–87', *Australian Geographical Studies*, vol. 26, no. 1, 1988, pp. 21–44.

Gentilli, J., 'Homologous peri-oceanic west coast climates in the southern hemisphere', in A. F. Pearce and D. I. Walker (eds), *The Leeuwin Current*, Perth, Royal Society of Western Australia, 1991, pp. 15–33.

Gentilli, J., 'Present climatic fluctuations in Western Australia', *Western Australian Naturalist*, vol. 3, 1952, pp. 155–65.

Gentilli, J., *Atlas of Australian Agriculture*, Crawley, UWA Text Books Board, 1941.

Gentilli, J., *Australian Climate Patterns*, Melbourne, Thomas Nelson, 1972.

Gentilli, J., *Australian Climates and Resources*, Perth, Whitcombe & Tombs, 1946.

Gentilli, J., *Climates of Australia and New Zealand*, New York, Elsevier, 1971.

George, R., McFarlane, D. and Nulsen, R., 'Salinity threatens the viability of agriculture and ecosystems in Western Australia', *Hydrogeology Journal*, vol. 5, no. 1, 1997, pp. 6–21.

Gibbs, W. J. and Maher, J. V., *Rainfall Deciles as Drought Indicators*, Melbourne, Bureau of Meteorology, 1967.

Giddens, A. and Pierson, C., *Conversations with Anthony Giddens*, Palo Alto, Stanford University Press, 1998.

Glynn, S., 'The transport factor in developmental policy: pioneer agricultural railways in the Western Australian wheat belt, 1900–1930', *Australian Journal of Politics and History*, vol. 15, no. 2, 1969, pp. 60–78.

Glynn, S., *Government Policy and Agricultural Development*, Nedlands, UWA Press, 1975.

Goodall, H. and Cadzow, A., *Rivers and Resilience*, Sydney, UNSW Press, 2009.

Goodall, H., 'Riding the tide: indigenous knowledge, history and water in a changing Australia', *Environment and History*, vol. 14, no. 3, 2008, pp. 355–84.

Government of Western Australia, *Securing Our Water Future: a state water strategy for Western Australia*, Perth, Government of Western Australia, 2003.

Government of Western Australia, *State Water Plan*, Perth, Dept of Premier and Cabinet, 2007.

Green, N., 'Aborigines: the changing scene', in L. Hunt (ed.), *Yilgarn*, Southern Cross, Shire of Yilgarn, 1988, pp. 125–48.

Green, N., *Broken Spears*, Perth, Focus Education Services, 1984.

Gregory, J. A., '"Let our watchword be 'order' and our beacon 'beauty'": achieving town planning legislation in Western Australia', in R. Freestone (ed.), *Cities, Citizens and Environmental Reform*, Sydney, Sydney University Press, 2009, pp. 173–99.

Gregory, J. A., 'Protecting middle-class suburbia: an ideal space for the citizens of interwar Perth', *Studies in WA History*, vol. 17, 1997, pp. 77–91.

Gregory, J. A., *City of Light*, Perth, City of Perth, 2003.

Griffiths, T. and Sherratt, T., 'What if the northern rivers had been turned inland?', in S. Macintyre and S. Scalmer (eds), *What If? Australian History as it Might Have Been*, Carlton, Melbourne University Press, 2006, pp. 234–54.

Haebich, A., '"Clearing the wheat belt": erasing the Indigenous presence in the southwest of Western Australia', in A. Dirk Moses (ed.), *Genocide and Settler Society*, New York, Berghahn Books, 2004, pp. 267–89.

Haebich, A., 'European farmers and Aboriginal farmers in south Western Australia, mid-1890s–1914', *Studies in WA History*, vol. 8, 1984, pp. 59–67.

Haebich, A., 'Nuclear, suburban and black', in T. Rowse (ed.), *Contesting Assimilation*, Perth, API Network, 2005, pp. 201–20.

Haebich, A., *For Their Own Good*, Nedlands, UWA Press, 1992.

Haebich, A., *Spinning the Dream*, North Fremantle, Fremantle Press, 2008.

Hall, T., *The Life and Death of the Australian Backyard*, Collingwood, CSIRO, 2010.

Hallam, S. J., *Fire and Hearth*, Canberra, Australian Institute of Aboriginal Studies, 1975.

Hancke, S. H. and Davis, R. K., 'Demand management through responsive pricing', *Journal of the American Water Works Association*, vol. 63, no. 9, 1971, pp. 555–60.

Hartley, R. G., *River of Steel*, Bassendean, Access Press, 2007.

Hatton, T. J., Ruprecht, J. and George, R. J., 'Preclearing hydrology of the Western Australian wheatbelt: target for the future?', *Plant and Soil*, vol. 257, 2003, pp. 341–56.

Havel, J. J., 'The effects of water supply for the city Perth, Western Australia, on other forms of land use', *Landscape Planning*, vol. 2, 1975, pp. 75–132.

Hayman, P. and Cox, P., 'Drought risk as a negotiated construct', in L. C. Botterill and D. A. Wilhite (eds), *From Disaster Response to Risk Management: Australia's National Drought Policy*, Dordrecht, Springer, 2005, pp. 113–26.

Head, L. et al., 'A fine-grained study of the experience of drought, risk and climate change among Australian wheat farming households', *Annals of the Association of American Geographers*, vol. 101, no. 5, 2011, pp. 1,089–1,108.

Heathcote, R. L., 'Managing the droughts? Perception of resource management in the face of the drought hazard in Australia', *Vegetatio*, vol. 91, 1991, pp. 219–30.

Hertzler, G., 'Prospects for insuring against drought in Australia', in L. C. Botterill and D. A. Wilhite (eds), *From Disaster Response to Risk Management: Australia's National Drought Policy*, Dordrecht, Springer, 2005, pp. 127–38.

Hewitt, K., 'The idea of calamity in a technocratic age', in K. Hewitt (ed.), *Interpretations of Calamity from the Viewpoint of Human Ecology*, Boston, Allen & Unwin, 1983, pp. 3–32.

Hodge, J. M. *Triumph of the Expert,* Athens, Ohio University Press, 2007.

Hollick, M. J., *The Management of Water Supplies in Western Australia*, Nedlands, UWA Department of Civil Engineering and Department of Politics, 1983.

Holling, C. S., 'Resilience and stability of ecological systems', *Annual Review of Ecology and Systematics*, vol. 4, 1973, pp. 1–23.

Holmes, K., 'Growing Australian landscapes: the use and meanings of native plants in gardens in twentieth-century Australia', *Studies in the History of Gardens and Designed Landscapes*, vol. 31, no. 2, 2011, pp. 121–30.

Holmes, K., 'In her master's house and garden', in P. Troy (ed.), *A History of European Housing in Australia*, Oakleigh, Cambridge University Press, 2000, pp. 164–81.

Home, R. W., 'Rainmaking in CSIRO: the science and politics of climate modification', in T. Sherratt, T. Griffiths and L. Robin (eds), *A Change in the Weather*, Canberra, National Museum of Australia, 2005, pp. 66–79.

Hopper, S. D. and Gioia, P., 'The southwest Australian floristic region: evolution and conservation of a global hot spot of biodiversity', *Annual Review of Ecology, Evolution and Systematics*, vol. 35, 2004, pp. 623–50.

Hughes, G., 'Meeting the challenge of climate variability in a major water supply system', *Water Science and Technology: Water Supply*, vol. 3, no. 3, 2003, pp. 201–7.

Hunt, H. A., Taylor, G. and Quayle, E. T., *The Climate and Weather of Australia*, Melbourne, Commonwealth Bureau of Meteorology, 1913.

Hunt, H. E., 'Address', in *Seminar H2O: domestic extravagance*, Nedlands, UWA, 1975, pp. 1–13.

Hunt, H. E., *Perth's Early Water Supplies*, Perth, Institution of Engineers Australia (WA), 1984.

Hunt, S-J. and Bolton, G., 'Cleansing the dunghill: water supply and sanitation in Perth 1878–1912', *Studies in Western Australian History*, vol. 2, 1978, pp. 1–17.

Hunt, S-J., *Water, the Abiding Challenge*, Perth, Metropolitan Water Board, 1980.

Hunter, L., 'Climate and landscape', in L. Hunt (ed.), *Yilgarn*, Southern Cross, Shire of Yilgarn, 1988, pp. 11–54.

Hussey, K. and Dovers, S., 'Trajectories in Australian water policy', *Journal of Contemporary Water Research and Education*, no. 135, 2006, pp. 36–50.

Hutton, D. and Connors, L., *A History of the Australian Environment Movement*, Melbourne, Cambridge University Press, 1999.

Indian Ocean Climate Initiative (IOCI), *Climate Variability and Change in South West Western Australia*, Perth, IOCI, 2002.

IOCI, *Towards Understanding Climate Variability in South Western Australia, Research Reports on the First Phase of the Indian Ocean Climate Initiative*, East Perth, IOCI Panel, 1999.

Jennings, P., 'A decade of wetland conservation in Western Australia', in R. Giblett and H. Webb (eds), *Western Australian Wetlands*, Perth, Black Swan Press, 1996, pp. 149–66.

Jones, R. and Tonts, M., 'Rural restructuring and social sustainability: some reflections on the Western Australian wheatbelt', *Australian Geographer*, vol. 26, no. 2, 1995, pp. 133–40.

Kaïka, M., 'Interrogating the geographies of the familiar: domesticating nature and constructing the autonomy of the modern home', *International Journal of Urban and Regional Research*, vol. 28, no. 2, 2004, pp. 265–86.

Kelsall, K. J., 'The Comprehensive Water Supply Scheme', *Journal of Agriculture (Western Australia)*, vol. 18, no. 3, 1977, pp. 68–72.

Kimberley Water Resources Development Advisory Board, *Report of the Kimberley Water Resources Development Advisory Board*, Perth, Kimberley Water Resources Development Office, 1993.

Kurz, T. et al., 'The ways that people talk about natural resources: discursive strategies as barriers to environmentally sustainable practices', *British Journal of Social Psychology*, vol. 44, 2005, pp. 603–20.

Laing, I. A. F., 'Farm dams in the wheatbelt', in *Wheatbelt Water Supply Seminar*, Perth, Water Research Foundation of Australia, WA State Committee, 1977, pp. 2–10.

Laing, I. A. F., Pepper, R. G. and McCrea, A. F., *Problem Districts for On-Farm Water Supply in South Western Australia*, Perth, Dept of Agriculture, 1988.

Langford-Smith, T., 'Water supply in the agricultural areas of Western Australia', *Australian Geographer*, vol. 5, no. 6, 1947, pp. 115–56.

Laws, A. T., 'Restructuring the water industry in Western Australia to better manage the state's resources', in *Hydrogeology and Land Use Management*, Bratislava, International Association of Hydrogeologists, 1999, pp. 17–22.

Layman, L., 'Development ideology in Western Australia 1933–1965', *Historical Studies*, vol. 20, no. 79, 1982, pp. 234–60.

Le Page, J. S. H., *Building a State*, Leederville, Water Authority of Western Australia, 1987.

Loh, I. C., 'Appendix 1: the history of catchment and reservoir management on Wellington Reservoir Catchment W.A.', in P. Laut and B. J. Taplin (eds), *Catchment Management in Australia in the 1980s*, Canberra, CSIRO Division of Water Resources, 1989, pp. 202–23.

Loh, M. and Coghlan, P., *Domestic Water Use Study in Perth, Western Australia 1998–2001*, Leederville, Water Corporation, 2003.

Lowe, G. (ed.), *Greenhouse88 – Planning for Climatic Change: Western Australian conference proceedings*, Perth, WA Water Resources Council and Environmental Protection Authority, 1989.

Maddock, J., *Westonia*, Westonia, Shire of Westonia, 1998.

Marsden, J. and Pickering, P., *Securing Australia's Urban Water Supplies*, Camberwell, Marsden Jacob Associates, 2006.

Matthews, J. J., *Good and Mad Women,* Sydney, George Allen & Unwin, 1984.

Mauger, G., *Planning Future Sources for Perth's Water Supply*, Leederville, Water Authority of WA, 1987.

McDonald, E., Coldrick, B. and Christensen, W., 'The green frog and desalination: a Nyungar metaphor for the (mis-) management of water resources, Swan Coastal Plain, Western Australia', *Oceania*, vol. 78, no. 1, 2008, pp. 62–75.

McDonald, E., Coldrick, B. and Villiers, L., *Study of Groundwater-related Aboriginal Cultural Values on the Gnangara Mound, Western Australia*, Perth, Estill Associates, 2005.

McFarlane, D., *Context Report on Southwest Water Resources for Expert Panel Examining Kimberley Water Supply Options*, Canberra, Water for a Healthy Country National Research Flagship, CSIRO, 2005.

McManus, P. and Pritchard, B., 'Introduction', in B. Pritchard and P. McManus (eds), *Land of Discontent*, Sydney, UNSW Press, 2000, pp. 1–13.

Metropolitan Water Authority, *Domestic Water Use in Perth, Western Australia*, Perth, Metropolitan Water Centre, 1985.

Mitchell, B. and Hollick, M., 'Integrated catchment management in Western Australia: transition from concept to implementation', *Environmental Management*, vol. 17, no. 6, 1993, pp. 735–43.

Morgan, L., *Climate Change and Adaptation in South West Western Australia: Phase One of Action 5.5, State Greenhouse Strategy*, Perth, Dept of Agriculture and Food (WA), 2007.

Morgan, R., 'Dry horizons: the responses of Western Australian water managers to the enhanced greenhouse effect in the late 1980s', *History Australia*, vol. 8, no. 3, 2011, pp. 158–76.

Morgan, R., '"Fear the hose": an historical exploration of sustainable water use in Perth gardens, 1970s', *Transforming Cultures eJournal*, vol. 5, no. 1, 2010, <http://epress.lib.uts.edu.au/ojs/index.php/TfC/issue/view/87/showToc>, (Accessed: 28 September 2013).

Morgan, R., 'A thirsty city: an environmental history of water supply and demand in 1970s Perth', *Studies in WA History*, vol. 27, 2011, pp. 81–97.

Muir, C., Rose, D. and Sullivan, P., 'From the other side of the knowledge frontier: Indigenous knowledge, social-ecological relationships and new perspectives', *Rangeland Journal*, vol. 32, 2010, pp. 259–65.

Murray, D., 'Land settlement and farming systems', in L. Hunt (ed.), *Yilgarn*, Southern Cross, Shire of Yilgarn, 1988, pp. 267–350.

Nash, L., *Inescapable Ecologies*, Berkeley, University of California Press, 2006.

Newbey, K., *Land Use Planning of the North Fitzgerald Area*, Perth, Author, 1982.

257

Nicholls, N., 'Climatic outlooks, from revolutionary science to orthodoxy', in T. Sherratt, T. Griffiths, and L. Robin (eds), *A Change in the Weather*, Canberra, National Museum of Australia Press, 2005, pp. 18–29.

Nicholls, N., 'Sea surface temperatures and Australian winter rainfall', *Journal of Climate*, vol. 2, 1989, pp. 965–73.

Nicholls, N. and Lavery, B., 'Australian rainfall trends during the twentieth century', *International Journal of Climatology*, vol. 12, no. 2 1992, pp. 153–63.

O'Connor, R., Bodney, C. and Little, L., *Preliminary Report on the Survey of Aboriginal Areas of Significance in the Perth Metropolitan and Murray River Regions*, East Perth, Heritage Council of WA, 1985.

O'Hara, I., 'The role of the Metropolitan Water Board in the management of the groundwater resources', in B. R. Whelan (ed.), *Groundwater Resources of the Swan Coastal Plain*, Perth, CSIRO, 1981, pp. 393–406.

Pakulski, J. and Tranter, B., 'Environmentalism and social differentiation: a paper in memory of Steve Crook', *Journal of Sociology*, vol. 40, no. 2, 2004, pp. 225–6.

Pakulski, J. and Crook, S., 'Introduction: the end of the green cultural revolution?' in J. Pakulski and S. Crook (eds), *Ebbing of the Green Tide?*, Hobart, University of Tasmania, 1998, pp. 1–21.

Paton, D., Kelly, G. and Doherty, M., 'Exploring the complexity of social and ecological resilience to hazards', in D. Paton and D. Johnston (eds), *Disaster Resilience*, Springfield, Charles C Thomas, 2006, pp. 190–212.

Pearman, G. I., 'Preface', in G. I. Pearman (ed.), *Greenhouse, Planning for Climate Change*, East Melbourne, CSIRO Publications, 1988, pp. ix–xii.

Peck, A. J. and Allison, G. B., 'Groundwater and salinity response to climate change', in G. I. Pearman (ed.), *Greenhouse, Planning for Climate Change*, East Melbourne, CSIRO Publications, 1988, pp. 238–51.

Peel, M., 'Between the houses: neighbouring and privacy', in P. Troy (ed.), *A History of European Housing in Australia*, Melbourne, Cambridge University Press, 2000, pp. 269–86.

Pen, L. J., *Managing Our Rivers: a guide to the nature and management of the streams of south-west Western Australia*, East Perth, Water and Rivers Commission, 1999.

Pigram, J. J., *Issues in the Management of Australia's Water Resources*, Melbourne, Longman Cheshire, 1986.

Pittock A. B. et al., 'Appendix: climate change in Australia to the year 2030 AD', in G. I. Pearman (ed.), *Greenhouse, Planning for Climate Change*, East Melbourne, CSIRO Publications, 1988, pp. 737–40.

Pittock, A. B., 'Actual and anticipated changes in Australia's climate', in G. I. Pearman (ed.), *Greenhouse, Planning for Climate Change*, East Melbourne, CSIRO Publications, 1988, pp. 35–51.

Pittock, A. B., 'Climatic change and the patterns of variation in Australian rainfall', *Search*, vol. 6, no. 11–12, 1975, pp. 498–504.

Pittock, A. B., 'Recent climatic change in Australia, implications for a CO2-warmed Earth', *Climatic Change,* vol. 5, 1983, pp. 321–40.

Powell, J. M., *An Historical Geography of Modern Australia,* Melbourne, Cambridge University Press, 1991.

Powell, J. M., *Watering the Western Third: water, land and community in Western Australia, 1826–1998,* Leederville, Water and Rivers Commission, 1998.

Power, S., Sadler, B., and Nicholls, N., 'The influence of climate science on water management in Western Australia, lessons for climate scientists', *Bulletin of the American Meteorological Society,* vol. 86, 2005, pp. 839–44.

Reiger, K., *The Disenchantment of the Home,* Melbourne, Oxford University Press, 1985.

Ritter, D., 'Trashing heritage: dilemmas of rights and power in the operation of Western Australia's Aboriginal heritage legislation', *Studies in WA History,* vol. 23, 2003, pp. 195–208.

Robin, L., 'Battling the land and global anxiety: science, environment and identity in settler Australia', *Philosophy, Activism, Nature,* no. 7, 2010, pp. 3–9.

Robin, L., 'Ecology: a science of empire?', in T. Griffiths and L. Robin (eds), *Ecology and Empire,* Melbourne, Melbourne University Press, 1997, pp. 63–75.

Robin, L., 'New science for sustainability in an ancient land', in S. Soerlin and P. Warde (eds), *Nature's End,* New York, Palgrave Macmillan, 2009, pp. 188–214.

Robin, L., *How a Continent Created a Nation,* Sydney, UNSW Press, 2007.

Royal Commission on the Agricultural Industries of Western Australia, *Progress Report of the Royal Commission on the Agricultural Industries of Western Australia on the Wheat Growing Portion of the Southwest Division of the State,* Perth, Govt. Printers Office, 1917.

Royal Commission on the Agricultural Industries of Western Australia, *Second Progress Report of the Royal Commission on the Agricultural Industries of Western Australia on the Selected Portions of the South-West Coastal Districts,* Perth, Govt. Printers Office, 1918.

Ruprecht, J. K., Bates, B. C., and Stokes, R. A., *Climate Variability and Water Resources Workshop, a Summary of Outcomes,* East Perth, Water and Rivers Commission, 1996.

Ryan, B. F. and King, W. D., 'A critical review of the Australian experience in cloud seeding', *Bulletin of the American Meteorological Society,* vol. 78, no. 2, 1997, pp. 239–54.

Sadler, B., 'Water resource and land use problems in Western Australia', in D. H. Falkenborg, H. F. Heady and J. P. Riley (eds), *Watershed Management on Range and Forest Lands: proceedings of the fifth workshop of the United States/Australia Rangelands Panel,* Logan, UT, Utah Water Research Laboratory, 1976, pp. 13–30.

Sadler, B., 'Water supply and alternate sources', in B. A. Carbon (ed.), *Groundwater Resources of the Swan Coastal Plain,* Perth, CSIRO, 1976, pp. 37–60.

Sadler, B. and Cox, B., 'Water resources management: the socio-political context', *Nature and Resources*, vol. 22, 1986, pp. 12–19.

Sadler, B., Mauger, G. W., and Stokes, R. A., 'The water resource implications of a drying climate in south-west Western Australia', in G. I. Pearman (ed.), *Greenhouse, Planning for Climate Change*, East Melbourne, CSIRO Publications, 1988, pp. 296–311.

Sadler, B. S., 'State water planning in Western Australia: trends and future directions', in W. D. Sewell, J. W. Handmer and D. I. Smith (eds), *Water Planning in Australia*, Canberra, ANU, 1985, pp. 161–82.

Sadler, B. S. and Field, C. A. R., *South West Regional Water Planning Study: working report*, Perth, PWD, 1973.

Seddon, G., *Landprints*, Melbourne, Cambridge University Press, 1997.

Seddon, G., *Swan Song*, Nedlands, UWA Centre for Studies in Australian Literature, 1995.

Select Committee on Salinity, *Report on Salinity in Western Australia: discussion paper*, Perth, The Committee, 1988.

Sherratt, T., 'Human elements', in T. Sherratt, T. Griffiths and L. Robin (eds), *A Change in the Weather*, Canberra, NMA Press, 2005, pp. 1–17.

Smith, D. I., *Water in Australia*, Melbourne, Oxford University Press, 1998.

Smith, K., 'Trends in water resource management', *Progress in Physical Geography*, vol. 3, 1979, pp. 236–54.

Smith, S. T., 'A logical approach to water resource utilisation in the wheatbelt', in *Wheatbelt Water Supply Seminar*, Perth, Water Research Foundation of Australia, WA State Committee, 1977, pp. 2–7.

Snooks, G. D., 'Development in adversity 1913–1946', in C. T. Stannage (ed.), *A New History of Western Australia*, Nedlands, UWA Press, 1981, pp. 237–65.

Soerlin, S. and Warde, P., 'The problem of the problem of environmental history: a re-reading of the field', *Environmental History*, vol. 12, 2007, pp. 107–30.

Sofoulis, Z., 'Big Water, everyday water: a sociotechnical perspective', *Continuum*, vol. 19, no. 4, 2005, pp. 445–63.

Southern, R. L., 'The Atmosphere', in B. J. O'Brien (ed.), *Environment and Science*, Crawley, UWA Press, 1979, pp. 183–226.

Stannage, C. T., *The People of Perth*, Perth, Perth City Council, 1979.

State Salinity Council, *The Salinity Strategy: natural resource management in Australia*, Perth, Government of Western Australia, 2000.

Statham, P., 'Swan River Colony 1829–1850', in C. T. Stannage (ed.), *A New History of Western Australia*, Nedlands, UWA Press, 1981, pp. 181–210.

Statham, P., 'Western Australia becomes British', in P. Statham (ed.), *The Origins of Australia's Capital Cities*, Oakleigh, Cambridge University Press, 1989, pp. 121–40.

Steffen, W., *The Critical Decade: climate science, risks and responses*, Canberra, Climate Commission Secretariat, 2011.

Stephens, D. et al., 'Experiences in the use of climate information, and its communication in 2002/03, from the perspective of the Department of Agriculture, WA', in N. Plummer et al. (eds), *DroughtCom Workshop*, Vol. 2, 2003, Melbourne, Bureau of Meteorology, pp. 42–5.

Stokes, R. A. et al., *Perth's Water Future: a vision for the water supply of Perth and Mandurah to 2050*, Leederville, Water Authority of WA, 1995.

Syme, G. J. and Kantola, S. J., 'Investment in private bores: underground water usage from a household perspective', in B. R. Whelan (ed.), *Groundwater Resources of the Swan Coastal Plain*, Perth, CSIRO, 1981, pp. 453–76.

Syme, G. J., Kantola, S. J. and Thomas, J. F., 'Water resources and the quarter-acre block', in R. Thorne and S. J. Arden (eds), *People and the Man Made Environment*, Sydney, University of Sydney, 1980, pp. 182–201.

Taylor, V. and Trentmann, F., 'Liquid politics: water and the politics of everyday life in the modern city', *Past and Present*, no. 211, 2011, pp. 203–14.

Thomas, J., *Water in the Australian Economy*, Parkville, Australian Academy of Technological Sciences and Engineering, 1999.

Tilbrook, L., 'A chronology of the Swan River Colony 1829–1840', in S. Hallam and L. Tilbrook (eds), *Aborigines of the Southwest Region 1829–1840*, Nedlands, UWA Press, 1990, pp. xiv–xvii.

Tonts, M., 'Some recent trends in Australian regional economic development policy', *Regional Studies*, vol. 33, 1999, pp. 581–6.

Tonts, M., 'Spatially uneven development: government policy and rural reform in the wheatbelt of Western Australia', *Anthropological Forum*, vol. 14, no. 3, 2004, pp. 237–40.

Tonts, M., 'State policy and the yeoman ideal: agricultural development in Western Australia, 1890–1914', *Landscape Research*, vol. 27, no. 1, 2002, pp. 103–15.

Toussaint, S., 'Aboriginal resistance and the maintenance of identity: Nyungars and the state', *Social Analysis*, no. 32, 1992, pp. 16–30.

Toussaint, S., 'For whom the Fitzroy River flows: a fluctuating analysis of social and environmental sustainability and incremental sovereignty', in D. Ghosh, H. Goodall and S. H. Donald (eds), *Water, Sovereignty and Borders in Asia*, Hoboken, Routledge, 2007, pp. 174–87.

Toussaint, S., Sullivan, P. and Yu, S., 'Water ways in Aboriginal Australia: an interconnected analysis', *Anthropological Forum*, vol. 15, no. 1, 2005, pp. 61–74.

Troy, P., 'Conclusion', in P. Troy (ed.), *Troubled Waters*, Canberra, ANU Press, 2008, pp. 187–210.

Utting, M., *Windows to the Southern Skies*, Perth, Murdoch University, 1991.

WA Greenhouse Taskforce, *Western Australian Greenhouse Strategy*, Perth, WA Greenhouse Taskforce, 2004.

WA Water Symposium, *Our Water Future*, Perth, WA Water Symposium, 2002.

Wahlquist, Å., *Thirsty Country*, Crows Nest, Allen & Unwin, 2008.

Walter, J., *What Were They Thinking? The politics of ideas in Australia*, Sydney, UNSW Press, 2010.

Water and Rivers Commission, *Environmental Management of Groundwater Abstraction from the Gnangara Mound 2000–2003: triennial report to the Environmental Protection Authority*, East Perth, Water and Rivers Commission, 2004.

Water and Rivers Commission, *Perth Groundwater Atlas*, East Perth, Water and Rivers Commission, 1997.

Water Corporation, *Desalination – Creating New Water Sources: a strategic review of desalination possibilities for Western Australia*, Leederville, Water Corporation, 2000.

Water Corporation, *Perth Residential Water Use Study 2008/2009*, Perth, Water Corporation, 2010.

Water Corporation, *Source Development Plan 2005–2050: an overview*, Leederville, Water Corporation, 2005.

WAWA, *Perth's Water Future, a water supply strategy for Perth and Mandurah to 2021 with a focus to 2010, overview*, Leederville, WAWA, 1995.

WAWA, *Sources Development Plan 1988 Review*, Leederville, WAWA, 1988.

WAWA, *Water Conservation Plan 1987/89*, Leederville, WAWA Water Resources Directorate, 1987.

Webster, K., 'Groundwater management on the Swan Coastal Plain: an overview', in G. Lowe (ed.), *Swan Coastal Plain Groundwater Management Conference Proceedings*, Leederville, WA Water Resources Council, 1989, pp. 21–30.

Webster, K., 'Profile of Australian water use with reference to domestic water use in Perth', in *Proceedings of the National Workshop on Urban Water Demand Management*, Perth, WA Water Resources Council, 1986, pp. 75–94.

Webster, K., 'Water resources', in R. T. Appleyard (ed.), *Western Australia into the Twenty-first Century*, Perth, St George Books, 1991, pp. 325–46.

Weller, R., *Boom Town*, Crawley, UWA Publishing, 2009.

Western Australian Parliament, *Western Australian Parliamentary Debates (WAPD)*, Perth, Govt Printer, 1890–2001.

White, B., 'The importance of climate variability and seasonal forecasting to the Australian economy', in G. Hammer, N. Nicholls and C. Mitchell (eds), *Applications of Seasonal Climate Forecasting in Agricultural and Natural Ecosystems*, Dordrecht, Kluwer Academic Publishers, 2000, pp. 1–22.

White, D. H. and Karsseis, L., 'Australia's National Drought Policy: aims, analyses and implementation', *Water International*, vol. 24, no. 1, 1999, pp. 2–9.

White, D. H., Collins, D. and Howden, M., 'Drought in Australia: prediction, monitoring, management and policy', in D. A. Wilhite (ed.), *Drought Assessment, Management, and Planning: theory and case studies*, New York, Kluwer, 1993, pp. 213–36.

Wilhite, D. A., 'Drought policy in the US and Australia: a comparative analysis', *Water Resources Bulletin*, vol. 22, no. 3, 1986, pp. 425–38.

Wilhite, D. A. and Buchanan-Smith, M., 'Drought as hazard: understanding the natural and social context', in D. A. Wilhite (ed.), *Drought and Water Crises*, Boca Raton, FL, Taylor and Francis, 2005, pp. 3–29.

Wilhite, D. A., Hayes, M. J., and Knutson, C. L., 'Drought preparedness planning: building institutional capacity', in D. A. Wilhite (ed.), *Drought and Water Crises*, Boca Raton, FL, Taylor and Francis, 2005, pp. 93–136.

Williamson, D. R., 'Statistics of water use', in *Seminar H2O: domestic extravagance*, Perth, University of Western Australia, 1975.

Theses and dissertations

Morgan, R., 'Running Out? An environmental history of climate and water in the southwest of Western Australia, 1829 to 2006', PhD Thesis, University of Western Australia, 2012.

Toussaint, S., 'Nyungars in the city: a study of policy, power and identity', MA Thesis, University of Western Australia, 1987.

Webber, K., 'Romancing the machine: the enchantment of domestic technology in the Australian home, 1850–1914', PhD Thesis, University of Sydney, 1997.

INDEX

www.ingramcontent.com/pod-product-compliance
Lightning Source LLC
Chambersburg PA
CBHW020341270326
41926CB00007B/265